D1188301

Lewis Morris, 1671–1746

A New York State Study

GOVERNOR LEWIS MORRIS (ca. 1726), oil on canvas by John Watson (1685–1768). *The Brooklyn Museum, Dick S. Ramsay Fund, John Hill Morgan.*

Lewis Morris
1671–1746

A Study in
Early American Politics

EUGENE R. SHERIDAN

SYRACUSE UNIVERSITY PRESS   1981

Copyright © 1981 by SYRACUSE UNIVERSITY PRESS
SYRACUSE, NEW YORK 13210

Winner of the New Jersey Historical Commission's first Alfred E. Driscoll Prize.

Library of Congress Cataloging in Publication Data

Sheridan, Eugene R.
  Lewis Morris, 1671–1746.

  (A New York State study)
  Bibliography: p.
  Includes index.
  1. Morris, Lewis, 1671–1746. 2. New Jersey —
Politics and government — Colonial period, ca. 1600–
1775. 3. New York (State) — Politics and govern-
ment — Colonial period, ca. 1600–1775. 4. New
Jersey — Governors — Biography. 5. Judges — New York
(State) — Biography. I. Title. II. Series.
F137.M63S47   974.9'02'0924 [B]   81-14531
ISBN 0-8156-2243-0   AACR2

Manufactured in the United States of America

For Sylvia

EUGENE R. SHERIDAN received the M.A. and Ph.D. in American history from the University of Wisconsin. He was a National Historical Publications Commission Fellow in Advanced Documentary Editing with the Adams Family Papers at the Massachusetts Historical Society, and served as assistant and associate editor of *Letters to Delegates to Congress, 1774–1789,* at the Library of Congress. He is now associate editor of the *Papers of Thomas Jefferson* at Princeton University.

Contents

Preface

$\mathcal{S}$INCE THE END OF THE SECOND WORLD WAR scholars have greatly enriched and considerably revised our understanding of the nature of early American politics. Studies by Robert and Katherine Brown, Jackson Turner Main, and Chilton Williamson, indicating that colonial America had a larger electorate, greater economic opportunity, and higher social mobility than earlier writers had assumed, have led many historians to abandon the old Progressive interpretation of colonial politics as a simple struggle between the forces of aristocracy and democracy. Instead scholars are now groping their way toward a new synthesis which describes early American politics in terms of a series of conflicts among rival elite groups set within the context of a deferential society. In addition, the works of Bernard Bailyn, Edmund S. Morgan, and Gordon Wood, emphasizing the role of political ideology as a factor in the American Revolution, have led to a renewed interest in the significance of ideology in the conduct of prerevolutionary politics. Ideas and principles, often dismissed by Progressive historians as little more than convenient camouflage for supposedly more basic social or economic interests, are now recognized as important determinants of human behavior in their own right. Indeed, Bailyn has gone so far as to argue that one strand of political thought—that produced by the English opponents of Sir Robert Walpole—was a primary element of early eighteenth-century American politics: "primary in the sense of forming assumptions and expectations,

ix

of furnishing not merely the vocabulary but the grammar of thought, the apparatus by which the world was perceived." Finally, the studies of James Henretta, Stanley N. Katz, and Alison G. Olson, analyzing the Anglo-American dimension of the colonial political system, have provided historians with a sophisticated understanding of the subtle interaction between English and American politics. Colonial political leaders, it now appears, were as sensitive to shifts in English party politics and the decisions of the imperial administration as colonial merchants to the passage and enforcement of parliamentary economic regulations.

In the present work I have endeavored to analyze and describe the political career of Lewis Morris in the light of these historiographical trends. Morris was an assertive and combative landed aristocrat whose long and stormy political career in New York and New Jersey ought to make historians wary of trying to fit colonial political life into an all-embracing synthesis, for whereas his career in New York reflects the model of competition among rival factions of the provincial elite now in favor among many scholars, his career in New Jersey is more reminiscent of the struggle for political power between different classes that was emphasized by Progressive historians. Morris was also a thoughtful and articulate man whose intellectual and political gyrations reveal that colonial America had a richer and more complex ideological universe than that suggested by the current emphasis on the significance of English Opposition thought.

Furthermore, Morris figured prominently in imperial as well as provincial history, undertaking two crucial missions to England at widely different times — the first near the end of the reign of William III and the second during the heyday of Sir Robert Walpole — and serving for the last eight years of his life as royal governor of New Jersey. As a result, his career provides an excellent case study of the interaction between English and American politics that was such a marked feature of the colonial period. Above all, however, Morris was a fascinating character in his own right, so that although I have tried to keep these general historical issues in view, my main concern has been to trace the development of the man of whom Herbert L. Osgood wrote: "No one in the course of his life illustrated better the inconsistencies and conflicts in colonial relations than did Lewis Morris."

At the outset I should note that I have not written a full-scale biography of Morris because the materials for such a study do not exist. There is a considerable corpus of Morris papers still extant, but these papers reveal only the outlines of such topics as his family life, business affairs, cultural interests, and religious beliefs. I have summarized much of this material in the first chapter of this work in an effort to draw a personal portrait of Morris, and in later chapters I have also discussed his religious views, social attitudes, and political thought. Otherwise I have focused my attention on Morris' political career, not only because I believe this is where his main historical significance lies, but also because the nature of my sources obliges me to do so.

In quoting from primary sources I have reproduced the words exactly as they were written, except for lowering superscript letters, and have made no effort to call attention to misspelled words. On the other hand, I have modernized Old Style dates, changing February 1, 1715/16, for example, to February 1, 1716.

In the course of writing this study I have incurred many obligations which it is now my pleasure to acknowledge. Both David S. Lovejoy and Stanley N. Katz supervised my doctoral dissertation at the University of Wisconsin on which this book is based, giving generously of their time and knowledge in the process. James Morton Smith and Merrill M. Jensen also gave my dissertation the benefit of a good critical reading. Thanks to the efforts of all four men, the present book is a much better work than it would have been without their help.

Gerard W. Gawalt read portions of the revised manuscript and allowed me to avail myself of his extensive knowledge of American legal history. Norman S. Fiering and Stephen Saunders Webb both read the revised manuscript in its entirety and made a number of perceptive suggestions for improving it. I am particularly indebted to Professor Webb for his detailed comments and suggestions.

Mrs. Lawrence M. C. Smith, in a characteristic act of generosity, gave me access to her valuable collection of Lewis Morris papers. Patricia U. Bonomi and Alison G. Olson provided me with copies of some of their writings on colonial New York when these were otherwise unavailable to me.

The research for this book has been financed, in part, by grants from the American Philosophical Society, the Colonial Dames of Wisconsin, the Ford Foundation, and the New Jersey Historical Commission. It has also been greatly facilitated by the able assistance of the dedicated staffs of the John Carter Brown Library, Colonial Williamsburg, Inc., County of Essex Record Office, Historical Society of Pennsylvania, Henry E. Huntington Library, Library of Congress, Lincolnshire Archives Committee, New Jersey Historical Society, New-York Historical Society, New York Public Library, Public Record Office, Franklin D. Roosevelt Library, and Rutgers University Library. I owe a special debt of gratitude to the New Jersey Historical Commission for awarding my manuscript the first Alfred E. Driscoll Prize, which helped to make the publication of this book possible.

I am deeply grateful to my parents for their constant support and encouragement. My daughter Maureen was always a source of joy and delight during the writing of this book. My greatest debt, however, is to my wife Sylvia. Without her unfailing support, informed criticism, and diligent typing, I might never have completed this study. It is, then, to her that I dedicate this book.

Spring 1981   Eugene R. Sheridan

Lewis Morris, 1671–1746

⤜ 1 ⤝

"One Poor Blossom"

LEWIS MORRIS WAS BORN IN NEW YORK CITY on October 15, 1671, the only child of Richard and Sarah Pole Morris, who had come to New York from Barbados the year before. Industrious genealogists, sometimes too quick to credit their families with ancestors they did not actually have and virtues they did not really possess, have traced the origins of the Morris family to Rys, a legendary medieval Welsh warrior. Rys, we are told, displayed such tremendous bravery and daring in helping Henry II of England to conquer Ireland in the twelfth century that he won the name of Great Rys, which in Welsh is Maury Rys, and which down through the centuries was transformed into Morris.[1]

It is doubtful that Lewis Morris was a descendant of the warrior Rys, but it is true that the father who begot him and the uncle who raised him to manhood came from a Welsh family which lived on an estate called Tintern in Monmouthshire, England. Richard Morris, born in 1616, was "a man full of strength and vigor, inured to hardships," who had a pleasing prose style and a keen interest in science. He fought on the side of Parliament during the English Civil War and attained the rank of captain in an infantry regiment. After the establishment of the Commonwealth, he migrated to Barbados where he joined his older brother, Lewis Morris, Sr., a well-to-do sugar planter. During his stay on Barbados, Richard married Sarah Pole, a resident of the island, who shortly after her death was deeply mourned by a friend as "a virtuous young woman in the prime

1

of life," and who almost a century later was improbably described by one of her grandsons as a "Daughter to the Lt of the Tower" of London. In the late 1660s he made several trips to New York, acting as a factor for his brother and seeking a new home for them. Richard and Sarah finally settled permanently in New York in 1670 when he purchased for himself and his brother a 520-acre tract of land in what is now the southern part of Bronx County that became the nucleus of the family estate in this colony. Richard worked as a merchant and attorney in New York until death suddenly struck down him and his wife in the summer of 1672, leaving their "lovely, healthy child" Lewis, who was still less than a year old, in the hands of some guardians appointed by the provincial government. Young Lewis was not destined to grow up without the care of a family of his own, however, for when Lewis Morris, Sr., learned of the deaths of his brother and sister-in-law and their survival by, as a family friend quaintly informed him, "but one poor blossom, of whom yet there may be great hope," he decided to come to New York in order to bring up his nephew and take over the family estate.[2]

When Lewis Morris, Sr., finally arrived in New York in September 1673 he was already seventy-two years old and able to look back on a long and varied career as a West Indian adventurer, Barbadian sugar planter, and Quaker proselyte. He began his West Indian career in the 1630s by entering the service of the Providence Company, an organization headed by a group of influential English Puritan leaders, including such notables as John Pym and the Earl of Warwick, whose colony on the island of Santa Catalina off the coast of modern Nicaragua began as a holy experiment and ended as a base of operations against Spanish shipping. Morris, Sr., helped to perpetuate this anti-Spanish tradition by serving as master of one of the ships which took part in Captain William Jackson's bold raids against Jamaica and the Spanish Main between 1642 and 1645, a stirring enterprise which fired the imaginations of Englishmen and led to Oliver Cromwell's even more famous Western Design a decade later. After the completion of Jackson's expedition, Morris, Sr., returned to England and distinguished himself at the reduction of the Scilly Islands by parliamentary forces in 1651. In gratitude for his "good service in Scilly," the Council of State awarded £100 to Morris, Sr., and recommended him to Sir George Ayscue, who was about to lead a fleet against the royalist-controlled island of Barbados. Morris, Sr., accompanied Ayscue's expedition to Barbados and was wounded while leading a raiding party before the Barbadian government finally agreed to recognize parliamentary authority in 1652.[3]

At this time Morris, Sr., decided to end his life of wandering and settle down in Barbados. He acquired a sugar plantation named "Apes hill" and after some initial difficulties became a successful planter. Eventually his estate expanded to include 400 acres worked by 200 slaves, thus placing him in the top rank of the island's planter elite. As his wealth increased, so also did his social prestige, until both were threatened by his conversion to Quakerism sometime after the Restoration. Although the circumstances surrounding the elder Morris' decision to become a Quaker are unknown, the fervor with which he embraced his new faith was remarkable. He repeatedly bore public witness to his beliefs; corresponded with George Fox, the founding father of Quakerism, and William Penn, perhaps the most influential and certainly the most famous of the sect's second-generation leaders; and he became renowned among Friends as "the famous Coll Lewis Morris . . . of Barbados."[4] The Barbadian authorities were less enthralled by the old planter's religious conversion, though at first they reacted to it with nothing more than amused contempt. Contempt turned to anger, however, when Morris, Sr., refused to pay church dues, support ministers, or provide men and horses for the militia, and in 1669 he was struck with the first of a series of fines that eventually cost him more than 16,000 pounds of sugar. He suffered for his religion in other ways as well, and in one otherwise obscure case he found an intercessor in the person of no less a figure than the crypto-Catholic Secretary of State Arlington, whom he thanked effusively for saving him from being "opprest by a weked and unjost Man who had hoeps of enriching himselfe by my Ruing under the pretens of Riet, and layed that to my Charg I was not guilti of."[5] But whatever else Arlington's intercession accomplished for the elder Morris, it certainly did not teach him discretion. He continued to bear public witness to his faith and to incur fines for refusing to support the church, the ministry, and the militia. Since the brothers Morris had considered leaving Barbados as early as the middle of the 1660s, it is not surprising that Morris, Sr., decided to seize the opportunity created by Richard Morris' death to move to New York and leave behind the "weked and unjost" men who, it seemed to him, were bent on taking advantage of his faith to deprive him of his fortune.

After settling in New York, the elder Morris displayed a remarkable spirit of enterprise for a man his age. He worked as a merchant and a landholder, engaging in trade with England and the West Indies and making a series of "good improvements" on his land. Not content with merely developing the 520-acre tract he and his brother had acquired in partnership, he obtained a 1,400 acre addition to it from Governor Edmund Andros in 1676. He named the enlarged estate Morrisania, and it was this property for which his nephew gained manorial status more than twenty years later.[6]

Nor did Morris, Sr., restrict his interests to New York. In 1675 he and Cornelius Steenwyck, a New York merchant who was said to be the second richest man in that colony, formed a partnership to own and operate the Tinton Iron Works in Shrewsbury, East Jersey. Tinton was one of only about a dozen ironworks erected in seventeenth-century America, and of these it was the largest and most complex. The works themselves were located on a 3,900-acre tract that Morris obtained from the proprietary government of East Jersey and named Tintern—which was soon corrupted to Tinton—Manor in honor of his ancestral home in England. Here manufacturing and agriculture were carried on by a mixed labor force of black slaves and white indentured servants. Bog iron was turned into an assortment of iron products in a hammer forge fueled by charcoal. At one point as many as twenty-five servants and sixty slaves were employed at Tinton, and between 1675 and 1683 Morris, Steenwyck, and some of their Jersey associates invested £8,680 in the iron business—an investment the prudent Morris sought to protect by obtaining some advantageous economic concessions from the proprietor and assembly of East Jersey. Steenwyck died in 1684, and afterward Morris, Sr., became sole proprietor of Tinton, in which capacity he acquired another 2,300 acres of land so that at the time of his death the estate contained 6,200 acres. By enlarging and improving Morrisania in New York and acquiring Tinton in East Jersey, the elder Morris laid the material foundations for young Lewis Morris' subsequent political career.[7]

Morris, Sr., prepared the way for his nephew in another respect as well. In colonial America economic success and social prestige frequently led to political power. The elder Morris is a case in point. A firm supporter of the Duke of York's government in New York and the proprietary regime in East Jersey, he was rewarded for his loyalty in 1683 with prestigious appointments to membership in the New York Council as well as the East Jersey Council and Court of Common Right. Morris, Sr.'s, advanced age precluded active participation in the political affairs of either province, but in a political system where access to appointive office often passed from father to son, his service in these bodies facilitated Lewis Morris' subsequent entry into political life, especially in East Jersey.

And what of that "one poor blossom" the elder Morris had come to New York to raise? Lewis Morris' early life is largely wrapped in obscurity, but what little is known about it suggests that his uncle was far more successful in developing the family estate than in bringing up the heir to it according to his expectations. This was only to be expected when one considers that young Lewis' most impressionable years were also highly unsettling ones. He lost both his mother and his father before he was a year old and then spent the next two years under the supervision of two different sets of guardians appointed by English and Dutch officials. He received another rude shock in 1673 when his home was plundered by family servants and foreign soldiers, and afterward lived for two more years with a nurse whom his uncle employed to care for him while the old gentleman made the transition from Barbados to New York. These experiences understandably turned Morris into a defiant, high-spirited, rebellious child who was not disposed to submit tamely to his septuagenarian uncle or his uncle's younger wife, Mary, whom family tradition has vilified as a low-born woman who deliberately set uncle against nephew in an effort to deprive the youngster of part of his rightful inheritance. Perhaps Morris would have been better behaved if his uncle had given him some of the love he had missed by the untimely deaths of his parents, but the old Quaker was a stern man who did not display affection easily and consequently his nephew gave him little of it in return.[8]

Lewis particularly resisted the elder Morris' efforts to raise him according to the precepts of George Fox. For this purpose Morris, Sr., employed two tutors—Hugh Coppathwait, who was described by an eighteenth-century historian as "a Quaker zealot," and George Keith, the fiery Quaker apologist who later became an Anglican and denounced the doctrines of Friends as vigorously as he had once defended them. Neither man seems to have had much success with the boy, and Coppathwait in particular became the butt of his scorn. Years later Morris liked to regale his friends by describing how once as a lad he hid himself in a tree and, affecting to be a voice from heaven, almost convinced Coppathwait to journey to the wilderness of northern New York to bring the good news of the gospels to the Mohawks. Although the sophisticated, nominally Anglican Morris found this anecdote amusing, it also indicates his resentment of his Quaker upbringing.[9]

Morris' youthful rebelliousness manifested itself in other, more serious ways as well. As the boy grew older, his uncle charged, he was repeatedly guilty of "many and great miscarryages and disobedience towards me and my wife . . . and adhering to and advizeing with those of bad life and conversation." Admittedly, young Lewis was once discovered "Running of Races and playing at Nynne Pinns on the Sabbath day," but if this was typical of his youthful misdeeds, perhaps there was some merit in his belief that his aunt deliberately magnified his faults in order to discredit him in the eyes of his uncle and thereby deprive him of part of the family estate.[10] In any case Morris obviously got along badly with his aunt and uncle, and at length their relationship deteriorated to such an extent that he left home when he was about eighteen. Travelling by foot, he made his way to Virginia, where he took ship for Bermuda and from thence sailed to Jamaica. There he worked as a scrivener for about a year—hence his neat, precise handwriting—until finally his uncle learned of his whereabouts and sent a ship to fetch him home.

Morris arrived back in New York early in February 1691. It was good for him he returned home when he did, for his uncle died on February 14 and his aunt a week later, thereby raising the issue of who would inherit the family estate. In a will drawn up just a few days before his death, the old Quaker displayed great magnanimity to his prodigal nephew by bequeathing to him Tinton in East Jersey and a 1,500-acre tract of land on Long Island called Mattinicott, while leaving Morrisania and a home in New York City to his wife "her heirs and assigns forever." After Mary Morris' death, however, there was some question as to the disposition of her share of the estate. Morris firmly believed that it should revert to him, but his uncle's will was so worded that there was nothing in it to prevent any of Mary Morris' Barbadian relatives from contesting his claim. Fortunately for Morris, circumstances favored his effort to gain control of the entire estate. Mary Morris died intestate, and soon thereafter Morris learned from one of his uncle's executors that she had tampered with her husband's will after his death, most notably with the section governing the disposition of Morrisania in the event of her demise. Morris saw to it that this information was brought to the attention of the governor and council of New York when the will came before them for probate on May 8, 1691, and in consequence they decided to make Morris sole administrator of the whole family estate. During the next decade, Morris purchased releases from a number of his aunt's relatives in Barbados to avoid any litigation over his right to Morrisania, but long before that process was complete he had achieved his main objective, for at the age of nineteen he was in effective control of the estate his father had begun in New York and his uncle had expanded and extended into East Jersey.[11]

Morris' inheritance was a magnificent one by the standards of the time. He now possessed a 6,200-acre estate in East Jersey, a 1,920-acre estate in New York, a 1,500-acre tract on Long Island, and a home in New York City. He also owned a fully developed ironworks, a saw mill and a grist mill, and a share of the *Friends Adventure,* a ship that his uncle had used in conjunction with other New York merchants for trading ventures. He even inherited a seasoned labor force of sixty-six black slaves to work his various enterprises: "22 man negroes . . . 11 women . . . 6 boys . . . 2 garles . . . 25 children." Nor did this exhaust his patrimony. He was also the owner of a valuable assortment of personal property, including, among other things, family plate and jewelry, clothing, furnishings, books, gold coins, shop goods for trade, and farming tools. Morris estimated that his landed estates were worth £10,400—£6,000 for Tinton,

£4,000 for Morrisania, £400 for Mattinicott — and put the value of all his other personal property at £6,418. Contemporaries were equally impressed by Morris' inheritance. In 1692 an imperial official visited New York and reported that Morris "has the Greatest Estate in the Country." This statement is clearly an exaggeration — other New Yorkers owned more land than Morris — but certainly Morris was one of the wealthiest men in New York and New Jersey as the seventeenth century drew to a close.[12]

Morris' successful struggle to preserve the integrity of his family estate gained him membership in the landed aristocracies of New Jersey and New York, whose values he was to espouse and whose interests he was to defend throughout his life. His entrance into the ranks of the provincial elite was symbolized by his marriage in November 1691 to Isabella Graham, the daughter of James Graham, in a match that is said to have been arranged by the elder Morris shortly before his death. This marriage was a classic union of wealth and power — Morris' wealth and Graham's power. James Graham was a Scottish-born lawyer and merchant of moderate means who exercised tremendous political influence in New York. At the time of his daughter's marriage to Morris, Graham was serving as speaker of the provincial assembly and was soon to become recorder of the city and attorney general of the province of New York. During the 1690s he was also a close confidante and adviser to a succession of royal governors, including Richard Ingoldesby, Benjamin Fletcher, and the Earl of Bellomont, until in 1699 Bellomont broke with him and denounced him as "a right Scot, Cunning, but as false as hell and Corrupt, and besides, no lawyer." Marriage to one of Graham's daughters was a telling sign of the high social status Morris now enjoyed by reason of his great wealth.[13]

Morris' marriage was, by all accounts, a happy one. His new bride Isabella was an eighteen-year-old Scottish lass who apparently never lost her brogue. Plain in appearance, she more than made up for her lack of physical beauty by her great strength of character, so that she came to be justly celebrated as "a pattern of conjugal affection, a tender parent, a sincere friend, and an excellent economist." Though the marriage of Lewis and Isabella was not marked by any outward signs of great romantic passion, it was distinguished by a high degree of mutual love and tenderness. To Isabella, Lewis was always her "dear husband," and her constant concern for him was symbolized by the prosaic advice she gave to a son who accompanied him on a political mission to London in 1735–36: "Take all the Care you Can of your father and if its possible to prevaill with him not to Sett up Latte nor drink to freely of there mixt wine." To Lewis, Isabella was always "my good and deservedly well beloved wife," and toward the end of his life he strictly enjoined his children "to be kind, tender and affectionate to their mother, she having been always so to them." They remained a faithful and devoted couple for fifty-five years.[14]

Morris and his wife observed the biblical injunction to increase and multiply. During the first twenty-two years of their marriage Isabella gave birth to fifteen children of whom eleven—eight girls and three boys—lived to be adults.[15] Morris proved to be a loving father who could also be stern when he thought the occasion required it. Even after his children were fully grown, he frequently began his letters to them with the salutation "My dear child" and always signed himself "Your affectionate father." Yet he could also be highly caustic in dealing with a son he thought was performing inadequately as overseer of Tinton—"You are an excellent Husband man in the Opinion of your neighbours, and this tho I am very glad to heare, yet it doth not (I must own) so fully convince me of your Judgment in that Science as it doth of the Judgment of those that give the character"—and one of his daughters trembled at the displeasure she incurred when one of her beaus fell asleep while her father was holding forth at a family gathering.[16] Morris took a special interest in supervising the education of his children and made sure that all of them—girls as well as boys—learned how to read and write. In the process he also conveyed some of his own natural pugnacity to them. Benjamin Franklin, who knew Morris' youngest son, recorded in his autobiography that Morris encouraged "his Children to dispute with one another for his Diversion while sitting at Table after Dinner," and characteristically reflected that "the Practice was not wise, for in the Course of my Observation, these disputing, contradicting and confuting People are generally unfortunate in their affairs. They get Victory sometimes, but they never get Good Will, which would be of more use to them." But Morris' children did not share the good doctor's reservations about their father's peculiar pedagogical technique, and in general they retained a high regard for him throughout their lives. Once when Morris was away in England on a political mission one of his daughters regretted his absence because the family "know not what to do with-out him," and this remark seems to have typified the attitudes of his other children as well.[17]

Morris supported himself and his family largely through his landed estates. Unlike his uncle, he did not pursue a dual career as a landholder and merchant. In fact, Morris regarded mercantile life as an unworthy calling for a gentleman and despised most merchants as double-dealing tricksters who were constantly conspiring to cheat honest tillers of the soil by charging too much for the goods they sold to them and paying too little for the products they purchased from them. Accordingly, he devoted himself to the management of his estates at Morrisania and Tinton, secure in the belief that this was a more suitable occupation for a gentleman than working as a merchant. These estates were complex enterprises. On them Morris grew wheat, rye, barley, oats, and corn; produced butter, cheese, and cider; and raised cattle, pigs, hogs, sheep, and horses. After the needs of his family and slaves had been taken care of, he shipped his surplus production to New York City in a small sloop he owned and there sold part of it to city dwellers and the rest to local merchants, who exported it to the West Indies to feed the planters and slaves on the sugar islands. In addition, Morris ran a saw mill that turned lumber into board and a grist mill that ground grain into flour for customers in New Jersey and New York. Furthermore, for a time he continued operations at the Tinton ironworks, making plate and bar iron for a small clientele in the same two colonies, but production seems to have been sporadic, and the works themselves were probably shut down after 1715.[18] There are no known business records by which we might ascertain Morris' annual profits and losses from his various enterprises, but there is no reason to doubt that his estates enabled him to maintain an extremely comfortable standard of living.

Morris enjoyed the unique distinction of owning estates in both New Jersey and New York that were also manors. Lewis Morris, Sr., induced Sir George Carteret, the proprietor of East Jersey, to make Tinton a manor in 1676, though at the time Sir George failed to specify the rights appertaining to the estate. The elder Morris made up for this oversight in the following year when he persuaded Carteret to free Tinton from the obligation to pay quitrents for five years and taxes for seven years, to exempt Tinton workmen from arrest for debt and ordinary militia service, and to grant Tinton the right to hold a petty court to try small causes on the estate. Yet by 1691 some of these rights had expired and others had fallen into disuse, so that by the time Morris acquired control of it Tinton was a manor in little more than name only.[19]

Morris himself obtained manorial status for Morrisania and the rights he won for it were—at least on paper—far more impressive than any that had ever been exercised at Tinton. Morris petitioned Governor Benjamin Fletcher to make Morrisania a manor, and Fletcher, who was pursuing a policy of attracting the support of the local landed aristocracy for royal authority, granted his request in May 1697. At that time the governor issued a patent designating Morris as lord of the manor of Morrisania and investing him with feudal privileges that his putative ancestors among the Welsh nobility would not have scorned. As lord of Morrisania, Morris was entitled to hold a court leet to make ordinances for his tenants and present offenders against them and to erect a court baron to try cases involving tenants and disputes about manorial lands. He could also appoint stewards and authorize them to distrain the goods of tenants who failed to render him "the rents services and other sumes of money payable by virtue of the premisses" and employ "all other lawfull remedyes and means" to enforce his right to "all waifs Estrays wrecks deodands goods of felons happening and being forfeited within the said Lordship or Mannour of Morrisania." Moreover, he was given the right of advowson — the privilege of selecting a clergyman for any church on the manor — and the right to appoint his own officials to assess and collect taxes imposed by the provincial assembly. And in return for the grant of this battery of feudal rights he only had to pay the English crown a quitrent of six shillings every year on the feast of the Annunciation of the Virgin Mary.

But if in theory Morris possessed the rights of a medieval manor lord, in practice he behaved more like a typical substantial colonial American landholder. There is no evidence that he ever held a court leet or a court baron, he never exercised the right of advowson, and it is unlikely that he ever had occasion to use the right of distraint because at Morrisania he dealt primarily with slaves rather than tenants. In only one respect did Morris' lordship of Morrisania have any practical effect: it enabled him to keep Westchester County tax assessors and collectors off his estate. Otherwise Morris' status as a manorial lord in New Jersey and New York was chiefly significant as a symbolic recognition of his position as one of the leading landed aristocrats in these two colonies.[20]

Morris' estates were worked almost exclusively by black slaves. The sixty-six slaves he inherited from his uncle in 1691 probably made Morris the largest slaveholder in New York and New Jersey, and he seems to have owned roughly the same number of bondsmen until he relinquished the management of his estates to his sons after his appointment as governor of New Jersey in 1738.[21] Morris' slaves performed a wide variety of tasks. They planted and harvested his crops, cared for his livestock, worked at his mills, labored at his iron works, and attended to the personal needs of himself and his family. Morris sometimes hired seasonal white workers to assist with the harvest, but for the most part he relied on the labor of his slaves. In some respects Morris held relatively liberal views about slavery. He acknowledged the humanity of slaves in radical fashion by boldly asserting as chief justice of the supreme court of New York that slaves were men and that any black bondsman was justified in taking the life of a white man who threatened his master or mistress. He also courageously supported the work of Elias Neau, an Anglican catechist who gave religious instruction to New York City slaves, when, in the aftermath of the great servile revolt that shook the town in 1712, many other slaveholders opposed Neau as a subversive influence on slaves. Yet one should not exaggerate Morris' liberality as a slaveholder. He saw no contradiction between recognizing the humanity of blacks and depriving them of their freedom, nor is there any evidence that he ever allowed his own slaves to be Christianized. On the contrary, he believed that his bondsmen were "both Stupid and conceited and will follow their own way if not carefully looked to," and he warned a son he had placed in charge of Tinton that "negroes will Steale, I feare, in Spite of all your caution to prevent them."[22] This behavior may have been a manifestation of black resistance to the slave regime, but for Morris it merely reinforced his belief that without strict supervision his slaves were nothing more than perverse, shiftless, and childlike creatures. In brief Morris was that familiar colonial American social type—an aristocrat whose own freedom and prosperity largely depended upon depriving other men and women of theirs.

Morris used the leisure that the wealth produced by slave labor afforded him to pursue a wide range of cultural interests. Having received a meager education as a youth, he devoted much of his adult life to a relentless quest for knowledge, not only because he valued learning in itself, but also because he regarded it as an essential attribute for a gentleman of his station in life. In this sense he was an exemplar of the popular seventeenth-century belief that for a gentleman learning was "not only an additament, but ornament to gentry. No complement gives more accomplishment." Accordingly, Morris made himself proficient in Greek, Latin, Hebrew, and Arabic, and is said to have understood some "Oriental Languages," too. He became an avid reader and amassed a library of 3,000 books, "replete with learned Works in Law, Politics, Hist[or]y, Philo[sophy], the Sciences, [and] Theol[og]y." This achievement is particularly impressive when one considers that at the time of its greatest extent Morris' private library contained only 500 fewer volumes than the library of Harvard College in 1723.[23]

Part of Morris' library was destroyed during the American Revolution, and the rest was subsequently dispersed among descendants, but it is still possible to form some idea of his reading habits from scattered references in his writings.[24] Like so many other men of his time, Morris frequently turned to the ancient world for intellectual nurture. He was fascinated by classical mythology and was particularly drawn to the writings of ancient authors whose work reflected the dramatic period when the Roman Republic declined and gave way to the Empire. Thus he read Cicero, the soul of Roman eloquence; Vergil, the greatest of Rome's poets; Tacitus, the stern historian of Roman decay and Germanic virtue; Lucan, the epic poet of the civil war between Caesar and Pompey; and Josephus, the chronicler of the Jews of antiquity. He translated part of Lucan's *De bello civili* and greatly admired the grave eloquence of Tacitus. "I want my Tacitus much," he once wrote to one of his sons, "but no hassard in

Sending of it nor do not lend it on any Account to any body whatever for I know that country [New Jersey] too well to lend books in it. That is not a book fit to come into a country fellows hand to daub and dirty."[25]

Morris' love for the ancients did not blind him to the merits of the moderns. He enjoyed the plays of Shakespeare, the poetry of Milton, the plays and poetry of Addison, and was delighted by Montesquieu's witty satire on the ancien regime, *The Persian Letters*. He also read the work of lesser lights of English literature like Thomas Shadwell, a Restoration playwright and poet of uneven quality of whom it was said that "if Shadwell had burnt all he wrote, and printed all he spoke, he would have had more wit and humour than any other poet"; and George Granvill, a distinctly mediocre dramatist and poet whom Samuel Johnson justly described as an artist who "had no ambition above the imitation of Waller, of whom he copied the faults, and very little more."

Turning from literature to politics, Morris was familiar with the works of James Harrington, the celebrated author of *Oceana*, and Andrew Fletcher of Saltoun, a Scottish republican theorist. Moreover, he was a devoted reader of John Trenchard's and Thomas Gordon's *Cato's Letters* and Lord Bolinbroke's *Craftsman* essays, both of which warned of the dangers to English liberty stemming from Walpolean corruption— the first from a radical Whig and the second from a conservative Tory perspective. In history Morris' taste ran to Paul de Rapin-Thoyras' multivolume *History of England*, which dealt with the subject in terms of a constant struggle to protect ancient Saxon liberties against the encroachments of arbitrary power; John Oldmixon's *The History of England, during the reigns of the Royal House of Stuart*, which described that troubled dynasty from the viewpoint of a moderate Walpolean Whig; and Count Henri de Boulanvilliers' *An Historical Account of the Antient parliaments of France*, a French aristocrat's lament for the lost glory of his class. Morris shared the well-known eighteenth-century interest in exotic lands and cultures, and therefore he read Jean Baptiste Du Halde's *The General History of China* and Captain Alexander Hamilton's *A New Account of the East Indies*. Lastly, he was fascinated by problems of theology, and in his own spiritual life he moved from Quakerism to Anglicanism to Deism. This spiritual odyssey was reflected in his reading, which ranged from Anglican devotional tracts like William Beveridge's *The Excellency and Usefulness of the Common Prayer* to Deistic tomes like Marie Huber's *The Religion Essential to Man*, and included as well the writings of Thomas Chubb and Matthew Tindal, two of England's leading Deists. These examples, tantalizingly few as they are, suggest that on the whole Morris read both widely and well.

Morris' cultural interests were not confined to the languages he mastered and the books he read. He also had a deep love for music and poetry. He admired the work of Arcangelo Corelli, the first great violinist and violin composer, and learned himself how to play the fiddle. So fond was Morris of his fiddle that he sometimes played it on the most unlikely occasions. Once when he was chief justice of the supreme court in New York he went to Albany to hold a circuit court, drank too heavily the night before opening court, and slept till sunset of the following day. At length he was awakened by his servants accompanied by some of the people who had been waiting for him to hold court, and, upon being told the time of day, he exclaimed "how can that be . . . the sun is but just risen, and saying so he took up his Fiddle and played the Company a tune." It is doubtful that any of the witnesses to this impromptu concert consoled themselves with the thought that they were being entertained by an American Corelli, for as Morris humorously wrote about himself in another context: "He'll dispute with the masters of Musick in theire owne art but to hear him pforme is Enough to give you the Gripes."[26]

In addition to reading the works of major and minor poets of ancient and modern times, Morris also wrote poetry of his own. Written in the "broad Hudibrastic tradition,"[27] much of Morris' poetry dealt with political disputes in which he was personally involved, as in these lines excoriating the imperial administration's failure to respond to his complaints about Governor William Cosby during one of his missions to England:

> Complaints if just, are very shocking things,
> And not encourag'd in the courts of Kings.
> T' accuse your Chief, they'll construe to be meant
> A Side reflection on the Government:
> And Senders mostly will defend the Sent.
> If they perhaps deceiv'd abroad do send
> Some worthless wretch, or known one recommend,
> In either case the matter's much the same;
> The Recommendors can't be free'd from blame.
> Will therefore for their own sakes strive to shun
> A Censure well deserv'd for what they've done:
> And either hide his Conduct from the State,
> Or what they can't deny, will palliate.
> Will call you factious, turbulent, and Say
> You stirr'd the people up to disobey:
> That if such men as You be heard, there's none
> Henceforth will undertake to serve the crown.
> They'll to his acts wrong appellation give
> And call abuse of Power, Prerogative.

And if at hand convincing proofs you have
To shew your Chiefs no better than a Knave,
They'l not be heard, but put from day to day
They'l tire your patience out with long delay;
And when You've spent your little all in vain
You may, if You think fitt, go back again
And truly shew tis bootless to complain.[28]

In other poems Morris displayed a flair for social satire, as in these verses depicting the corruption he perceived in the society of Walpolean England during the same trip to London:

Most live by fraud and study to appeare
The true reverse of what they really are
By Shews beguile, to Virtue make pretence
And both deceive the fool and man of Sense
There's scarce such thing as friendship but in Name
Profit's the only Butt, at which most aim.
This to obtain, each man will cheat his Brother,
The Factors cheat the Merchants, They each other,
And if we dare believe what many say
Both Senates and their choosers vote for pay:
And both alike their Liberty betray.[29]

And still other poems reflect Morris' appreciation of the delights of the American scene, as in this excerpt from a poem about the perplexing problem of where to locate a new capital for New Jersey:

Shou'd you reside in the Hackinsack
You may have Rum and Sometimes Rack
Good mutton, Venison and veale
Geese, mallard, prover duck and trale
Tho company not so polite
As you wou'd wish to Spend a night
And Shou'd your choice be to reside
In Essex on pisayicks Side
That pleasing Stream will gratifie
By turns your pallat and your Eye
And with the neighbring lands aford
Plenty to grace a noble board
And tho no wine theres in its Stead
Mathoglin and the Sparkling mead

Wth. which regal'd you'll Sometimes meet
Wth. punning Jokes and Smutty wit
For English boyes and Belgicks fit.[30]

It would be absurd to claim that Morris is a major undiscovered talent in early American literature, but his poetry does occasionally display genuine literary ability and the mere fact that he took the trouble to write it is eloquent testimony of his devotion to the art.

Morris' love for the arts was matched by an interest in science. Like many other educated men of his day, Morris dabbled in natural science and produced some "curious Disquisitions into the works of Nature." One of Morris' friends in England urged him to send him some of these "Disquisitions" so that they could be communicated to the Royal Society. Morris never complied with this request, and it is probably just as well that he did not: he was once intrigued by the theory that the Red Sea had acquired its name because "twice a year it's cover'd with red Locusts drove into it by a strong wind from the Land." Still, Morris' fascination with natural science is an important indication of the breadth of his intellectual interests, and in this regard it is worth noting that when the English naturalist Peter Collinson was seeking support for the work of the American botanist John Bartram, Morris was one of those he turned to for help.[31]

As a result of his love of learning, Morris came into contact with some of the most erudite men in the Anglo-American world. Morris took great delight not only in acquiring knowledge but also in sharing it with others. As an eighteenth-century historian noted: "Being excessively fond of the society of men of sense and reading, he was never wearied at a Sitting, till the spirits of the whole company were dissipated." Thus William Penn met Morris during his last visit to America at the end of the seventeenth century and was impressed by his "Sense, fortune and education." Penn's agent and secretary James Logan, a noted bibliophile, Latin scholar, and natural scientist, met Morris several years later and became a lifetime acquaintance. James Alexander, a distinguished lawyer, mathematician, and polemicist, and Cadwallader Colden, a highly gifted historian, philosopher, and scientist, were both Morris' political allies and close personal friends during his political career in New York. Two of the most learned and refined royal governors of New Jersey and New York relied on Morris for political counsel and personal friendship: Robert Hunter, an intimate of Addison, Steele, and Swift, who collaborated with Morris in creating the first play written and published in the British colonies; and William Burnet, the well-read son of the famous Whig bishop and historian, Gilbert Burnet, who himself wrote theology with a Whiggish twist. All these men enjoyed Morris' company and John Chamberlayne — master of sixteen languages, fellow of the Royal Society, gentleman in waiting to Queen Anne, and an English correspondent of Morris' — probably spoke for all of them when he praised Morris for his delightful ability to discuss "the state of Philosophy, Belles Lettres &c." In sum Morris transformed himself from an unruly youth into a well-bred country gentleman who deserved the accolade that was bestowed on him slightly more than a decade after his death by the first historian of colonial New York: "He was a man of letters, and tho' a little whimsical in his temper, was grave in his manner and of penetrating parts."[32]

Husband, father, landed aristocrat, manorial lord, slaveholder, man of letters, amateur scientist . . . all these roles were important in Morris' life but his main historical significance lies in his extraordinarily long, rich, and complex career as a colonial political leader. Morris was drawn to political life by a combination of personal conviction, ambition, and temperament. To begin with, he was a dedicated elitist who believed as a matter of course that his wealth and social standing gave him the right to act as one of society's natural leaders and to be recognized as such by common people, fellow aristocrats, and imperial officials alike. Empire follows the balance of property, James Harrington had proclaimed to the seventeenth century, and from this Morris deduced that those who had the greatest material stake in society should have the largest say in the direction of its political affairs. In practice this meant for Morris that the landed aristocracy should play the dominant role in New Jersey and New York political life. Merchants, he believed, were too absorbed in the pursuit of private profit to consider the common good of society as a whole, and for him it was axiomatic that artisans, craftsmen, and farmers should follow the lead of those he deemed their social betters. In his view, only the landed aristocracy possessed the proper blend of wealth, prestige, learning, talent, and public spirit to provide effective political leadership for the people of the two provinces in which he owned estates.

Personal ambition reinforced Morris' elitist convictions and disposed him to participate in political life. Morris was not interested in accumulating great wealth or in devoting himself primarily to the disinterested pursuit of knowledge. Rather he was an intensely ambitious man who deeply craved the power and preferment to which he felt his aristocratic status entitled him. If he had lived in England and been of comparable rank, he might have satisfied this drive through service at court, in Parliament, or in the army, but as colonial America lacked a royal court and a standing army, he could only find an outlet for his ambitions in provincial politics.

Lastly, Morris was temperamentally suited for the public service toward which his personal ambition and political convictions led him. He acquired the habit of command through managing his slaves and did not shrink from exercising authority over freemen as well. He had an imposing bearing and stature, being considerably taller than most men of his time, and this reinforced the air of authority he exuded. Except among intimates, he had an austere demeanor and rarely displayed his gregariousness in public, but this was not a severe handicap in a society that was still highly deferential and in a political system where many of the choicest offices were appointive rather than elective, dependent on the favor of a royal or proprietary governor instead of the wishes of the populace. Above all, he was naturally assertive, bold, and combative, and seemed to thrive on controversy. During Morris' lifetime it was fashionable in the Anglo-American world to frown upon partisan strife as inherently inimical to the common good. Morris paid lip service to this convention in theory, but in practice he accepted competition between different social classes, economic interests, and political factions as part of the natural order of things and eagerly joined in the fray.

Contemporaries were quick to note Morris' aptitude for public affairs. In 1692 Edward Randolph, the imperial administration's most diligent watchdog in the colonies, met Morris during a visit to New York and was so impressed by his "good Genius and Capacity to serve their Majesties in the Government" that he recommended his appointment as a provincial councilor to William Blathwayt, the highly influential secretary of the Lords of Trade.[33] But Randolph's suggestion was ignored in England and Morris took no part in New York politics until the administration of Governor Robert Hunter eighteen years later. In the meantime, however, proprietary government in East Jersey was being reestablished upon the ruins of the Dominion of New England, and in 1692 Morris, like his uncle before him, became a member of the East Jersey Council and Court of Common Right, thereby launching a political career that lasted until his death more than half a century later.

✄ 2 ✄

"Morris's Inconsistencies"

Lewis Morris entered political life in 1692 and within a decade raised himself from the rank of an obscure member of the East Jersey Council to become one of the principal leaders of the proprietary party in New Jersey. The circumstances of the time, no less than his own native abilities, account for Morris' rise to a position of commanding influence in this colony. For proprietary government was in decay, in East Jersey as well as in West Jersey, weakened from within by formidable local groups antagonistic to the exercise of proprietary authority and threatened from without by imperial administrators determined to royalize all proprietary colonies in the empire. Unable to endure the strains imposed by the convergence of the forces of internal dissension and external coercion, proprietary government in the Jerseys collapsed at the end of the seventeenth century, and the proprietors from both divisions of the province surrendered their rights of government to the crown in 1702. It was the peculiar achievement of Lewis Morris to cooperate with the proprietors in royalizing New Jersey after he had first helped to make royalization imperative by subverting proprietary authority in East Jersey.

Morris' task was made easier because he began his career in New Jersey when the proprietary system there was on the verge of a crisis deeply rooted in its history. To begin with, the political authority of the New Jersey proprietors lacked legitimacy. In 1692 New Jersey consisted of two autonomous divisions, East Jersey and West Jersey, governed by two interrelated but legally distinct groups of English and Scottish proprietors, the East Jersey proprietors and the West Jersey Society, neither of which had a valid title to the rights of government they claimed. The proprietors and the Society both derived these rights from grants they had received, either directly or indirectly, from the Duke of York, the original proprietor of New Jersey, but since under English law only the king could rightfully delegate sovereignty to his subjects, the governing authority they exercised in East and West Jersey was highly questionable.[1]

The problem of proprietary political authority was aggravated in East Jersey by the conflict between the proprietors and the Nicolls patentees. The East Jersey proprietors claimed title to all the undivided land in their province and sought to require every freeholder to take out a proprietary land patent and pay them an average annual quitrent of two shillings per hundred acres. Eighty-five in number when Morris first entered public life, the East Jersey proprietors fell into two distinct categories—nonresident and resident. Whereas the nonresident proprietors, who consisted primarily of Scots and English Quakers and were led by William Dockwra, their diligent secretary and register, formulated proprietary policies with the aim of maximizing the profits on their investment in East Jersey, the responsibility for executing these policies rested with the resident proprietors, most of whom came from north of the Tweed and hence were known as the Scottish proprietors. The Scottish proprietors and Andrew Hamilton, a former Edinburgh merchant who was appointed governor of East Jersey in 1692 by the nonresident proprietors, made up the East Jersey Board of Proprietors, which distributed land, collected quitrents, and settled boundary disputes in the province.

The Nicolls patentees vigorously denied the proprietors' title to all the soil in East Jersey and refused to pay quitrents to them. The patentees, fiercely independent Puritan farmers from New England and Long Island who had founded the settlements of Elizabethtown, Woodbridge, Piscataway, Newark, Middletown, and Shrewsbury in Essex and Monmouth counties, claimed no less than 750,000 acres in East Jersey on the basis of two magnificent land grants that Governor Richard Nicolls of New York had made in 1664 and 1665 before he learned that the Duke of York had conveyed New Jersey to Sir George Carteret and Lord John Berkeley, the predecessors of the proprietors Morris served. Although York subsequently disavowed the Nicolls grants, the patentees continued to regard them as valid and therefore refused to take out proprietary patents or pay proprietary quitrents for their lands. As a result, when Morris assumed his first public office East Jersey politics revolved around the rivalry between the proprietary and the antiproprietary parties, with the former consisting of the Scottish proprietors led by Governor Hamilton and such freeholders as recognized their rights to the soil and the latter of the Nicolls patentees and other freeholders who were also averse to obtaining proprietary patents or paying proprietary quitrents.[2]

The issue of proprietary governing rights was exacerbated in West Jersey by tensions between the West Jersey Society and the local Quaker population. The West Jersey Society was an organization of forty-eight London merchants and gentlemen which in 1692 purchased the government of West Jersey and twenty of the one hundred proprieties (or shares of land) into which the province was divided from Dr. Daniel Coxe, an Anglican land speculator. Coxe also sold the Society two of East Jersey's twenty-four proprieties, thus linking it with the East Jersey proprietors — a process that was illustrated by the Society's appointment of Andrew Hamilton as governor of West Jersey several months after his selection as governor of East Jersey.

Although the Society was primarily interested in fostering the commercial development of West Jersey and selling its land there, from the start it was viewed with misgivings by West Jersey Quakers. Led by Samuel Jennings, a resident proprietor, the Friends believed that they should exercise the rights of government since they had settled the province two decades before on the understanding that these rights came with the purchase of the soil. They also feared the Society as a potential threat to their control of the provincial government and were apprehensive lest it fail to cooperate with the West Jersey Council of Proprietors, an organization of resident proprietors somewhat like the East Jersey Board of Proprietors, in the orderly distribution of land in the province. The Society unwittingly confirmed the Quakers' worst apprehensions by its unfortunate choice of American business agents, most notably Jeremiah Basse. Basse, a former Anabaptist minister who served as the Society's business agent from 1692 to 1695, clashed with the Council of Proprietors and formed a coalition consisting of Anglican employees of the Society and local members of the Church of England that was anxious to wrest control of the provincial government from the Friends. Thus while in East Jersey proprietary authority was threatened by the clash between the Scottish proprietors and the Nicolls patentees, in West Jersey it was endangered by the polarization of the province into Anglican and Quaker factions.[3]

Commercial rivalry with New York and the imperatives of English colonial policy constituted the final elements in the crisis of the proprietary regime at the outset of Morris' political career. In regard to the former, the East Jersey proprietors' wish to spur the commercial development of their province by making Perth Amboy a free port inevitably brought them into conflict with New York governors and merchants, who wanted to continue the traditional practice of requiring ships entering or leaving East Jersey to pay customs at New York City—the governors because they did not want to diminish their revenues and the merchants because they were eager to thwart a potential rival. Although James II decreed in 1687 that ships could sail directly to East Jersey without first having to drop anchor in New York, after the Glorious Revolution, New York resumed the practice of exacting customs from vessels sailing to or from East Jersey, notwithstanding strenuous protests by the proprietors. Perth Amboy's uncertain status exacerbated relations between East Jersey and New York and, perhaps more importantly, lessened the prestige of the East Jersey proprietors in the eyes of the people they presumed to govern.[4]

Whereas the issue of Perth Amboy touched only East Jersey, English colonial policy affected both parts of the Jerseys. As tensions rose between England and France and the two countries became involved after the Glorious Revolution in the first of a series of global conflicts that lasted until Waterloo, a number of imperial administrators became convinced of the need to royalize proprietary governments in order to facilitate the defense of the colonies and the enforcement of the Acts of Trade. In response to this impulse toward imperial centralization, East and West Jersey were added to the Dominion of New England in 1688, and four years later they narrowly escaped being incorporated into New York. But it is crucial to note that the imperial administration allowed the East Jersey proprietors and the West Jersey Society to govern their respective provinces on the understanding that they would preserve order in them and ensure that the Jerseys contributed to the defense of the strategically vital province of New York when needed. Failure to meet either of these conditions was bound to raise anew the vexed question of the validity of proprietary political authority in the Jerseys—and this at a time when certain key imperial administrators like William Blathwayt and Edward Randolph were inclined to favor the abolition of all proprietary governments in the colonies.[5]

Lewis Morris entered into this tangled web of doubtful authority, disputed land titles, intercolonial rivalry, and imperial centralization when he became a member of the East Jersey Council on September 14 and a judge on the East Jersey Court of Common Right on October 4, 1692. Morris was offered these appointments by Andrew Hamilton, and his acceptance of them indicates that even at this early date he favored the faction which the governor headed. The proprietary party attracted Morris' support for several reasons. Morris was a landed aristocrat who believed that his wealth and social prestige entitled him to act as one of the natural leaders of society. "Its much better to be Govern'd by the Head then the feet," he once observed, using metaphorical language that would have won the approval of most medieval political thinkers, and there was no doubt in his mind that the landed aristocracy constituted the intelligent part of the body politic.[6] The proprietary party, which numbered among its ranks most of East Jersey's fledgling landed aristocrats, was therefore a natural haven for a man of Morris' status and views. In addition, Morris, though not a proprietor himself, did have proprietary patents for his lands in East Jersey and so had every reason to support proprietary rights to the soil. Finally, it was only natural for the ambitious Morris to attach himself to the party which controlled the path to preferment and power in East Jersey.

Morris supported proprietary authority as a councilor and a judge during Governor Hamilton's administration. As a councilor he helped to draft legislation protecting Perth Amboy's right to free port status against encroachments by New York and tried in vain to persuade the provincial assembly to provide the governor with an adequate revenue. As a judge he displayed a concern for the protection of proprietary property rights, most notably in the celebrated case of *Fullerton* v. *Jones*. In an effort to annul the Nicolls grants, the resident proprietors, acting in the name of James Fullerton, brought an ejectment suit against Jeffrey Jones, a Nicolls patentee from Elizabethtown, in the Court of Common Right on October 11, 1693, Morris' first day on the bench. Morris and his fellow justices intermittently listened to arguments on both sides for almost two years before sending the case to the jury on May 11, 1695, with instructions to the jurors to bring in "a Speciall Verdict" which had been agreed upon by the opposing lawyers in the suit. Instead the jurors disregarded these instructions and found in favor of Jones. Morris and his colleagues on the bench, "being either of the Number of the said Proprietors or by them appointed," promptly reversed the jury's verdict and handed down a decision in favor of Fullerton, thus denying, in effect, the validity of all Nicolls patents and setting a precedent for the use of similar suits against other patentees. But this victory for the proprietors was short lived. In 1697 the Privy Council in England reversed the court's decision in *Fullerton* v. *Jones,* emboldening the people of Elizabethtown to ask the king to annex them to New York and accentuating the already serious strains in the proprietary system.[7] Still, in all these instances Morris played no more than a secondary role. He did not move to the forefront of East Jersey politics until after the proprietors from both divisions of New Jersey, having misinterpreted the Act of Trade passed in 1696 to mean that Scots could not hold offices of trust in the colonies, replaced Hamilton as governor with Jeremiah Basse.

The advent of Jeremiah Basse brought the crisis of proprietary government in New Jersey to a head and marked the beginning of Morris' rise to power. Basse, a former Anabaptist preacher and business agent of the West Jersey Society, labored under two serious handicaps even before he arrived in America. He failed to obtain the approval of the king that was required of colonial governors under the terms of the recently passed Act of Trade, although he concealed this fact from the proprietors and decided to try to govern without it. Basse's decision to proceed without royal approval was nothing less than foolhardy because it threatened to raise in heightened form the explosive question of the legitimacy of proprietary political authority in New Jersey. Basse also left England in the belief that the imperial administration was about to recognize Perth Amboy's right to free port privileges. In this he was mistaken, and his subsequent efforts to defend this right embroiled him in a conflict with the New York authorities which complicated his position in East Jersey in strange ways.[8]

Morris appears to have viewed Basse's replacement of Hamilton with misgivings from the start. Basse reached East Jersey on March 31, 1698, his arrival having been preceded by a letter from the proprietors to Hamilton and the provincial council announcing that Basse was coming to America with royal approval and that Perth Amboy was a free port at last. Basse met with Hamilton and the council early in April, and when Hamilton discovered that Basse did not have the requisite royal approbation he attempted to dissuade him from acting as governor. Basse brushed aside Hamilton's warnings and Hamilton left the issue up to his council to decide. The councilors deliberated for two days and on April 7 four of them—Andrew Bowne, Samuel Dennis, John Bishop, and James Dundas—met and agreed to accept Basse as governor. Morris did not attend this meeting, and from his absence it is legitimate to infer that he had grave reservations about Basse's authority to act as governor of East Jersey.[9]

Morris' reservations about Basse soon turned into open defiance. After his acceptance by the East Jersey Council, Basse went to West Jersey to proclaim his authority. There he encountered vigorous opposition from the Quaker-dominated assembly, which refused to recognize him as governor because of his lack of royal approval and whose leaders subsequently urged the people of West Jersey to discountenance the holding of courts under his authority. Shaken by these events, Basse returned to East Jersey determined to prevent the outbreak of similar acts of defiance there. Accordingly he reorganized the East Jersey Council and Court of Common Right on May 7 and 9, eliminating Morris from both bodies. Basse probably relieved Morris of these offices because of Morris' failure to support his assumption of the governorship the month before. If so, Basse little reckoned on the response of the fiery spirit he had thus offended. For the ambitious Morris, dismissal from office was insulting enough, but to be excluded by a governor whose own authority was so questionable and whose social status was so inferior to his own—"A Brewers clerke . . . Infamous to ye Last degree" was one of Morris' milder characterizations of Basse—was intolerable. From the moment Basse deprived him of his offices, Morris became the governor's implacable enemy and resolved to bring his administration in East Jersey to an end.[10]

Morris wasted no time. Two days after his dismissal Basse and the new justices gathered together to open a session of the Court of Common Right in Perth Amboy. Before they could proceed to business Morris, his sword dangling at his side, dramatically strode into the courtroom and demanded to know "by what Authoritie they kept Court." By the authority of the king, Basse replied. Morris vigorously denied this, clearly implying that the governor's lack of royal approbation left him with no authority to hold a new court, much less to reconstitute the membership of the old one. Basse, somewhat taken aback by Morris' "Saucy Language," sarcastically inquired if anyone else shared his skepticism about the legitimacy of the court's authority. "One and all," Morris defiantly replied. Unwilling to tolerate further insubordination from Morris, the governor ordered the constables in the courtroom to arrest him. No sooner did Basse issue this command than a number of spectators echoed Morris' defiant cry: "One and all! One and all! One and all!" As the constables advanced toward him, Morris grasped hold of his sword and voiced his defiance, "saying I wish I could see the man that dare meddle with me." Bloodshed was averted only by the timely intervention of an obscure onlooker who grabbed Morris and prevented him from drawing his sword. Morris was then arrested, fined £50 for denying the court's authority, and ordered to be held in custody until he paid his fine.[11] Nevertheless, he had set in motion a pattern of protest against proprietary authority in East Jersey that lasted until the provincial government was royalized four years later.

After his release Morris broadened his opposition to Basse into a systematic attack on the entire proprietary regime in East Jersey. Now that his once promising political career had been cut short by Basse, Morris, who to all appearances had served the proprietors faithfully for the past six years, became convinced that proprietary government must give way to royal government. Therefore he decided to encourage the movement for the annexation of East Jersey to New York which was being spearheaded by the Nicolls patentees of Elizabethtown. Since Morris also owned a landed estate in New York, and since his father-in-law, James Graham, was still on good terms with the Earl of Bellomont, the governor of that province, he may well have concluded that the path to preferment and power would be easier to follow in royal New York than in proprietary East Jersey.

Morris unleashed his attack on the proprietors in the first of his so-called "Red-hott" letters, written to the people of Elizabethtown on July 13, 1698. In this letter Morris denied the legitimacy of proprietary political authority, accused the proprietors of maladministration, and urged the royalization of East Jersey. With unerring accuracy, Morris pointed out the fundamental weakness of the proprietary regime: the illegitimacy of proprietary government. The proprietors, whom Morris now described as "base inconsiderable Persons," had no right to govern East Jersey because they had never received a valid delegation of sovereign authority from the king. The rights of government, he pointed out, were "only Granted to the Duke and cou'd not be Granted by him to them, especially it cou'd not be purchased by them as a Property: for if it cou'd be Purchased by 24, they might divide & subdivide and so we shall have 24 or 2400 parts, for they pretend to have purchased both, and they claim these parts as their property as well as the Governmt." Besides, Morris argued, in an effort to ridicule the proprietors' pretentions, "if the King (of whom they pretend to have Purchased) can sell any part of his Governmt. he can sell the whole, to a Subject or to foreigner (for I know no Law that restrains the one & tolerates the other) and so may sell the Kingdom of England to the King of France to morrow: and it seems to me a Contradiction to have the Property of the Governmt. and at the same time be a Subject."

Even if the proprietors had a valid right to govern East Jersey, Morris continued, there were enough abuses in the proprietary system to justify an end to proprietary rule. Proprietary-appointed judges could not administer justice impartially in cases involving disputes between the proprietors and the people, and it was absurd to expect other proprietary-appointed officials to enforce the verdicts of local juries against the proprietors. Uncultivated proprietary lands were not subject to the payment of taxes, thus heightening the burden of taxation borne by local freeholders, and quitrents constituted an unjust tax which drained needed money out of the province. Nor was this all. Some of the proprietors were Quakers whose pacifism threatened to leave the colony "naked and defenceless, a Prey to any bold Intruder," and many proprietary policies and pronouncements were contradictory. The proprietors had promised not to re-survey lands held for seven years or more, yet such lands were constantly being subjected to this process. And, Morris wondered, if Parliament had excluded Scots from offices of trust in the colonies, why had the proprietors removed Governor Hamilton but retained Secretary Thomas Gordon and Surveyor General George Willocks, who were also Scots? In fact, Morris asserted, sacrificing objectivity to rhetorical effect, the record of proprietary government in East Jersey was one of unrelieved gloom. "I wou'd be glad to hear any one of their Admirers instance but any one good thing the Proprietors have done for the Countery, show where they have performed any of the many promises they have made in their Concessions, and by their Governours. What trust, what faith is there in them? what truth in their letters? where is their Integrity? Justice, honesty and fair dealing with the Countery? Instance you that [can], for I cannot."

Since the proprietors had no legal right to govern, and since their administration was riddled by so many abuses, Morris concluded that royal government was East Jersey's only hope. The proprietors had frequently argued that their government would be less burdensome to the people of East Jersey than the king's, but Morris dismissed this claim with scorn. If the people of East Jersey were to buy out the proprietors' quit-rent claims or refuse to provide their governor with a revenue, Morris maintained, the proprietors would quickly drop their objections to royal government, "for God knows they care not one straw whether the King or the Devil has the Govermt. if they have the money in it." Therefore he applauded Elizabethtowners for recognizing the desirability of East Jersey's annexation to New York, offered to help them in any way he could, and exhorted them to remember: "We to our Selves are gods, they thrive who dare / And fortune is a foe to Sloathfull Prayer."[12]

Morris' flirtation with the antiproprietary party in East Jersey proved to be short lived. There is no evidence that Elizabethtown ever responded to his offer of assistance, and only three years after writing this "Red-hott" letter he journeyed to England to join with the proprietors in defending before the Board of Trade some of the very proprietary rights he had so sharply denounced in that document. The origins of this dramatic change in Morris' attitude, which led some of his later political adversaries to charge that during this period "Morris's Inconsistencies . . . made him Almanzor like change Parties," must be sought in an unexpected reversal of alliances occasioned by a recurrence of the conflict between East Jersey and New York over the status of Perth Amboy.[13] Despite the fierce opposition he encountered in both parts of New Jersey, Basse consistently defended Perth Amboy's right to serve as a free port. This inevitably involved him in a dispute with the Earl of Bellomont, who insisted, in obedience to instructions from the Board of Trade, that ships bound for or leaving from Perth Amboy had to pay customs at New York. Eventually Basse decided that this controversy could only be resolved by an English court, and so in November 1698 he maneuvered Bellomont into seizing at Perth Amboy and bringing to New York the *Hester,* a sloop jointly owned by Basse and his brother-in-law John Lofting, whose cargo of barrel staves was valued by one source at £70 sterling. Bellomont offered to return the *Hester* as soon as New York customs were paid and, when Basse refused to pay them, was chagrined to realize that the New Jersey governor planned "to try in Westminster Hall whether Perth Amboy be a port or no, and to sue me for damages for bringing away the ship Hester." But to do this Basse needed money, and in order to obtain it he decided in December to call a meeting of the East Jersey Assembly, unaware of Bellomont's boast that since the people of East Jersey "do not own Basse's authority, and for fear they should call it more publickly in question, he dares not call an Assembly."[14]

Bellomont's prediction that holding an assembly would create new sources of difficulty for the much troubled Basse turned out to be correct. Morris ran for a seat in the assembly from Monmouth County, where Tinton Manor was located. His opponents castigated him as a "Pentioner" of New York and denounced his advocacy of East Jersey's annexation to that province. They also accused him of knowing beforehand of Bellomont's plan to seize the *Hester* and charged that he wanted to introduce Anglican ministers into heavily Nonconformist East Jersey. As a result of these accusations, Morris lost his bid for an assembly seat by one vote. Morris himself attributed his defeat to the almost unanimous opposition of local Quakers and implied that they were strongly influenced by the allegation that he was bent on bringing Anglican ministers into the province, but it is also likely that his harsh criticism of the pacifism of Quaker proprietors in the "Red-hott" letter cost him the votes of many Friends.[15] In any case, Morris was temporarily relegated to a spectator's role when the assembly convened at Perth Amboy for its first meeting under Basse on February 21, 1699.

The ensuing three-week legislative session brought about a startling political realignment in East Jersey as Basse broke with the resident proprietors and Morris gravitated back to the proprietary fold. Basse soon realized that in order to obtain the funds he needed to bring the *Hester* case to trial in England he would have to accede to the wishes of the antiproprietary deputies who dominated the assembly. These deputies were eager to secure the passage of a bill to rectify a decision of the Court of Common Right that threatened to prevent many freeholders from legally conveying their land to their heirs, and they also favored two other bills that were designed to limit proprietary influence in the assembly and curtail the power of the Board of Proprietors. Although the resident proprietors wanted Basse to reject all three bills, the governor disregarded their wishes and gave his assent to them. In return, the assembly approved a bill granting Basse £675 — the largest appropriation in East Jersey history — to finance an appeal of the *Hester* case to England, with the money to be derived from a tax on uncultivated land. Ignoring an instruction from the proprietors in England that forebade the taxation of such land, Basse approved the £675 Act on March 13 and then promptly adjourned the assembly. Thus as the legislators prepared to return to their homes, East Jerseyites were treated to the curious spectacle of a proprietary governor who had thrown in his lot with the antiproprietary party in pursuance of a goal—free port status for Perth Amboy—that the proprietors had been trying to achieve for years.[16]

Even as Basse and the antiproprietary party were entering into an alliance of convenience, Morris and the resident proprietors were reaching an accommodation. In the midst of the legislative session George Willocks, the proprietary surveyor general who represented Perth Amboy and was the leading proprietary spokesman in the assembly, was expelled from the lower house because of his opposition to the antiproprietary measures that most of his colleagues in that body favored. Shortly afterward some of the resident proprietors approached Morris and asked him to run for the seat Willocks had been obliged to vacate. Morris yielded to their entreaties and thus ended the estrangement that had developed between them after his dismissal from office by Basse. The resulting alliance was not as incongruous as many contemporaries believed. With the antiproprietary party disposed to cooperate with Basse, Morris, whose opposition to the governor remained unflagging, was in danger of finding himself in the position of a leader without a party; and with Willocks expelled from the assembly, the proprietors, who still hoped to block the passage of antiproprietary legislation, found themselves a party in search of a leader in that body. Mutual convictions reinforced mutual need. Morris still denied that Basse was entitled to act as governor and continued to maintain that royal government was needed in East Jersey. The resident proprietors now shared Morris' opposition to Basse and had concluded as early as 1695 that under certain conditions royal government would be preferable to proprietary rule in East Jersey. As for the immediate task at hand, Morris and the proprietors agreed that it was essential to secure Morris' election to the assembly so he could mobilize opposition among the members to Basse's request for funds to finance an appeal to England. Morris considered this necessary because of his professed belief that Basse only intended to use this money to make up for the loss he had sustained from the seizure of the *Hester,* and the proprietors also hoped that if Morris convinced the deputies to deny these funds to Basse, the governor would retaliate by rejecting the antiproprietary bills the lower house favored.[17]

The crafty governor and his new allies gave Morris no chance to put this strategy into effect. When Morris and his supporters gathered in Perth Amboy for the special election that Basse had scheduled for March

11, the governor, pleading a defect in the document, suddenly withdrew his electoral writ about fifteen minutes before polling time. Morris went ahead with the poll despite Basse's action and was chosen to fill Willocks' vacant seat, but the assembly refused to admit him because he lacked the necessary writ. Basse issued another writ for a poll to be held two days later and once again Morris was elected. This time, however, the assembly refused to seat him because the deputies claimed that English law required him to be a resident of Perth Amboy. Morris sought to assure the assembly that residency requirements for deputies were unheard of in East Jersey and asserted that if they had existed in England few members of the revolution convention of 1689 would have been legally entitled to hold their seats. Unmoved by Morris' arguments, the deputies adhered to their decision to deny him his seat. In the meantime Basse adjourned the legislature before Morris could try a third time to gain admittance to the assembly.[18]

Having failed to sway the assembly, Morris embarked upon a systematic campaign to persuade the nonresident proprietors to dismiss Basse and to incite the people of East Jersey to nullify the £675 Act. Accordingly he prepared a letter to the English proprietors criticizing Basse on the grounds that "instead of Keeping up the honr of Governmt as was his duty he has upon all Occasions basely Prosstituted it." In support of this grave accusation he charged that Basse had failed to defend Perth Amboy's port privileges, unfairly alleging that the seizure of the *Hester* was the result of the governor's cowardice rather than the first step in a settled design to vindicate Perth Amboy's right to free port status. More to the point, Morris scored Basse for violating "Our Rights and Priviledges . . . in the highest degree" by arbitrarily interfering with Morris' election to the assembly. And in a final thrust that was well calculated to impress the proprietors, he took the governor to task for violating their ban on the taxation of unimproved land.[19]

Morris next turned his attention to the task of mobilizing popular opposition to Basse. Thus Morris and Surveyor General Willocks appeared before the town meetings of Newark and Elizabethtown on April 21, urging them to oppose the £675 Act and winning their support for Morris' letter to the proprietors. Four days later, Morris, Willocks, and the proprietary secretary, Thomas Gordon, persuaded the Perth Amboy town meeting to approve Morris' letter and exhorted it to refrain from paying the taxes imposed by the £675 Act, arguing that there was no guarantee Basse would actually use the money to appeal the *Hester* case in England. And in June the town of Freehold also signified its approval of Morris' letter.[20]

Morris and Willocks were so successful in stirring up popular opposition to the £675 Act that Basse haled them before the provincial council on May 10, several days before the assembly was due to reconvene in order to amend some of the more objectionable features of that law, and ordered them to post £300 as security for their good behavior pending their trial before the Court of Common Right in the fall on a charge of sedition. After some hesitation, both men refused to comply with Basse's order, and Morris in particular had the effrontery to deny that he had ever given the governor cause to doubt his good behavior. Consequently Basse had the two firebrands incarcerated in the Monmouth County jail at Woodbridge. However, their period of confinement was unexpectedly brief, because early in the morning of May 13, a mob from Elizabethtown armed with "Clubbs Staves and other weapons" broke into the jail, released them, and left the building in shambles. Morris and Willocks never fell into Basse's hands again and thus avoided having to stand trial for sedition.[21]

Morris and Willocks' escape set the stage for their last great acts of defiance against Basse's administration. Returning to Perth Amboy and finding the governor himself away in West Jersey, they directed the full force of their fury against the provincial council, which had assented to their arrest. To this body they dispatched a threatening note on the afternoon of May 16: "We are now able (God be thank'd) to treat with you any way you think fit; if you had valued either your own or the Welfare of ye Government, your procedures had been more calme; Your day is not yet out, & it is yet in your Power to follow the things that make for peace, & if you do not, at your door lye the Consequence, Our friends will not suffer us to be put upon." Morris and Willocks' own inclination toward harmony and peace was highly conjectural. At the very time the council was considering their note, they were on board a sloop in Perth Amboy harbor *"Firing Guns as by way of Defiance to the Government."*[22]

Morris followed up this comic opera display by addressing the second of his "Red-hott" letters to the council. In it he excoriated the council for its decision to accept Basse's authority despite the governor's lack of royal approval and claimed that as a result "most of your Acts of Governm't have been unlawfull." He ridiculed the council for defending what he perceived to be Basse's cowardice in the *Hester* affair, alleging that in this as in many other instances the governor had "basely prostituted the Honr: of Government. & made E: Jersey contemptible in the eyes of its neighbours." Morris also rebuked the council for approving a letter Basse had written to the English proprietors accusing Hamilton of arbitrary rule, an indication perhaps that he was looking forward to Hamilton's return as Basse's successor. But much as Morris despised Basse's supporters, he scorned Basse even more, and he concluded by denouncing the governor who had dismissed, imprisoned, and humiliated him as a Jacobite, a religious fanatic, a fornicator, and a cheat.[23]

Morris and Willocks' dramatic defiance of Basse's administration accomplished its objective. The deputies did not amend the £675 Act, and it is unlikely the act itself was ever enforced. They also refused to heed the council's request for assistance in taking precautionary measures against the vague threats made by Morris and Willocks, preferring instead to adjourn themselves on May 18. By the time the assembly ended, Basse had been thoroughly discredited in East Jersey. "All or the greatest part of the people do not think themselves oblidged to obey Our Governor," observed the royal collector in Perth Amboy, "he, as they say, not having the Kings Approbac'on."[24]

Morris' opposition to Basse was at least partially responsible for Andrew Hamilton's return as proprietary governor of East and West Jersey in December 1699. Hamilton, like Basse before him, lacked royal approval, but in this case there was an extenuating circumstance which convinced Morris to support his authority. In the preceding April the Board of Trade had decided to mount a legal challenge to the East Jersey proprietors' rights of government, and since then the English proprietors themselves, though they opposed this particular suit, had concluded that it would be in their best interests to negotiate a surrender of their governing rights to the crown in exchange for guarantees of their property rights. The Board of Trade could not recommend Hamilton for approval to the king without tacitly recognizing the very proprietary rights to govern it was planning to contest in court, and so instead it informally agreed to allow Hamilton to govern without royal approval until this issue was judicially determined in England. Morris, who was pleased at the prospect of royal government in East Jersey, was willing to accept Hamilton as governor on these terms and, while remaining out of office himself, to encourage his friends to support the governor too.[25]

Morris' willingness to accept Hamilton's authority as governor was not widely shared in East Jersey. The governor's lack of royal approval soon led him into many of the same difficulties his predecessor had experienced. In March 1700, angry mobs, familiar with Morris' example, disrupted county courts in Elizabethtown, Piscataway, and Middleton, disavowing their authority and physically abusing the judges. Then in the following month 240 residents of East Jersey sent a petition to the king that criticized the proprietors for sending Hamilton to America without royal approval and asked for his removal. And in May Hamilton was obliged to dissolve the assembly when the deputies, incited by Andrew Bowne and John Royce, who had been two of Basse's staunchest supporters in the council, began to raise embarrassing questions about his failure to obtain royal approbation.[26]

Beset by opposition from almost every side, Hamilton turned to Morris as the only person with the ruthless determination needed to enforce respect for gubernatorial authority in East Jersey and made him president of the provincial council in June. In accepting this office Morris vigorously denied that there was any parallel between his earlier opposition to Basse and the current opposition to Hamilton. In his view the former had been a legitimate protest by one of the natural leaders of society against a governor who had failed of his own accord to obtain the royal approval required to validate his authority, whereas the latter was an illegitimate protest led by men Morris deemed his social inferiors against a governor who had only been denied royal approval because of the imperial administration's legal challenge to the proprietors' rights of government. The "mob," in Morris' opinion, had no right to judge Hamilton's qualifications, and since the king had not yet thought fit to replace Hamilton with a royal governor, he maintained "it was the peoples duty to sit still and obey, there being no other End in Asserting an Authority than ye publique good."[27] Hamilton's opponents may be forgiven for rejecting this tortuous distinction, but in any case almost from the moment he assumed office Morris gave them fair warning of what to expect. "He had taken an Office uppon him & . . . he would goe through with itt," he told some neighbors in Shrewsbury, "& if any man Resisted him he would Spill his blood or he should Spill his, for he made no scruple of Conscience." Lest there be any doubters, he reiterated "that he would quell the opposite party . . . or he would imbrew the Province in blood."[28]

Morris was almost as good as his word. Acting with dispatch to reestablish Hamilton's authority in Monmouth County, one of the chief centers of resistance, Morris and Hamilton placed a trusted supporter in the office of county sheriff. The sheriff tried to arrest Richard Salter, an antiproprietary leader, but Salter was rescued by some neighbors who gave the hapless sheriff a good drubbing in the process. Salter and his cohorts, emboldened by this incident, then planned to break into the Middletown jail on July 19 and rescue a local freeholder who had been imprisoned for his opposition to Hamilton. Morris learned of this plan and resolved to forestall it, hoping to make an example of the instigators. Hence Morris and Hamilton arrived at Middletown on the 19th with a force of about 50 men and found themselves confronted by an angry crowd of more than 150 farmers armed with sticks. A bloody clash seemed inevitable until some local justices of the peace suddenly revealed that they had already released the prisoner the farmers had come to set free, whereupon both groups withdrew.[29]

This near tragedy spread shockwaves of alarm throughout East Jersey. Middletown sent representatives to confer with other towns in Essex and Middlesex counties and received assurances of support for continued opposition to "Morris & the rest that assert & would endeavour to set up Col. Hamiltons arbitrary & illegal power." Elizabethtown, the bulwark of opposition to the proprietors, issued a call for unified resistance to Morris and Hamilton in East Jersey, and Elizabethtown, Middletown, and Piscataway warned Morris and other supporters of the governor that unless they began "to Sit Still and be quiet till his Majesty's pleasure Concerning us be known," they would be forced to answer "for the mischiefs you have done and are doing the province." Morris tried to convince the people of Elizabethtown in a final "Red-hott" letter that there was no contradiction between his past opposition to Basse and his present support of Hamilton, but they rejected this contention and threatened to "tear [him] to pieces" if he ever set foot in their town again.[30] Two Basse partisans took ironic comfort in the thought "that throughoutt the province theare is six to one against owneing Col Hamilton Governor and almost all biterly against Morris, whome they looked uppon as the first man as Indeed he was that opposed Government."[31]

But Morris' worst humiliation was yet to come. On March 25, 1701, as Morris, Hamilton, and three other judges were holding court in Middletown to try a suspected pirate, they were interrupted by an armed mob of seventy or eighty men who denied their authority to hold court and seized their prisoner. Morris and his colleagues drew their swords and advanced on the mob in an effort to recapture the man, but instead they only succeeded in wounding two of the rescuers. This so enraged the rest of the mob that they seized the five officials and held them under guard for four days until it became apparent that the wounded men were going to recover.[32] This incident understandably made a profound impression on Morris. It convinced him as nothing else had that East Jersey was in the grip of political anarchy and that rule by "men of the best figure and Estates" was seriously threatened by those he considered the "Verry dreggs and rascallity of the people."[33] He now realized that the restoration of social order and the perpetuation of rule by the landed elite in East Jersey was more than ever dependent on decisions made in England, where the proprietors and the imperial administration were still far from agreement on terms for the royalization of the colony. Consequently he decided to take part in these negotiations in behalf of the resident proprietors, and so in May 1701, he set sail for England and headed into the unfamiliar world of Anglo-American politics.

⪜ 3 ⪛

"Their Champion Goliath"

Lewis Morris arrived in England early in July 1701, and took up lodgings at Newburgh House in the St. James Park section of London near Whitehall, the seat of the imperial administration. He brought with him a letter of recommendation from William Penn, with whom he had become acquainted during Penn's most recent sojourn in America, in which Penn extolled him as "a Gentleman of good Substance both in E Jersey and N York and of ye first Rank as well in Sense as Quality." Penn, who was a leading proprietor in East and West Jersey as well as Pennsylvania, could have given Morris access to some of the most prominent Whig and Tory leaders of the time and may have expected him to safeguard his interests in all three colonies against attacks by the Board of Trade, but there is no evidence that Morris ever utilized any of Penn's English political connections or transacted any business for him during his stay in England. Instead, Morris focused his attention on New Jersey affairs throughout his London mission and sought to bring about the surrender of proprietary government to the crown in such a way as to restore order in the colony, secure the political dominance of the landed aristocracy, and obtain the appointment of Andrew Hamilton as the province's first royal governor.[1]

Soon after his arrival in London Morris met with the East Jersey proprietors and learned that the situation in England was even more complex than the one in East Jersey. To begin with, the Board of Trade was anxious to royalize the governments of East and West Jersey but uncertain how to go about it. After threatening in 1699 to request an English court to determine the legality of proprietary government in East Jersey, the Board then began to negotiate with the East Jersey proprietors for the surrender of their governing rights to the crown. However, these negotiations were broken off in January 1700 as a result of the Board's refusal to accept free port status for Perth Amboy as a condition of surrender. Having failed to achieve the royalization of East Jersey through negotiations, the Board next embarked upon a campaign to convince Parliament to royalize the governments of all chartered and proprietary colonies in the interests of more effective colonial defense and more efficient enforcement of the Acts of Trade. In this endeavor the Board received the diligent assistance of Morris' old nemesis Jeremiah Basse, who had returned to England in 1700 determined to compel the East Jersey proprietors and the West Jersey Society to surrender their rights of government to the king, though this did not deter him from bringing the *Hester* case before the Court of King's Bench and winning a decision that established Perth Amboy's right to freedom from interference by New York. Acting as the spokesman for the East Jersey antiproprietary party and the West Jersey Anglicans, Basse vigorously supported the Board's proposal to resume colonial charters both as a witness before Parliament and as the author of a public letter to a member of it. Yet despite the testimony of Basse and other prerogative men in favor of this policy, the House of Lords failed to pass a Resumption Bill in June 1701 because of the opposition of English Quakers, who mistakenly regarded this measure as an Anglican thrust aimed at Protestant dissenters in America, and the Board's own failure to make an effective case for imposing stricter controls over the colonies. Although Morris sympathized with the Board's wish to establish royal government in New Jersey, he preferred to achieve this through direct negotiations between the Board and the proprietors because this method seemed more likely than an act of Parliament to produce a settlement that would be favorable to the interests of his party in East Jersey.[2]

Morris also discovered that in addition to tactical uncertainty on the part of the Board of Trade he would have to reckon with internal disunity among the East Jersey proprietors. In the previous year the Scottish proprietors in East Jersey had accused William Dockwra, the proprietary secretary and register in England, of a variety of corrupt practices and repudiated his authority. This, in turn, had precipitated the division of the nonresident proprietors into two opposing factions: the English East Jersey proprietors and the London East Jersey proprietors. The English proprietors, a minority group led by Dockwra and supported by Peter Sonmans, who himself laid claim to the largest single share of East Jersey proprieties — five and one-quarter of the original twenty-four, entered into a strange alliance with the antiproprietary party in East Jersey and sought to break the power of the Scottish proprietors by appealing to prejudice against Scots in the colony and in England. They also complicated the political situation in East Jersey even more by appointing Andrew Bowne, an erstwhile supporter of Jeremiah Basse, as governor of the province in March 1701. The London proprietors, a majority group headed by Joseph Ormston, an English merchant whose marriage to Peter Sonmans' sister had led him to dispute Sonmans' claim to all five and one-quarter proprieties, apparently resented the autocratic control over the formulation of proprietary policies to which Dockwra had become accustomed and consequently supported the authority of Hamilton as governor and the interests of the Scottish proprietors. The English proprietors and the London proprietors both agreed on the necessity of surrendering their governing rights in exchange for protection of their property rights, but owing to Morris' ties with the Scottish proprietors and support for Hamilton, he was more disposed to align himself with the London proprietors than their rivals.[3]

Lastly, Morris' talks with the proprietors revealed that any negotiations with the imperial administration would now involve West Jersey as well as East Jersey. In March 1701, the West Jersey Society had formally decided that in view of the disorders then prevailing in West Jersey it would be in its best interests to relinquish its governing authority to the crown. But like the East Jersey proprietors, the West Jersey Society approached this task beset by internal dissensions. Shortly after Morris' arrival in England, Dr. Daniel Coxe conveyed to his son, Daniel, Jr., all the property in New Jersey he had sold to the Society almost a decade before, thus forcing the Society to defend its title to its American lands at the same time it was preparing to give up its political authority over them. In the ensuing dispute Morris sided with the Society against the younger Coxe because the Society shared Morris' goal of securing the appointment of Hamilton, its American business agent, as New Jersey's first royal governor.[4]

After meeting with the proprietors, Morris took advantage of the first opportunity that arose to reopen negotiations between them and the Board of Trade. On July 18 the Board received two petitions from a number of inhabitants of East and West Jersey criticizing Hamilton's administration and calling upon the king to take the government of New Jersey into his hands. The Board read these petitions and then summoned Morris, whom it knew of as "a gentleman lately come from those parts," to appear before it and comment on them. Morris met with the Board four days later and boldly assured it that the signers of the petitions were "generally men of the least consideration in those Provinces" and hence could not be trusted. He also revealed that he had been in contact with the East Jersey proprietors and stated that he was about to meet with the West Jersey Society in order to persuade both to surrender their claims to the rights of government. In this way Morris sought to create a role for himself as the indispensable mediator between the Board and the proprietors.[5]

Not content with a mere verbal repudiation of Hamilton's critics, Morris obtained copies of the two petitions and composed a detailed refutation of them which he submitted to the Board on August 5. In doing this he sought not only to vindicate Hamilton but also to impress the Board with the urgency of resuming discussions with the proprietors. Morris admitted that Hamilton was governing New Jersey without royal approval, but he argued that resistance to him for that reason was unwarranted because the Board itself had assured the governor he could serve in America without the king's approbation as long as proprietary political authority was under challenge in England. He then pointed out that many of the signers of one of the anti-Hamilton petitions had taken part in the disruption of the East Jersey judicial system after the governor's return to America in 1699 and asserted that such men deserved exemplary punishment for their behavior rather than a hearing for their complaints, especially the perpetrators of "yt Remarkable Ryot, or rather Rebellion" at Middletown in which Morris himself had recently been subjected to such ignominious treatment. In addition to tarring Hamilton's American opponents with the brush of sedition, Morris also tried to destroy their English agent's credibility with the imperial administration. Thus he skillfully stressed the incongruity between Basse's current pretensions as a prerogative man and his previous decision to govern New Jersey without royal approval and laid the blame for much of the colony's subsequent political instability on that fateful judgment. But in defending Hamilton, Morris had no wish to absolve the proprietors of their share of responsibility for the political crisis in New Jersey. With one faction of proprietors supporting Hamilton as governor of East Jersey and another backing Andrew Bowne, Morris sarcastically observed, "Att this rate my Lords, we may have New Governours, by every Ship from England." In fact, since "Government is prostituted in ye Hands of such people," proprietary rule was no longer tolerable and royalization was imperative to restore order in New Jersey. Yet until this had been achieved, Morris advised the Board, it was essential either to grant Hamilton interim royal approval or to commission a new governor "under ye broad Seale" — advice the Board ignored.[6]

Having thus disposed of Hamilton's opponents in America and their chief spokesman in England, Morris joined with the East and West Jersey proprietors in drawing up a set of conditions for yielding their rights of government to the crown which was embodied in a memorial submitted to the Lords Justices on August 12. In this the proprietors reaffirmed the legality of their political authority, but announced their willingness to give it up in return for "all reasonable Privileges, which are necessary to preserve their civil Rights and the Interests of the Planters." Since the proprietors' main concern was to obtain security for their property rights in New Jersey, they asked for confirmation of their rights to the soil and the collection of quitrents, the sole right to purchase land from the Indians, and the right to appoint special officials to record and survey their land grants. The East Jersey proprietors in particular were probably responsible for requests to invalidate all land claims based only on Indian titles and to require all freeholders to possess proprietary patents for their lands. The proprietors also opposed the suggestions made by some English officials for annexing East Jersey to New York and West Jersey to Pennsylvania, and wanted instead to unite these provinces into a separate colony with appropriate safeguards for the interests of each. Thus they advocated the establishment of a general assembly and provincial supreme court to meet alternately at Burlington and Perth Amboy, the grant of equal representation to East and West Jersey in the provincial assembly and council, and the creation of a separate system of inferior courts for each division of the province. The proprietors were sensitive as well to the need to make New Jersey a more attractive place for future settlement. To this end they asked the Lords Justices to grant liberty of worship and the right to hold public office to all Protestants, to bestow free port status on Perth Amboy in East Jersey as well as Burlington and Cohansey in West Jersey, and to authorize the assembly to enable Quakers to substitute affirmations for oaths.

Up to this point the proprietary terms of surrender probably would have been much the same if Morris had never left America, but his influence is readily apparent in the provisions dealing with the qualifications for voters and assemblymen as well as the apportionment of seats in the assembly. Before Morris arrived in England the proprietors had largely ignored these issues, judging from the surrender terms they had previously offered to the crown and the Board of Trade.[7] But after he conferred with them they asked the Lords Justices to restrict membership in the assembly to freeholders owning at least 1,000 acres of land in New Jersey and to limit the franchise in assembly elections to freeholders possessing no less than 100 acres. These arrangements were obviously intended to secure the political dominance of the landed aristocracy and to protect the interests of the Scottish proprietors against their lower and middle class opponents. Few members of the antiproprietary party in East Jersey were able to lay claim to 1,000 acres, so that under this system they would almost be reduced to voting for proprietary party assembly candidates or none at all. Yet the proprietors sought to impose even further restrictions on popular participation in the New Jersey political system by requesting that all assemblymen be elected at large except for two each from Perth Amboy and Burlington. By electing most representatives at large rather than from specific districts it would be possible for the Scottish proprietors, given the cooperation of a willing sheriff, to make it difficult for their opponents to vote by having the poll conducted in a relatively inaccessible place, which is exactly what happened during the first assembly election held in New Jersey under royal government.[8] It is doubtful that the Quaker party in West Jersey, which could rely on popular support at the polls, would have approved of these proposals, but Morris was dealing with the West Jersey Society in London, and the Society's knowledge of the province it governed was imperfect at best.

The proprietors also asked for the right to nominate New Jersey's first royal governor, but it soon became apparent that they were deeply divided over their choice for this office. Two days after the presentation of their offer of conditional surrender, representatives of the West Jersey Society and the London East Jersey proprietors, following Morris' earlier example, petitioned the Lords Justices for interim royal approval of Hamilton as governor of New Jersey. William Dockwra and the London East Jersey proprietors, who still favored Andrew Bowne, were not among the signers of this petition. This was the signal for a spirited struggle over the nomination of the colony's first royal governor which crystallized the factions, English as well as American, that dominated early eighteenth-century New Jersey politics and created a pattern of alliances that lasted almost until the administration of Governor Robert Hunter a decade later. In this contest the London proprietors and the West Jersey Society joined forces to support Hamilton, who was also backed by the Scottish proprietors and the West Jersey Quakers. Opposed to them were the English proprietors, improbably allied with the antiproprietary party in East Jersey, and Jeremiah Basse, who also represented the East Jersey antiproprietary party as well as the West Jersey Anglicans. But Basse worked independently of Dockwra's faction and sought to thwart Hamilton's supporters by enlisting the aid of William Blathwayt, the most influential member of the Board of Trade at this time. Morris, who was acting as the English agent of the Scottish proprietors, aligned himself with the London proprietors and the West Jersey Society, and his subsequent efforts in behalf of all three groups earned him the title of "their Champion Golia[t]h."[9]

Morris quickly emerged as a leading spokesman for Hamilton's appointment and the proprietors' conditional surrender. On August 27 Morris and Sir Thomas Lane of the West Jersey Society appeared before the Board of Trade, to which the Lords Justices had referred the terms of surrender proposed by the proprietors, and were subjected to some searching questions about some of the proprietary requests. The Board expressed reservations about uniting East and West Jersey into one colony and voiced concern that granting three free ports to New Jersey might have adverse economic effects on New York and Pennsylvania. Board members also wanted an explanation of the proprietary requests for high property qualifications for assemblymen, equal representation in the council for East and West Jersey, and the right to nominate the first governor under crown rule. Morris and Lane's answers to these inquiries are not known, but apparently they were unpersuasive because one week later Morris appeared before the Board in company with William Dockwra of the English proprietors, Joseph Ormston of the London proprietors, and Edward Richier, the West Jersey Society treasurer. They then tried to convince the Board that the terms they sought were reasonable, being intended "only to secure their right in those things, which are a matter of property, and that they are unanimous in their desire to surrender the Government to his Majesty and submit the circumstances thereof to H.M. pleasure." Dockwra shattered this pleasing show of proprietary unity by criticizing the proposal to continue Hamilton as governor until the surrender had been consummated and asked instead for interim royal approval of Bowne. This led to a heated exchange with Morris and his proprietary allies that ended with an agreement by both sides to submit separate lists of nominees for governor and councilors for the Board's consideration.[10]

But even before the proprietors revealed their lack of unity over Hamilton, Jeremiah Basse had taken steps to prevent the Scot's continuance in office after the surrender of proprietary government. Basse established contact with Lord Cornbury, the Tory nobleman who recently had been appointed governor of New York through the influence of William Blathwayt and the Earl of Nottingham, and persuaded him to take a critical view of proprietary rule in New Jersey. He then turned to Blathwayt and offered him some compelling reasons for combining the governorships of New Jersey and New York in one official. Basse urged this extraordinarily influential imperial bureaucrat "to procure such a man to be [New Jersey's] Governor as may, by being wholly disengaged from any of the parties, be most likely to distribute equal justice to them" and suggested Cornbury as the ideal choice for this office. The noble lord's appointment, Basse cleverly argued, would not only restore tranquillity in New Jersey and safeguard the interests of New York but would also serve the larger purposes of the imperial administration "by Preventing the frequent desertions of Souldiers, from the companies, & Mariners from his Majesty's Ships of Warr [in New York] & Would Obstruct the defrauding of his Majesty of his Customes by Landing goods in East Jersie & be no mean Cheque on the Illegal trade of Pensilvania." These arguments were well calculated to impress Blathwayt, who was personally well disposed toward Cornbury and always ready to exalt the interests of strategically vital New York over those of her less important neighbors, but unfortunately Basse chose an unpropitious moment to advance them. The Tory failure to react more vigorously to the threat posed to England by the accession of a Bourbon to the Spanish throne lessened Nottingham's influence with the king and made it impolitic for Blathwayt to solicit another colonial appointment for Cornbury at this time. Nevertheless, if the seeds sown by Basse fell on rocky ground in the final months of William's reign, they were destined to flourish in more fertile soil in the early months of Anne's.[11]

Unaware of Basse's overtures to Blathwayt and Cornbury, Morris continued his efforts to win the Board of Trade's approval for conditional surrender and Hamilton's appointment. Thus on September 13 he submitted a memorial to the Board in justification of the proprietary surrender terms Board members had expressed reservations about the month before. Morris argued that the creation of a separate colony of New Jersey was vital to the interests of the proprietors and the inhabitants alike because otherwise the incorporation of East and West Jersey into New York and Pennsylvania would give the proprietors insufficient time to "Adjust their matters in them, and fix their titles, both to their Own land, and to the Persons they have made grants to." Hamilton's appointment as New Jersey's first royal governor would also be to the proprietors' advantage, Morris contended, because his knowledge of proprietary business affairs was unrivalled and if "ye People thinke [the proprietors] have Interest Enough, to recommend a Governour . . . it will make them cautious, of Invading their Proprieties." Then, after insinuating that free ports in New Jersey would not be economically detrimental to other colonies and maintaining that equal representation on the provincial council was necessary to prevent the domination of one section of the colony by the other, Morris vigorously defended the heart of his plan for preserving rule by the landed aristocracy. Restricting membership in the assembly to freeholders with at least 1,000 acres, he asserted, was a qualification "only modally different, from ye House of Commons in England," and besides the Board had to consider that "The Proprietors and Several Persons in that country, have large tracts of Land, and if every body were admitted (though of Never so little worth) to be Lawmakers, those Persons of best Estate in ye Countrie, and ye Proprs Interests, would be at ye disposall of ye tag, rag, and Rascallity." Morris reiterated that the proprietors' main concern was to obtain security for their property in New Jersey, but warned that unless the Board satisfied them on this score they would break off negotiations and take their case either to Parliament or the Court of King's Bench. In view of the Board's failure to obtain parliamentary approval of the Resumption Bill and the court's decision in favor of the proprietors in the *Hester* case, this was not a threat Board members could afford to take lightly.[12]

At the same time Morris gave the Board a petition in favor of Hamilton's appointment as governor and a list of nominees for the provincial council. This petition, which Morris drafted and which was signed by him in behalf of the Scottish proprietors, by Joseph Ormston in behalf of the London proprietors, and by five members of the West Jersey Society, stoutly maintained that the proposed appointment of Hamilton enjoyed overwhelming support among proprietors in England and America and was opposed "by none but Mr. Dockwra, and a small number of the meaner sort, who Sides wth. one Bowne." The list of candidates for the council, which also reflected the views of the by now firm alliance among the Scottish proprietors, the London proprietors, and the West Jersey Society, contained seventeen nominees consisting essentially of Hamilton supporters like Morris and resident proprietors like John Johnston for East Jersey, as well as local Quakers like Samuel Jennings and Anglican employees of the Society like Daniel Leeds for West Jersey. In order to satisfy itself about the characters of these men, the Board was advised to consult with, among others, Sir Edmund Andros, a former governor of New York, Joseph Dudley, a native Bay colonist who was soon to become governor of his home province, George Keith, Morris' old tutor who was about to begin a new career in America as an Anglican missionary, and Adolph Philipse, a New York merchant who two decades later became Morris' most cunning political adversary in that province.[13]

While the Board of Trade pondered the merits of the proprietary surrender proposals, Morris found time to become a member of the Society for the Propagation of the Gospel in Foreign Parts. The SPG was a new Anglican missionary organization which had been chartered by the king the month before Morris' arrival in England. Its members included Thomas Tenison, the gentle archbishop of Canterbury, Henry Compton, the militant bishop of London, Thomas Bray, the indefatigable champion of Anglican expansion in America, and a whole host of lesser clerics, nobles, and merchants. The Society aimed to strengthen existing Anglican churches in the colonies and draw religious dissenters there into the Anglican fold. It also sought the conversion of American Indians, but it soon became apparent that its main goal was to win over dissenters, and in this sense it can be seen as part of the last great wave of centralization which surged through the empire before the middle of the eighteenth century. Morris, a devout Anglican at this time in his life, welcomed the founding of the SPG. He too believed that its main function should be to win back American dissenters to the established church, and in the Keithian Quakers of New Jersey and Pennsylvania, separated from the main body of Friends by doctrinal differences which inclined many toward the church of Hooker and Laud, he saw a bountiful crop for the Society's missionaries to harvest. Hence when the Society sent out inquiries about the state of religion in the colonies, Morris eagerly responded with a long memorial about New Jersey and Pennsylvania which so impressed Society members that on September 19 they chose him as their first American member.[14]

Morris painted an exceedingly bleak picture of religious life in New Jersey and Pennsylvania for the SPG. He pointed out that in East Jersey there was a multiplicity of Protestant groups, including Anabaptists, Baptists, Congregationalists, Dutch Calvinists, Lutherans, Presbyterians, and Quakers, but only about twelve Anglican communicants, and he noted that although the church was making some progress in West Jersey and Pennsylvania, the dominant religion in those provinces was still Quakerism. As a zealous Anglican Morris deplored this profusion of creeds, though he never denied the right of others to hold religious beliefs different from his own, and as a landed aristocrat he was prone to attribute the obstreperousness of Jersey farmers to their New England ancestry and Puritan faith. But if the present expansion of Anglicanism in New Jersey and Pennsylvania was hindered by the existence of a variety of sects, its future prospects appeared even dimmer to Morris, for among the rising generation in both provinces he perceived an alarming rate of ignorance, debauchery, and religious indifference. In order to reverse the trend toward irreligion he discerned among younger Americans, and at the same time convert their generally dissenting parents, Morris urged the SPG to persuade the English government to appoint only Anglicans as colonial governors and magistrates, to convince Parliament to bestow on colonial Anglicans "some peculiar privileges above others," and to provide the American church with a steady flow of trained clergymen by requiring Anglican priests to preach for three years in the colonies before receiving a benefice in England. Most of Morris' proposals seemed more likely to strengthen the prejudices of dissenters against the Anglican church than to convince them of the truth of its teachings, and perhaps for this reason the SPG did not adopt them.[15]

Meanwhile the Board of Trade completed its report on the proposed royalization of New Jersey and forwarded it to the Lords Justices on October 2. After giving an unfavorable analysis of proprietary rule, the Board concluded that the Duke of York had had no authority to delegate governmental rights to the East and West Jersey proprietors and recommended the appointment of a royal governor for New Jersey with all due speed. In regard to whether the proprietors' surrender of their "pretended Right to Governmt" should be conditional or unconditional, the Board was ambiguous. On the one hand, it proposed to create in New Jersey "a regular Constitution of Government . . . in as full and ample manner as . . . any Plantation under Governours appointed by his Majesties immediate Commission," but on the other, it advised the Lords Justices to allow the proprietors to review the royal governor's draft commission and instructions. The Lords Justices approved this report and instructed the Board to prepare the necessary commission and instructions, whereupon Board members spent more than a month working on these documents before they were ready to be presented to the proprietors on November 14.[16]

Morris and his proprietary allies must have been pleased with the Board's handiwork because the draft instructions contained most of the significant concessions they had requested for surrendering the rights of government. Accordingly East and West Jersey were joined together as one colony and granted equal representation in the council and the assembly, with the latter to hold alternating sessions at Burlington and Perth Amboy. Domination of provincial politics by the landed aristocracy was apparently ensured by excluding from membership in the assembly freeholders with less than 1,000 acres of land, limiting the franchise in assembly elections to freeholders with 100 or more acres, and requiring the election at large of all assemblymen save those from Perth Amboy and Burlington. However, the assembly was empowered to alter these conditions if it saw fit to do so. Nor did the Board ignore the proprietors' wish for security of property. The new governor was instructed to approve assembly acts confirming proprietary rights to the soil and the collection of quitrents and to oppose any tax by that body on unimproved lands. He was also ordered to permit proprietary recorders and surveyors to go about their work freely, to come to the aid of proprietary quitrent collectors when necessary, and to allow only proprietors or their agents to buy land from the Indians. Finally, freedom of worship was granted to all Protestants, Quakers were allowed to hold public office and, subject to assembly approval, to use affirmations instead of oaths, and the colony's right to free ports was confirmed.[17]

So great was the similarity between these instructions and the terms requested by the proprietors in August that it is difficult to accept the Board of Trade's later contention that the surrender of proprietary government in New Jersey was unconditional.[18] In a narrow sense the Board's contention was correct — the actual instrument of surrender signed by the proprietors in April 1702 made no mention of conditions — but in a larger sense it was misleading, as the concessions to the proprietors embodied in the governor's instructions indicate. Certainly informed contemporaries believed the proprietors surrendered conditionally, and the Board itself admitted as much on one occasion. Morris assumed the surrender was conditional and referred almost as a matter of course to "the terms and conditions agreed upon at the surrender." William Penn sadly concluded "the surrender was knavishly contrived to betray the people," clearly implying his own belief in its conditional nature. And the Board conceded that its subsequent decision to select the members of the provincial council from lists of nominees prepared by the proprietors "was in some measure a condition upon which they have surrendered," a remark which applied with equal force to the concessions made in the gubernatorial instructions. Nor are the Board's motives for agreeing in effect to a conditional surrender far to seek. New Jersey was still in a state of political chaos and, with England and France hovering on the brink of war over the issue of the Spanish succession, it was necessary to restore order by ending proprietary government there as soon as possible. Board members may also have hoped that by offering concessions to the New Jersey proprietors which did not conflict with imperial interests or policies they could induce other chartered and proprietary colonies to seek similar settlements and thus realize the goal of royalizing colonial governments throughout the empire. The Board was especially eager to royalize one of the proprietary colonies after the failure of the first Resumption Bill, and in this respect Morris' threat to break off negotiations and appeal the proprietors' case to Parliament or an English court unless their principal surrender terms were met probably had a significant effect on the Board's final decision to accept these terms.[19]

Once the Board of Trade had granted the major conditions sought by Morris and the proprietors, attention shifted to the makeup of the provincial council and the appointment of the governor. The council was a crucial branch of colonial government because of the advice it could give the governor and the power it had to amend bills passed by the assembly, and in recognition of its importance the proprietors temporarily composed their differences in order to secure the appointment of councilors who were mutually satisfactory to all of them. Thus on December 5 Thomas Lane and Paul Docminique of the West Jersey Society and William Dockwra and Peter Sonmans of the English proprietors gave the Board separate but identical lists of nominees for councilors from East Jersey, consisting of three Hamilton supporters — Morris, Samuel Leonard, and William Sandford — two Hamilton opponents — Andrew Bowne and Samuel Walker—and one neutral—William Pinhorne. Scottish proprietors were conspicuously absent from both lists, which was undoubtedly the price exacted by Dockwra's faction for supporting the remaining nominees. The list submitted by Lane and Docminique, whose organization owned land in both parts of New Jersey, also contained the names of six proposed councilors from West Jersey, comprising the same mixture of local Quakers—Samuel Jennings, George Deacon, and Francis Davenport—and Anglicans who had been in the Society's employ—Edward Hunloke, Daniel Leeds, and Thomas Revell—that had already been offered to the Board in September. All twelve men were subsequently approved by the Board for membership on the council, another striking example of the Board's willingness to accommodate the wishes of the proprietors.[20]

Although Morris continued to urge the Board of Trade to agree to Andrew Hamilton's appointment as governor after the Board had approved the proprietor's conditions for surrender and their nominees for the council, his efforts proved unavailing in the face of continued proprietary disunity over the Scot's candidacy and the determination of William Blathwayt to obtain this office for Lord Cornbury. Blathwayt, who had taken no part in the Board's negotiations with the proprietors since Morris' arrival in England, reentered them at the end of 1701 as the Board was preparing to advise King William about the surrender of proprietary rights of government in New Jersey. Disregarding Morris' arguments in Hamilton's behalf, the Board counseled the king to accept the proposed surrender of the proprietor's political authority and to appoint a governor unconcerned in the factional strife in New Jersey, justifying the latter recommendation with a reference to the failure of the proprietors to agree among themselves on a candidate for this office. Although this was the main reason for Hamilton's rejection, Blathwayt's wish to replace him with Cornbury was probably also a factor.[21]

Apparently unaware of the Board's representation to the king, or its subsequent approval by the Privy Council, Morris made a last desperate attempt to induce the imperial administration to support Hamilton. Meeting with Dockwra in February 1702, Morris mendaciously assured him that he and his proprietary allies were abandoning their backing of Hamilton's candidacy. Then, hoping that he had lulled Dockwra's suspicions, Morris quietly prepared a petition to the king in favor of Hamilton which was eventually signed by himself in behalf of the Scottish proprietors as well as by sixty-four members of the London proprietors and the West Jersey Society. Whether such a transparent subterfuge would have achieved its purpose even if everything had gone according to plan may well be doubted, but everything did not. Before the petition could be presented to the king, William III died on March 8, necessitating a redrafting of the document for submission to the queen instead, but then, when it was finally sent to Anne, "unhappily," as William Penn noted, it "was wrapt up in the surrender, so that it was not read, and Dockwray and Sonmans getting air of it by the next day, came with a counter one and annexed reasons, that stops the affair."[22]

After this anticlimax Morris decided that the time had come for him to return to America. He had played a key role in negotiating a settlement with the imperial administration that seemed destined to restore order in New Jersey and ensure the dominance of the landed elite. He had failed, it is true, to secure Andrew Hamilton's appointment as the province's first royal governor, but not for want of effort. Besides, he had been away from his devoted wife and family for almost a year and had expended £1,000 of his personal fortune during his stay in London, which was a heavy drain even on his considerable resources. Thus in behalf of the resident East Jersey proprietors he signed the formal surrender of proprietary government and accompanied the other proprietors when they presented it to Queen Anne on April 17.[23] Morris was always extremely proud of his role in bringing about the royalization of New Jersey and later boasted it "may with no great Improprietie of Speech be calld an Enlarging [the queen's] dominions." With New Jersey now officially a royal colony, Morris set sail for home at the end of April aboard a ship that also carried George Keith, who was returning to the new world as an Anglican missionary, and Joseph Dudley, a fellow member of the SPG who had recently been appointed governor of Massachusetts. The ensuing voyage was a pleasant one, and Keith was so delighted by the level of conversation at mealtime that he likened it to "a colledge for good discourse, both in matters theological and philosophical."[24]

While Morris' ship carried him across the Atlantic, the last phase of the surrender process was played out in England. After Morris' departure, the London proprietors and the West Jersey Society continued to press for Hamilton's appointment as governor in spite of opposition from the English proprietors. The imperial administration had no intention of making this appointment, but in an effort to conciliate the proprietors, William Blathwayt and the Earl of Nottingham, the dour High Church secretary of state whom Whigs had derisively nicknamed "Dismal," arranged to appoint Morris as temporary executive head of New Jersey "to look into the affairs of the Jerseys and to examine matters till a Governor be sent," thus finally removing Hamilton, who had been serving as acting governor since the surrender.[25]

When Morris' commission arrived in America, one close observer of Jersey affairs mistakenly concluded he had actually been made the regular governor of the colony, and Morris himself believed this was only the prelude to his appointment to that office as a reward for his role in royalizing New Jersey. Neither could have been more mistaken. The indefatigable Blathwayt was already at work paving the way for Lord Cornbury to become governor of New Jersey, writing the noble lord on May 8 that although the proprietors still wanted the governorship for Hamilton, "in my poor opinion that Governmt would be more properly in your Ldps hands." By combining the governorships of New York and New Jersey in one man Blathwayt doubtless hoped to protect New York against serious commercial competition from New Jersey, to guarantee that New Jersey would contribute to New York's defense in time of war, and to prevent the use of New Jersey as a haven for deserters from the four independent companies of English soldiers and the Royal Navy ships stationed in New York.[26] The resurgence of the Tory party after Queen Anne's accession made this an ideal time for accomplishing Blathwayt's purpose. With Morris' temporary appointment, the way was open for the Earl of Clarendon, Cornbury's father, and the Earl of Rochester, Cornbury's uncle, to use their influence with the queen, their niece, to obtain the governorship of New Jersey for the noble lord. Clarendon, the only Tory statesman of any consequence not to recognize the queen as his lawful sovereign, had far less power than Rochester, an influential High Church leader, but their combined solicitations were more than enough to win Anne's approval of Cornbury as governor of New Jersey in July 1702 despite her low regard for her cousin. As a result of this decision, New Jersey and New York were jointly administered for thirty-five years until Morris himself finally became the former's first separate royal governor in 1738.[27]

Not only was Morris never seriously considered to serve as governor of New Jersey at this time, but even his appointment to the provincial council was challenged. In August Dockwra sought to alter the membership of the council, which had already been agreed upon by the proprietors and the Board of Trade, in favor of the East Jersey antiproprietary party and the West Jersey Anglicans. He enlisted the support of the Earl of Nottingham in this effort and induced him to propose to the Board a radical change in the personnel of the council involving, among other things, Morris' dismissal from this body because of his leadership "of the Scotch & Quaker factions concerned sundry years in ye divisions, & incendiary Parties, that has brought those Provinces into such Confusion of Governmt., Injustice to ye Proprietors and aversion of ye Planters & Inhabitants." The West Jersey Society vigorously opposed the proposed changes and the Board, jealous of its right to nominate colonial councilors, rejected them as well because they were contrary to its compact with the proprietors, though it did agree to add Robert Quary, a royal official in charge of the vice-admiralty court in Philadelphia, as an *ex-officio* member of the council to assist his campaign against smugglers.[28]

Meanwhile Morris arrived safely in America about the middle of June 1702 and began to extend his influence throughout New Jersey. In accordance with the plan devised by Blathwayt and Nottingham, he assumed temporary control of the colony's administration until the proclamation of Cornbury's authority, which did not occur until August 1703. During his tenure Morris was distressed by conditions in New Jersey, which he described as "the receptacle of abundance of rogues, that Cannot be safe anywhere Elce. . . . being without Law and gospell having neither Judge or priest," and vindictive toward his political adversaries. If the opponents of Hamilton who had brought New Jersey to the brink of anarchy were left unpunished, Morris warned imperial administrators in a frank admission of his elitist views, their pernicious example would surely spread to other colonies, for "the common People never concidering the true natures and circumstances of things . . . blindly coppy, and generally after (and Outdo) the worst Originalls." Still smarting over the treatment he had received from the Middletown mob the year before, and convinced that a show of strength was necessary to win respect for the queen's newest government, Morris urged the Board of Trade to visit exemplary punishment on the rioters, bitterly observing that "to see men of the best figure and Estates in ye Province, daily insulted by crowds of the most necessitous Scoundrells, the scum and dreggs of mankind, is no small temptation to resentment." Fortunately for the "scum and dreggs," Morris' vengeful counsel was ignored in England.[29]

Morris' term of service as New Jersey's interim chief executive was an important period of his career in several other respects. His role in bringing about the colony's royalization on terms favorable to the interests of the Scottish proprietors enabled him to replace Hamilton as the political leader of this faction. Morris appeared before the East Jersey Board of Proprietors on December 1, 1702, and gave its members an account of "the terms and conditions agreed upon at the surrender." The proprietors were so grateful for the concessions he had helped to win from the imperial administration that they granted him a new patent that reduced the quitrent on his lands to the token payment of a pint of spring water a year, absolved him of the obligation to pay any quitrents for which he had fallen into arrears, and awarded him a large tract of new land in East Jersey. This was a welcome boon to Morris in view of the large sums of money he had spent in England.[30]

Morris acquired new ties with the West Jersey Society as well as confirming his old ones with the Scottish proprietors. In April 1703 death came to Andrew Hamilton, the Society's American agent, and in July of that year Morris was chosen by the Society to succeed him. As the Society's American business agent, Morris was responsible for selling its lands and collecting its quitrents. He held this office for thirty-three years, and although in time his lax business practices made him the despair of his employers, they were deterred from dismissing him sooner by an awareness of his great political power in New Jersey. Before Morris' business laxity became apparent, however, this appointment gave him access to important officials of the Society who had influence with the imperial administration such as Sir Thomas Lane, who served as mayor and alderman of London, Paul Docminique, a Whig member of Parliament who was appointed to the Board of Trade in 1714, and Edward Richier, a London merchant who frequently represented the Society before the Board. These English connections proved to be of prime importance in Morris' New Jersey political career because of their ability to induce the imperial administration to act in ways that furthered his goals in America. Morris' appointment as the Society's agent also brought him into close contact with West Jersey Quakers, whose cooperation on the West Jersey Council of Proprietors he needed for the orderly sale of the Society's land in that division, and enabled him to take a seat on the East Jersey Board of Proprietors to oversee the Society's property in that section of the colony. As a result, he became directly concerned in East as well as West Jersey affairs for the first time in his career.[31]

Morris also maintained cordial relations with the SPG and emerged at this time as the foremost patron of the Anglican church in New Jersey. He always welcomed George Keith into his Shrewsbury home and frequently accompanied Keith to Quaker meeting houses in New Jersey to lend support to that worthy's efforts to convert Friends to the Anglican faith. Keith was highly impressed by his former pupil's religious zeal and reported to the Bishop of London: "Colonel Morris is a very good friend to the Church and a promoter of it, and was very kind and assistant to us, and is very regular in his family, and his Lady is a very pious and good Woman. His family is a little Church; he useth the Communion Prayer in his family daily, and on Sundays his neighbours come to his house, as to a Church."[32] Morris also corresponded regularly with the SPG, endorsing the view that "if the Church can be settled in New England it pulls up Schisme in America by the roots, that being the fountain that supplyes with Infectious Streams the rest of America," and arguing that many souls in East Jersey could be won for the church if only the Venerable Society sent the province a regular missionary "above fourty, of Piety, of good Learning, well skilled in the various points of Controversy, and in Circumstances above Dependance."[33] Morris' concern for the cause of

Anglican expansion in America won him the regard of John Chamberlayne, the cosmopolitan secretary of the Venerable Society who was also one of Queen Anne's gentlemen of the Privy Council. Like the West Jersey Society, Chamberlayne proved to be a valuable English patron to Morris in times of political crisis in America.[34]

As leader of the Scottish proprietors, agent of the West Jersey Society, member of the SPG, and a royal councilor in New Jersey, Morris had traveled far since his entry into public life a decade before. He had risen from relative obscurity to assume a position of great influence in New Jersey and to become part of the wider Anglo-American world. Now it remained to be seen if he could preserve intact the settlement between the proprietors and the imperial administration that he had helped to forge during his London mission.

≤ 4 ≥

"Tricks upon Tricks"

HE ROYALIZATION OF NEW JERSEY ended an inefficient and unpopular form of proprietary government and restored a measure of order in the province. But the institution of crown government did not efface the underlying sources of political conflict which had strained the proprietary system to the breaking point, and in fact it introduced new elements of discord which combined with the older antagonisms to make the conduct of politics in early eighteenth-century New Jersey a phenomenon of fantastic complexity. Within the context of this increasingly more elaborate political system, Morris strove to secure the ascendancy of the proprietary interest by implementing the settlement between the proprietors and the imperial administration which he had helped to negotiate during his stay in England. Ultimately Morris failed to achieve the political dominance of New Jersey by a small group of landed aristocrats as envisioned in this settlement, but he did succeed in maintaining the proprietary party as a cohesive force in spite of several severe setbacks to its fortunes and in acquiring new political skills which were destined to serve him in good stead after 1709, when his involvement in New York political life began to take precedence over his participation in New Jersey affairs.

Morris' political world on the eve of royal government was very different from the one he had entered a decade before. In East Jersey Nicolls patentees continued to dispute with Scottish proprietors over land titles and quitrents, while in West Jersey Quakers remained alert lest Anglicans deprive them of the right to hold public office and subject them to the rigors of an efficient militia system. Yet with the advent of royal government these traditional antagonisms were no longer carried out in a vacuum, for the dimensions of political conflict were significantly enlarged by the creation of a common assembly for East and West Jersey. This led to the formation of a new, provincial-wide pattern of political alignments which had been foreshadowed during the recent struggle over the nomination of New Jersey's first royal governor. Morris and the Scottish proprietors, who needed a counterweight to offset the more numerous Nicolls patentees, aligned themselves with the West Jersey Quakers, who welcomed their support because of the hostility to Friends among the Puritan patentees and the high repute in which Morris was held by the Anglican SPG. At the same time, a similar process took place between the patentees and the West Jersey Anglicans, who both shared a strong aversion to Quakers and a keen desire for a more open political system than the one Morris had helped to arrange while in England.[1]

The creation of a genuinely provincial system of political alliances in New Jersey was complicated by the impact on the colony of the rivalries among the various groups of proprietors residing in England. William Dockwra and the English East Jersey proprietors kept up their paradoxical alliance with the Nicolls patentees in an effort to wrest control over the distribution of land and collection of quitrents in East Jersey from the Scottish proprietors, though the patentees wished to do no more than break the political power of the Scots. In turn, Joseph Ormston's London East Jersey proprietors and the West Jersey Society continued to back the authority of the Scottish proprietors to grant land and collect quitrents. Furthermore the West Jersey Society sought to safeguard its lands in the other division of the province against the claims of Daniel Coxe, Jr., by supporting Morris, its American business agent, and his Quaker allies, who controlled the West Jersey Council of Proprietors. In response Coxe, Jr., attempted to make good his claims by supporting the aspirations of West Jersey Anglicans. The interaction between these competing English proprietors and the existing local factions in New Jersey brought into being two broad transatlantic coalitions which for the sake of convenience can be designated as the proprietary and antiproprietary parties. The first consisted of the Scottish proprietors and the Quakers as well as the London proprietors and the West Jersey Society. The second included the Nicolls patentees and the West Jersey Anglicans in addition to the English proprietors and the Coxe interest. Whereas the proprietary party was generally in favor of maintaining the settlement Morris had helped to negotiate with the imperial administration, the antiproprietary party was opposed to the restrictive political system this arrangement entailed and dubious about the right to hold public office it conferred upon Quakers.[2]

Morris' political universe was further altered by the subtle interplay between English party politics and local factionalism. The surrender of proprietary government took place against the background of the onset of the War of the Spanish Succession and the renewal of party strife between Whigs and Tories. The proprietary and antiproprietary parties both tried to take advantage of the "rage of party" in England to influence the imperial administration in their favor. With Dockwra as its chief English spokesman, the antiproprietary party rapidly developed an affinity for the Tories, who were more sympathetic than the Whigs to complaints about Scots and Quakers. Unlike its rival, the proprietary party had ties with both English parties. Morris' appointment as the West Jersey Society's business agent gave him access to the Whigs through such Society leaders as Paul Docminique, who had served as a Whig M.P. for London in the 1690s, and his membership in the SPG put him into contact with Tories like John Chamberlayne. Moreover, West Jersey Quakers had great confidence in Robert Harley, the moderate Tory leader who was much more sympathetic to dissenters than his High Church colleagues. Thus although English party politics during Queen Anne's reign affected New Jersey, political alignments in that colony did not precisely reflect the Whig-Tory cleavage.

Within the framework of a political system grown more complex through the formation of new alliances among local factions, their interaction with competing groups of English proprietors, and the influence of English politics, Morris set out to maintain the political dominance of the landed aristocracy and protect the economic interests of the Scottish proprietors and the West Jersey Society by preserving the compact between the proprietors and the imperial administration. Since the terms of this agreement were embodied in the queen's instructions to the governor, it was the governor to whom Morris turned in the first instance to realize his aims.

Edward Hyde, Lord Cornbury, was the scion of one of England's most distinguished families. His grandfather, the first Earl of Clarendon, had accompanied Charles II into exile and founded the Tory party. His father, the second Earl of Clarendon, and his uncle, the Earl of Rochester, faithfully adhered to the first earl's High Tory creed. The second Clarendon's fidelity to the principles of divine right and nonresistance was so marked, in fact, that it forebade him to acknowledge either William and Mary or Anne as his lawful sovereigns. Rochester's conscience was not as tender on these points as his brother's, and his recognition first of William and Mary and then of Anne enabled him to retain his position as one of the leaders of the High Church Tories.

Politically, Cornbury followed in the footsteps of his uncle rather than his father. It was Cornbury, no doubt prompted by John Churchill, later Duke of Marlborough, who led the first important defection of English soldiers to William of Orange in 1688. Cornbury's hopes for preferment from William were initially dashed by his vote for a regency in the Convention Parliament, and during the 1690s he obtained no higher office than that of M.P. for Christchurch. At the same time he also temporarily lost the favor of his royal cousin, Princess Anne, because of his refusal to accompany her husband on the Irish campaign in 1690.

Anne never completely overcame her distaste for Cornbury, but this did not always work to his disadvantage. In 1701, while King William familiarized Anne and John Churchill, her trusted friend and confidential adviser, with the network of alliances he had constructed to deny European hegemony to Louis XIV, William Blathwayt and the Earl of Nottingham took advantage of the reconciliation between the Houses of Orange and Stuart to arrange Cornbury's appointment as governor of New York. Then after Anne's accession to the throne in the following year her uncles, Clarendon and Rochester, prevailed on her to make her cousin governor of New Jersey as well. Anne, who was reportedly reluctant to have Cornbury present at court, may have consented to this appointment to help ensure that his stay in America would be a long one.

Cornbury brought with him to America certain attitudes that threatened to make cooperation with Morris and the proprietary party difficult. Before leaving England he had formed an unfavorable opinion of the administration of the proprietors in New Jersey, and this probably inclined him to view the proprietary party with suspicion from the start. He was also deeply hostile to Quakers, a key element in the proprietary coalition, believing that they constituted a serious obstacle to effective colonial defense. On the other hand the social and political prestige attached to the name of Hyde did not prevent Cornbury from falling into debt during William's reign, and there can be little doubt that his willingness to serve the crown in America was motivated primarily by a wish to profit from his office. Eager to enrich himself, Cornbury might be susceptible to the influence of the wealthier proprietary party. Averse to Quakers, he might be drawn into the orbit of the less well-to-do antiproprietary party. But it was an ill omen for Morris that only the latter faction could appeal to the noble lord's desire for self-aggrandizement and bias against Quakers simultaneously.[3]

Morris and the Scottish proprietors were the first local faction to approach Cornbury, and they did so in a way that was as cynical as it was direct. Acutely aware that the security of their property rights and the continuation of their political power depended upon the faithful execution of the governor's instructions from the queen, they decided to bind Cornbury to their side by offering him a bribe. This unseemly task was entrusted to John Johnston, a resident proprietor who was also a physician. Johnston met with Cornbury in New York during the summer of 1703 and told him that the proprietors "expected him to be their Governor and that they had obtain'd from the Queen some Terms on surrender of their Government which were to be given his Ldp. in his Instructions." He then added that he and his associates were willing to pay the governor £200 in return for his compliance with these instructions. Cornbury, who had not yet received his instructions for that office, piously replied that the queen had forbidden him to accept any "presents." Nevertheless he did agree to examine a copy of the instructions which Johnston had received from Morris and which he offered to leave with the governor before going back to New Jersey. Upon Johnston's return to New York shortly thereafter, Cornbury assured him that he would have no difficulty in carrying out the instructions. So pleased was Johnston by the governor's apparent willingness to cooperate with the proprietors that he neglected to give him the £200 "present." However, at the insistence of Morris and the Scottish proprietors, Johnston partially repaired this oversight by indirectly conveying £100 to Cornbury when he finally came to New Jersey to assume the government.[4]

Despite Cornbury's assurances to Johnston, Morris soon realized that it would be no easy matter to forge a working partnership between a High Tory governor and a local faction dominated by Scots and Quakers. Morris first met Cornbury when the governor came to Perth Amboy to proclaim his authority on August 10, 1703, and he accompanied him to Burlington for his first meeting with the provincial council three days later. At this meeting Morris became aware for the first time of some of the difficulties of his task. After Morris and all the other non-Quaker councilors present had taken the test and abjuration oaths from Cornbury, the governor proposed to administer them next to Samuel Jennings, Francis Davenport, and George Deacon, the only members of the Society of Friends on the council. But these three refused to swear the oaths and claimed the right of affirmation instead. This led Robert Quary, the *ex-officio* councilor who had welcomed Cornbury's appointment as the means of freeing New Jersey "from the tyranny of the Quakers, who are more inhuman than the Task Masters of Egypt," to inform the governor that while English law allowed Quakers to affirm when acting as witnesses in court, it did not exempt them from having to swear the oath of abjuration. Cornbury, who was as averse as Quary to allowing Quakers to hold public office, would have accepted this contention had it not been for Morris' prompt intervention. Realizing that Quary hoped to replace the three Quakers with West Jersey Anglicans, and fully aware of his own need to maintain an effective alliance between the Scottish proprietors and West Jersey Quakers, Morris promptly called Cornbury's attention to the fifty-third article of his instructions, which required him to admit Quakers into offices of trust regardless of their refusal to swear oaths. Since Morris' interpretation of this article was not open to doubt, the noble lord reluctantly overruled Quary and admitted the Quakers into the council.[5]

Morris' initial encounter with Cornbury made him determined to win control of the assembly and establish legal guarantees for certain proprietary rights before the governor turned against the proprietary party. Despite the high property qualifications for New Jersey voters and representatives, Morris left nothing to chance. After Cornbury had issued writs for the election of an assembly to meet in November 1703, Morris prevailed on him to appoint Thomas Gordon as high sheriff of Middlesex County in East Jersey. Once in office, Gordon, a Scottish proprietor who had replaced William Dockwra as proprietary register and secretary, did what was apparently expected of him: he rigged the election in favor of the proprietary party. Taking advantage of the fact that ten of East Jersey's twelve representatives were elected at large, Gordon attempted to discourage antiproprietary voters by deliberately holding the poll at an inconvenient location in Middlesex. In spite of this ruse more than 300 antiproprietary partisans appeared to vote on election day as opposed to about 40 proprietary supporters. Undisturbed by the odds against him, Gordon delayed the poll for as long as possible in an effort to thin the antiproprietary ranks. When this maneuver failed, he then "multiply'd Tricks, upon Tricks, till at last barefac'd he made ye returne contrary to the choice of the Country," with the result that at least half of the ten at-large assembly seats in East Jersey went to proprietary candidates in addition to the two seats for Perth Amboy. In the meantime the superb organization and skillful propaganda of the Quakers enabled them virtually to sweep the field in West Jersey without having to resort to the chicanery by which the Scottish proprietors had disgraced themselves. Thus the proprietary party dominated both the East and West Jersey delegations in the assembly which convened at Perth Amboy on November 8, but only at the cost of exacerbating the conflict between the Scottish proprietors and the Nicolls patentees.[6]

Morris' faction was so elated by its electoral victory that it became incautious and seemed to forget it still needed Cornbury's cooperation to achieve its goals. Despite the governor's call in his opening address for political harmony, financial support for the government, and confirmation of every proprietary right except that of government, the proprietary party chose to be vindictive to its opponents, generous to itself, and almost unmindful of the noble lord. On November 12 some East Jersey antiproprietary leaders submitted a petition to the lower house about the recent electoral irregularities. The representatives responded first by letting Thomas Gordon — of all people! — examine the petition and then by dismissing its complaints after only listening to the testimony of witnesses in favor of Gordon. Not content with this dubious vindication, Gordon retaliated against his critics by questioning the qualifications of Richard Hartshorne, an antiproprietary leader from Monmouth, whereupon the proprietary majority promptly excluded Hartshorne from his seat until he could prove he was duly entitled to hold it. This was a dangerous precedent to set, as the proprietary party later learned to its regret.

Once this challenge had been mastered, Morris turned to the task of creating additional safeguards for proprietary rights. In concert with George Willocks, his former partner in sedition against Governor Basse, he drew up a controversial act known as the "Long Bill" which won the assembly's approval on November 24. This measure invalidated the Elizabethtown and Monmouth grants of the Nicolls patentees, reasserted an old New Jersey claim to Staten Island, and denied the proprietors' obligation to pay almost £300 in quitrent arrears to the crown. It also confirmed proprietary land grants in East and West Jersey, called into question the legality of grants not sanctioned by the proprietors, and authorized the proprietors to distrain the goods of freeholders who refused to pay quitrents to them. Finally it terminated the practice whereby English and American proprietors held West Jersey lands in joint tenancy, leading some hostile observers to charge that this was deliberately designed to give the resident proprietors an unfair monopoly over the choicest tracts in that section. The assembly then provided further guarantees for proprietary rights by passing a bill that required anyone in New Jersey who wanted to purchase land from the Indians to obtain a special license from the proprietors and obliged everyone who had already made such a purchase to procure a proprietary patent for it.[7]

Despite Morris' efforts, Cornbury eventually approved the Indian Purchase Act but withheld his assent from the "Long Bill" because of the proprietary party's unwillingness to provide an ample revenue for the provincial government. Although the proprietary majority in the assembly proposed to raise £1,100 to repay some West Jersey creditors who had loaned money to Governor Hamilton during his last administration and £300 to reimburse representatives for their service during the present legislative session, at first it only offered Cornbury a one-year grant of £1,000 for the support of government. In Cornbury's view this sum was inadequate to his administration's needs, and he communicated his displeasure with it to Morris. Morris, who still hoped to win the governor's approval for the "Long Bill," tried to persuade his allies in the assembly to increase the proposed support grant to £1,500 a year, but to little avail. Proprietary assemblymen pointed out that £1,000 was £325 more than the largest previous appropriation in New Jersey history and insisted it was all the province could then afford, though they did agree to raise it for three years instead of one. In this way the proprietary party saved itself several hundred pounds and lost the favor of the governor whose cooperation was still essential to its continued success.[8]

The proprietary party's parsimony led Cornbury to explore the possibility of an alliance with its adversaries. With the governor's consent, Robert Quary held a series of talks just before the end of the assembly session with several antiproprietary leaders, who were infuriated by their cavalier treatment at the hands of the Scottish proprietors in the recent election and anxious to counter the threat to their land titles from Morris' "Long Bill." Quary assured these men that Cornbury would be willing to dissolve the existing assembly if they promised to be more considerate than the proprietary party of the government's financial needs. Richard Salter, the American agent of William Dockwra, and John Bowne, the brother of councilor Andrew Bowne, were the most receptive to Quary's overtures, and shortly after their meeting with him they began to lay plans for collecting contributions from antiproprietary freeholders to provide the governor with an inducement to hold new assembly elections. Meanwhile Morris and the Scottish proprietors, alarmed by Cornbury's sudden coolness toward them, dispatched the redoubtable Dr. Johnston to rekindle the governor's ardor for their cause with another £100 "present." But Cornbury was not to be won over so easily. Therefore he adjourned the assembly in December 1703 after assenting only to the Indian Purchase Act and hinting that the proprietors would never obtain the guarantees they sought for their rights unless they agreed to be more generous in providing funds for the government.[9]

Morris was angered by Cornbury's refusal to approve the "Long Bill." He regarded this as a breach of trust by the governor as well as a waste of £200 by the Scottish proprietors. After the adjournment of the assembly he stoutly maintained to all and sundry that the surrender of proprietary government in New Jersey had been conditional and that the concessions granted to the proprietors were embodied in Cornbury's instructions from the queen. Nowhere did these instructions require Cornbury to relinquish Staten Island to New Jersey or consent to what might be construed, however unfairly, as an attempt to defraud the West Jersey Society, but Morris preferred to ignore the more objectionable features of the "Long Bill" and dwell instead on the governor's alleged perfidy in disobeying his sovereign's commands. When Cornbury learned of Morris' grumbling, he confronted the cantankerous councilor and demanded to know the basis for his frequent assertions that the proprietary surrender to the crown had been conditional. This was something he had never been informed of by imperial authorities, Cornbury assured Morris, "to which mr. Morris replyd that it was true, that the Government was surrendered upon terms, and that if [the proprietors] could not have obtained those terms, they would not have surrendered at all." Asked to cite some of these terms, Morris pointed to the clauses in Cornbury's instructions dealing with the admission of Quakers to public office and the property qualifications for voters and assemblymen. Unimpressed, Cornbury sarcastically observed that Morris might just as well have cited the clause forbidding him to allow anyone except proprietors to purchase land from the Indians — only to be taken aback by Morris' impudent rejoinder that the queen need never have approved that clause because the land was already the proprietors' by virtue of the Duke of York's seventeenth-century grant. This confrontation ended with both men still adhering to their original positions and with the noble lord convinced that Morris "does give his tongue too great a liberty."

Morris' dispute with Cornbury about the nature of New Jersey's royalization was only one aspect of his steadily worsening relationship with the governor. They also clashed over the treatment of the rioters who had opposed Governor Hamilton in East Jersey after 1699. Morris, who still resented the indignities to which he had been subjected by some of these rioters, believed that they deserved to be punished for their actions and prevailed on Attorney General Alexander Griffith to file an indictment against them. But much to Morris' chagrin, these men never had to stand trial because Cornbury, wisely perceiving that such a trial would throw East Jersey into turmoil, ordered the indictment to be withdrawn.

Morris' relations with Cornbury were further exacerbated by profound differences in political philosophy. In several meetings with the governor Morris maintained that the people of New Jersey were entitled to all the rights of Englishmen and concluded that since they could not send representatives to Parliament their own assembly was inherently endowed with "the same Priviledges, Powers, and Authoritys as the House of Commons in England." Morris' views horrified Cornbury who denounced them as subversive of royal authority and rejoined that all colonial assemblies existed at the mere grace and pleasure of the crown and were "intended to be noe more than what every Corporation in England has, that is, to make Bylaws for the well gouverning of that Corporation." Morris informed Cornbury that he found these attitudes offensive, but in fact this exchange was really a reflection of a fundamental divergence of opinion between imperial officials and colonial Americans on the status of provincial assemblies which ultimately produced the American Revolution. It is one of the great ironies of Morris' career that his later attitude toward colonial assemblies closely resembled Cornbury's.[10]

While Morris and Cornbury drifted farther and farther apart, Richard Salter and John Bowne were busily soliciting contributions from disaffected freeholders in East Jersey to induce the governor to dissolve the proprietary-dominated assembly. Traveling from place to place in East Jersey, Salter and Bowne made the same appeal, though in different forms. "Now was the time," they urged some people, "to have their Liberties and Priviledges in chusing Assembly men and having Officers appointed to the good liking of the People and to be freed of their Quitrents if there were a sum of money raised to be privately disposed of to that end." "Now was the time," they exhorted others, "to have our agrievances Remedied, for my Lord . . . stood Inclin'd to the dissatisfied party, and that now was the time to prosecute the opportunity and make my Lord . . . a present of a piece of money of seven or eight hundred pounds and there was no question to be made but that it wou'd do that we should be confirm'd in our Rights and have such Officers both civil and Military as the People shou'd best like of." And to still others who objected that "it was very unjust and unreasonable that we shou'd buy with our money that which of Right belong'd to us," they argued "that it was customary in England so to do." Angered by the "Long Bill's" threat to their land titles, eager to eliminate current restrictions on voters and representatives, and determined to rid themselves of the "Scotch yoak," East Jersey freeholders contributed approximately £1,000 to Salter and Bowne's "blind tax," which was so designated because allegedly most of the contributors were unaware that their donations were going to be used to bribe Cornbury.[11]

Which side Cornbury chose to support now hinged on the actions taken by the assembly which reconvened at Burlington on September 1, 1704. However, at this critical juncture the proprietary party found itself deprived of Morris' services in the council, for on the eve of this legislative session his long simmering feud with Cornbury finally came to a head. As the governor was on his way to Burlington, he summoned Morris to meet with him in Perth Amboy to deal with an Indian accused of assaulting an English woman. Morris not only disregarded the governor's summons without offering him an explanation, but he also went to New York to handle some problems which had arisen on his Morrisania estate and remained there throughout the entire assembly session, again without offering any excuse. This cavalier behavior so annoyed Cornbury that he suspended Morris from the New Jersey Council at the end of September.[12]

In Morris' absence, Cornbury and the proprietary party reached a final parting of the ways. Cornbury opened the assembly by requesting passage of a generous Support Act, a reasonable Land Act, and an effective Militia Act. The proprietary-controlled assembly responded by offering to provide the provincial government with a three-year appropriation of £3,500, a sum the governor still considered inadequate, and by inadvertently offending the noble lord in several other ways as well. Thus proprietary representatives reintroduced the "Long Bill," which sought, among other things, to deprive New York of Staten Island; prepared a bill guaranteeing religious toleration to all Protestants, which seemed like an insulting lack of faith in Cornbury's willingness to obey the queen's instruction on this subject; and refused to pass a Militia Act, which only confirmed the governor's conviction that Quakers should not be allowed to hold public office. Consequently it was not surprising that when Salter and Bowne offered the proceeds from the "blind tax" to Cornbury through an intermediary, the governor accepted the money and dissolved the assembly on September 28, 1704. By this act he severed his ties with the proprietary party and destroyed Morris' best chance to have enacted into law some of the principal concessions he had persuaded the imperial administration to grant to the Jersey proprietors.[13]

Cornbury's decision to dissolve the assembly and to hold elections for a new one to meet six weeks afterward temporarily shook Morris out of his curious complacency. Confronted for the first time with the possibility that the assembly might be dominated by his political adversaries, he hastened to reclaim his council seat in order to defend the interests of the proprietary party. Meeting with Cornbury in New York, Morris denied he had deliberately absented himself from the recent legislative session out of disrespect for the governor and promised to attend to his conciliar duties more faithfully in the future. Cornbury thereupon accepted Morris' submission and restored him to the council.

Yet for a time it appeared that Morris had been unduly anxious about Cornbury's intentions. Despite Cornbury's open preference for their opponents, the Scottish proprietors and the West Jersey Quakers won a slim majority in the elections for the new assembly which first convened at Burlington on November 13, 1704. The proprietary party was able to count on the support of thirteen of the twenty-four representatives in this body, while the Nicolls patentees and Anglicans could rely on no more than eleven. Moreover, the selection as assembly speaker of Peter Fretwell, a long-time associate of the Quaker leader, Samuel Jennings, merely seemed to confirm the impression that Cornbury had blundered badly in turning against the proprietary party. Morris, for one, was so convinced of Cornbury's political impotence in New Jersey that he obtained permission from the governor to miss the opening of the session in order to complete his business at Morrisania, apparently assuming that no harm could come to the proprietary party as long as it dominated the assembly.[14]

If these were really Morris' calculations at this time, they were suddenly and unexpectedly upset. At this critical juncture Cornbury was saved from the necessity of dealing with a hostile assembly by what James Logan, a perceptive observer of New Jersey affairs, denounced as "the greatest breach of English privileges that has been heard of." Before the representatives were sworn in by the governor, Daniel Leeds and Thomas Revell, two West Jersey Anglican councilors mindful of the precedent set by Thomas Gordon the year before, claimed that three recently elected West Jersey Quakers — Thomas Gardiner, Thomas Lambert, and Joshua Wright — did not possess the 1,000 acres of land required for assembly membership. Cornbury promptly seized upon this opportunity to exclude the three Quakers from the assembly until they could prove they were duly qualified to serve in it, thereby transforming the antiproprietary party in a single stroke from a minority among twenty-four representatives to a majority among twenty-one. Even after the assembly itself declared the three Friends eligible for service in December, the noble lord professed to be skeptical of the evidence and refused for almost a year to admit them, prompting a Quaker leader in Pennsylvania to complain that "Cornbury carries it with a high hand in the Jerseys."[15]

In the meantime, the antiproprietary party, now in the ascendant, began to strike a series of near fatal blows against the settlement Morris had negotiated with the imperial administration. Led by John Bowne, Richard Hartshorne, and Richard Salter, the members of this faction first approved a two-year grant of £4,000 for the support of government and then decided to raise part of it by taxing unimproved land, which in the interests of the proprietors the queen had expressly exempted from taxation. Next they sought to protect themselves against any further efforts by Morris to call them to account for their rioting against Andrew Hamilton by passing a bill which in effect granted immunity to the former governor's opponents in East and West Jersey. Finally they tore up root and branch the institutional guarantees Morris had obtained for the purpose of perpetuating the political dominance of the landed aristocracy by enfranchising all freeholders, by giving access to membership in the assembly to this class, and by requiring the election of all assemblymen from specified districts. Only the various proprietary rights to the soil remained untouched.[16]

These abrupt changes in the fortunes of the proprietary party finally brought Morris back to New Jersey. Arriving in Burlington late in November, Morris found only one small cause for hope: Cornbury was disappointed by the failure of his new allies to offer greater financial support to the government and had not yet acted on any of the bills passed by the assembly. Morris tried to turn the governor's dissatisfaction to his own advantage by arguing in council that £2,000 a year was at least £500 less than what the government required, hoping that if Cornbury requested additional funding the assembly would refuse to grant it and the noble lord would retaliate by not approving any of the legislation passed by it. But this strategy was too transparent to succeed and actually reflected Morris' desperation at this time. An antiproprietary spokesman hastened to reassure Cornbury that £2,000 a year was all the province could afford to raise for the government, and the governor himself readily recalled Morris' earlier willingness to accept much lower support grants when they were offered by the proprietary party. Consequently Morris failed to dissuade Cornbury from assenting to the Support Act, which taxed unimproved land, the Immunity Act, which exempted Hamilton's opponents from prosecution, or the Election Act, which paved the way for a radical increase in popular participation in the provincial political process.[17]

Unable to protect the proprietary party against the fury of its opponents in the assembly, Morris was equally powerless to prevent an onslaught on West Jersey Quakers by their adversaries in the council. Shortly after Morris' return to Burlington, West Jersey Anglicans pushed a stringent militia bill through the council which, while exempting Friends from militia duty, subjected them to a series of fines for this "privilege" that were to be paid to the royal receiver general or provincial secretary and expended as the governor saw fit. Since Cornbury and Receiver General Peter Fauconnier, his personal and political confidant, were not models of probity, this measure was almost an open invitation to peculation. Yet most antiproprietary assemblymen were apparently still unaware of the darker side of the character of the governor with whom they were now aligned, and therefore they approved this legislative initiative by their conciliar allies.[18]

Morris' inability to stem the tide of antiproprietary legislation brought about a decisive break in his relations with Cornbury. Shortly before the assembly session ended on December 12, he abruptly left Burlington without requesting the governor's permission and made a brief trip to Philadelphia, though for what purpose is not known. Upon his return he deliberately stayed away from meetings of the council and, when asked why, tartly replied "he vallued not the Governor of a farthing." Cornbury quickly learned of this audacious remark and suspended Morris from the council for the second time in three months, indignantly explaining to his superiors in England that the recalcitrant councilor had "soe intirely given himself up to the Interests of the Proprietors, that he can see with no other eyes but theirs, and I can not say that they have always pursued the Interest of the Crowne."[19]

There was now no possibility that Cornbury would voluntarily observe the terms of the settlement between the Jersey proprietors and the imperial administration, but as yet Morris did not completely despair of preserving this compact. He still believed the proprietors had surrendered their rights of government to the crown conditionally and assumed in consequence that the imperial administration could be persuaded to order the governor to abide by the concessions it had made to the proprietors upon their surrender. Therefore in February 1705 he appealed to the West Jersey Society to use its influence with imperial officials to oblige Cornbury to carry out his instructions in accordance with the interests of the proprietors. If Cornbury was no longer willing to cooperate with the proprietary party freely, the only apparent alternative was to compel him to cooperate with it against his will.[20]

Morris' appeal to the West Jersey Society failed to achieve this ambitious goal. In response to Morris' entreaty, the Society submitted a memorial to the Board of Trade on April 17, 1705, which accused Cornbury of violating the compact between the proprietors and the imperial administration, called for the rejection of all the acts passed by the antiproprietary assembly, and asked for Morris' restoration to the council. In effect, the Society wanted the Board to force Cornbury to accept its own and Morris' interpretation of the royalization of New Jersey as well as all the corollaries to it. However, the Board waited seven months before replying to this memorial and when it did the results were dismaying to Morris and the Society. Although the Board informed the Society on November 14, 1705, that Morris would be restored to the council upon making due submission to Cornbury, it refrained from advising the queen to disallow the acts of the antiproprietary assembly and denied that the surrender of proprietary government in New Jersey had been conditional. In a narrow legal sense the Board was justified in describing the surrender of proprietary government as unconditional, but in view of the negotiations for the royalization of New Jersey Morris and the proprietors believed with equal justice that they had agreed to the crown's assumption of the colony's government in return for certain concessions and that these concessions had been embodied in Cornbury's instructions from the queen. In any case, the Board's insistence on the unconditional character of royalization destroyed the primary justification for the political course Morris had followed in New Jersey since the completion of his first London mission.[21]

While the West Jersey Society was unable at this time to assist Morris and the proprietary party in New Jersey, William Dockwra, Peter Sonmans, and Daniel Coxe, Jr., the leading antiproprietary party spokesmen in England, scored some notable successes for themselves and their political allies in America. To begin with, in April 1705, before a copy of the Election Act passed by the antiproprietary party had arrived in England, Dockwra, Sonmans, and Coxe prevailed on the Board to agree to an additional instruction to Cornbury which, in addition to stipulating that henceforth all New Jersey assemblymen had to be elected from specified towns or counties, enabled all those with 1,000 acres of land or £500 sterling in personal property to serve in the assembly and all those with 100 acres of land or £50 sterling in personal property to vote in provincial elections. This instruction effectively superseded the 1704 Election Act, and although it was more stringent than the latter in setting property qualifications for provincial voters and representatives, it too eliminated the highly restrictive political system Morris had helped to convince the imperial administration to create in the interests of the local landed aristocracy and the proprietors.[22] Encouraged by this success, Dockwra, whose English proprietors had already commissioned Sonmans to act as their agent and receiver in East Jersey, proceeded to induce the Board in the following month to recommend Sonmans to Cornbury for an appointment to the provincial council—an appointment the governor made after Samuel Jennings retired from that body in 1706. Finally Dockwra was instrumental in persuading the Board and the Privy Council in November 1705 to approve the appointment of three new councilors—Coxe, Jr., Roger Mompesson, and Richard Townley—whom Cornbury had nominated to fill the vacancies created by the deaths of Edward Hunloke, Samuel Leonard, and Samuel Walker. Since all three men were members of the Church of England who became firm supporters of Cornbury, their appointment tipped the balance of power on the provincial council in favor of the Anglican wing of the antiproprietary party. In fact the only setback Dockwra, Sonmans, and Coxe suffered during this period was their failure to convince the imperial administration to approve a proposal by Cornbury to exclude Quakers from public office in New Jersey, and this was due less to the opposition of the West Jersey Society than to the inexpedience of the measure itself.[23]

The failure of Morris' appeal to England was followed by a blow to the Scottish proprietors that finally convinced him of the futility of expecting cooperation from Cornbury on any terms. In August 1705 Peter Sonmans arrived in America with a commission from William Dockwra's English proprietors to serve as their agent and receiver general in East Jersey. This was a direct challenge to the Scottish proprietors, who for the past two decades had exercised exclusive control over the distribution of land and the collection of quitrents in East Jersey through their domination of the resident Board of Proprietors of which Morris himself was now a member. Cornbury, who was eager further to undermine Morris and the Scots, immediately recognized Sonmans' authority, ordered his subordinates to assist the newcomer in the performance of his duties, and obliged the Board to hand over its records to Jeremiah Basse, who had been appointed provincial secretary in 1704. As a result, the Board ceased to function for twenty years until it was reconstituted in 1725 with Morris as president, and the English proprietors assumed control over the disposal of land and the collection of quitrents in East Jersey.[24]

By the end of 1705 the compromise Morris had helped to work out between the Jersey proprietors and the imperial administration was largely in ruins, disregarded by Cornbury, disavowed in part by Dockwra's English proprietors, and disowned by the Board of Trade. The harmonious working relationship Morris had anticipated between the governor and the proprietary party had degenerated into mutual antagonism. The highly restrictive political system by which he had hoped to secure the ascendancy of the landed aristocracy had been replaced by a relatively more open one. Proprietary rights to the soil were still intact, but in East Jersey control over them had unexpectedly passed out of the hands of the Scottish proprietors and into those of the English proprietors. Quakers were victimized by a rigorous militia system, and Cornbury was bent on depriving them of their right to hold public office. The future of the proprietary party had seemed secure after Morris' return from England in 1702. Three years later its very existence appeared to be in jeopardy.

⪦ 5 ⪧

"To Obtain the Needful Certificats"

𝓗AVING TRIED AND FAILED to secure Lord Cornbury's support, Morris decided that his only recourse was to seek the governor's dismissal from office by the imperial administration. Despite the setbacks he and the proprietary party had recently received, Morris did not consider this to be an unrealistic goal. For he was convinced that in turning against the proprietary party Cornbury had sown the seeds of his own destruction. "As to my own character I know the gentleman [Cornbury] that gives it," Morris wrote after his second suspension from the provincial council, "He sails before the wind and tide, Tom Tinker's course, and needs not so much ballast as that I am forced to turn to windward. The common fate of such leeward bottoms is a lee shore where they lay their bones."[1]

Morris' forecast that Cornbury was sailing into serious difficulties was amply borne out by events. Even as the governor aligned himself with the antiproprietary party, his closest English patrons were losing power, thus leaving him vulnerable to opposition in New Jersey. Cornbury's father, the Earl of Clarendon, forfeited his chance to enjoy the favor of the queen by his refusal to acknowledge her as his rightful sovereign at the beginning of her reign. His uncle, the Earl of Rochester, whose High Church fervor had made his prospects for power seem so bright at Anne's accession, proved to be too much of a zealot for the moderate Harley-Godolphin-Marlborough ministry and was compelled to relinquish his position as lord lieutenant of Ireland in 1703. The Earl of Nottingham, whose patronage had been partially responsible for Cornbury's appointment as governor of New York, threatened in 1704 to resign as secretary of state for the southern department unless the queen dismissed the Whig members of her ministry and was greatly chagrined when Anne decided to accept his resignation instead of dismissing the Whigs. The once powerful William Blathwayt, who had been instrumental in securing both the governorships of New Jersey and New York for Cornbury, saw his own influence over colonial affairs wane as Marlborough's rose, until at length in 1707 he was dismissed from the Board of Trade. With the governor's English patrons out of power, Cornbury's position in America became correspondingly less secure. Early in 1706 Marlborough himself, who was still among the queen's most influential advisers, wanted to replace Cornbury with an English army officer named Richard Sutton, but he was apparently unable to take the matter up with Anne before his return to Europe for the spring campaign. Well might William Penn, writing from England on May 10, 1705, reassure James Logan, his business agent in Pennsylvania, that "Lord Cornbury, poor man, is so far from gaining points upon us [Quakers], that there is no argument left here to keep him there but the aversion they feel to have him home."[2]

How to overcome "the aversion they feel to have him home" and effect Cornbury's removal was the central problem confronting Morris between 1705 and 1708. In order to accomplish this it was desirable to offer an alternative to Cornbury as governor of New Jersey and essential to convince the imperial administration that he was incapable of governing the province effectively. The first condition was readily met. In November 1705 Morris and the Scottish proprietors persuaded one Major Douglas, an otherwise obscure army officer who was returning to England after a tour of duty with one of the four independent companies of English regulars stationed in New York, to solicit an appointment for himself as governor of New Jersey. But to facilitate Douglas' task and at the same time induce the home authorities to recall Cornbury, Morris and the proprietary party had to regain control of the provincial assembly so that they could send their complaints about the noble lord to England in the name of the freeholders of New Jersey. Accordingly Morris disdainfully refused to resume his place on the council as long as Cornbury remained in office and waited instead for an opportunity to win a seat in the assembly. For as a result of his defense against Cornbury of the rights and privileges of the assembly, Morris' second suspension from the council had been widely deplored in New Jersey, and he meant to take advantage of his newly won acclaim among the people to mobilize popular opposition to the governor in order to undermine his administration.[3]

Morris had to wait for almost a year and a half before he was able to enter the assembly. In protest against Cornbury's refusal in December 1704 to admit three Quaker representatives into this body, West Jersey Friends, who comprised all but one of the twelve representatives from that section, abstained from the legislative session scheduled to be held in May 1705, forcing the governor to postpone his meeting with the assembly until the following October. At that time Cornbury was obliged to admit the three Quakers, thereby restoring proprietary party control over the assembly by a slim margin. The members of this faction thereupon ignored the governor's request for defrayment of the expenses incurred by the government before the passage of the 1704 Support Act and instead proceeded to consider a bill designed to safeguard proprietary rights to the soil. This prompted Cornbury to adjourn the assembly, but when he returned to New Jersey to meet with it again in October of the following year, he found himself confronted by a massive boycott of representatives from both divisions of the colony which constrained him to order elections to be conducted for a new assembly early in 1707.

Cornbury's call for new elections came at a particularly propitious time for Morris and the proprietary party because the governor's popularity was sinking and the expiration of the Support Act passed in 1704 made him dependent on the forthcoming assembly for a new grant of revenue. As the abstention of representatives from East and West Jersey suggests, discontent with Cornbury was no longer confined to Scottish proprietors and Quakers. The Nicolls patentees of East Jersey and other small farmers throughout the province were also dissatisfied with him. The patentees had been deeply disillusioned by Cornbury's decision to support Peter Sonmans as proprietary agent and receiver general in East Jersey. It mattered not to them whether their land titles and refusal to pay quitrents were challenged by English or Scottish proprietors. They were equally averse to either group and had not contributed to the "blind tax" merely to replace one would-be set of overlords with another. Moreover, small farmers in general, patentees and otherwise, were adversely affected by the Support Act passed by the antiproprietary party and approved by Cornbury. Although this measure taxed the hitherto sacrosanct unimproved land of the proprietors, it also tended to aggravate the economic plight of New Jersey yeomen by levying a tax of £10 on every 100 acres of land and requiring its payment in silver. As the act went into effect when New Jersey's trade was unusually languid and her lack of specie acute, many farmers found it difficult to pay their taxes, so that, as Morris later observed, "the makers [of the act] who by laying of a tax on land thought it would fall easie upon their own party, who had but small tracts, found the success did by no means answer the expectations; for though it fell heaviest upon the men that had great tracts of land, yet they [were] better able to bear it, and their numbers were inconsiderable compared with the whole."[4]

Cornbury added to his unpopularity and strengthened the determination of Morris and the proprietary party to seek his recall by a series of imprudent displays of favor to his Anglican supporters. In April 1706 Cornbury granted a monopoly of the right to transport goods between Perth Amboy and Burlington to Hugh Huddy, a crony of Daniel Coxe, Jr. This led to an increase in carrying charges which farmers in particular could ill afford, thus accentuating their discontent with the governor. Two months later Cornbury refused to carry out an order from the queen granting control over the five and one-quarter East Jersey proprieties claimed by Peter Sonmans to Joseph Ormston, the leader of the London proprietors, and his wife Rachel, who was also Sonmans' sister. This enabled Sonmans to continue to sell proprietary lands and collect proprietary quitrents in East Jersey, greatly vexing Morris and the Scottish proprietors, who had expected to resume these functions themselves in consequence of the queen's order. Finally in November 1706 Cornbury sought to gratify the ambitions of Daniel Coxe, Jr., by ordering the West Jersey Council of Proprietors to desist from granting land to settlers in that part of New Jersey. The Council of Proprietors thereupon ceased to function for the remainder of Cornbury's administration, and Coxe made haste to dispose of some of the land he claimed from the West Jersey Society, thereby offending the Society's officers in England and providing Morris with an additional incentive for ridding New Jersey of the noble lord.[5]

By the end of 1706 Cornbury had alienated every important political faction in New Jersey with the exception of the West Jersey Anglicans. Yet just when he could ill afford to lose any more support, Cornbury further disgraced himself personally and impaired the prestige of his office by appearing in public dressed in women's clothing. Apparently Cornbury did not reveal his transvestism until after the death of his wife in August 1706, but the ultimate source of his abnormal behavior is less important than the fact that by succumbing to it when he did he further lowered his standing among the people of New Jersey.[6]

Morris and the proprietary party skillfully capitalized on popular discontent with Cornbury to win a resounding victory in the assembly elections held early in 1707. During this contest Morris and Samuel Jennings, the Quaker leader who had followed Morris' example and deliberately forsaken his seat on the provincial council to oppose the governor more effectively as a popularly elected representative, led the still firm alliance between the Scottish proprietors and the West Jersey Quakers. In each of their respective divisions of New Jersey, Morris and Jennings circulated printed pamphlets denouncing Cornbury's gubernatorial record and peculiar sartorial habits and warned the people that "all their libertys and propertys lay at stake." To ensure that voters did not go astray on election day the two men also handed out slates listing the names of preferred candidates and assured freeholders that "if they would choose of them, that then there should be no money raised for the support of Government nor any Militia Act past." These efforts to mobilize popular support paid off handsomely. Morris won election to the assembly from East Jersey, Jennings captured a seat in West Jersey, and the proprietary party as a whole won approximately three-fourths of the twenty-four assembly seats. With the proprietary party once again firmly in control of the assembly, Morris looked forward to using this body to further the efforts of Major Douglas to become Cornbury's successor in New Jersey, as Morris' friend and political ally John Johnston explained shortly before the assembly met to an East Jersey proprietor living in England:

> By this I have writ to Major Douglas. I'm very Sensible what he has undertaken will not be obtained without a great deal of Charge and pains, which in due time we shall all of us Hartily acknowledge. I send him Som new matter and to obtain the needful Certificats you may assure him no stone shall be left unturned. . . . I have not seen my friends since I recd Yours but have writt to them to prepare matters against the assembly . . . who I expect will answer what you desire if they be permitted to Sitt but if disolved we shall have the Same again.[7]

Almost as soon as Cornbury officially opened the new assembly on April 5, 1707, Morris and Jennings began to lay the groundwork for the noble lord's dismissal from office. Jennings was elected speaker of the assembly while Morris became in effect the floor manager in charge of spearheading the attack against the governor. So zestfully did Morris perform in this novel role that Cornbury subsequently charged he "caused all the resolutions of the House to be entred in the Journalls Nemine Contradicente when some Members were absent and others who were present dissented." Although Cornbury, acting in accordance with instructions from the Board of Trade, asked in his opening address for passage of a twenty-one year grant of revenue to the government, the assembly disregarded this request and instead formed itself into a committee of the whole on April 8, with Morris as chairman. The purpose of this committee was to investigate the grievances of the people of New Jersey against Cornbury in order to obtain the "needful Certificats" required to discredit him with his English superiors. Since this work could best be done in secret, Morris persuaded his colleagues in the lower house to ensure the confidentiality of their proceedings by replacing William Anderson, the assembly clerk appointed by the governor, with Thomas Farmer, an elected representative from West Jersey. Cornbury vigorously protested against the ouster of Anderson and admonished the assembly to pass laws instead of investigating grievances, but the determined representatives ignored this admonition and the hapless governor, acutely aware of his dependence on them for a new revenue, was obliged to relent.[8]

With Morris in the chair, the committee of the whole worked at its task for almost a month. Under his leadership it devoted no small part of its time to a relentless investigation of the so-called "blind tax." A number of East Jersey freeholders were taken into custody by the lower house's sergeant at arms and brought before Morris to testify about their knowledge of this matter. The assembly even ordered the high sheriff of Burlington to release a prisoner in his custody so that he could appear before Morris for this purpose. Morris himself attempted to compel John Bowne, an assemblyman from East Jersey who had been one of the collectors of the "blind tax," to give testimony, and when he refused, Morris had him expelled from the assembly. Despite Bowne's failure to cooperate, Morris managed to accumulate an impressive body of evidence from various contributors to the "blind tax" which tended to indicate that Cornbury had indeed been bribed to dissolve the proprietary-controlled assembly in 1704.[9]

By the time the committee completed its work on May 5, it had compiled a formidable number of grievances against Cornbury's administration which were promptly translated into a series of "needful Certificats." On this day the members of the lower house approved a petition to Queen Anne accusing Cornbury of having accepted a bribe from the anti-proprietary party, denouncing him for having arbitrarily excluded the three Quaker representatives from the assembly, and asking her to appoint a separate governor of New Jersey. Next they assented to a letter to the same effect from Speaker Jennings to Secretary of State Harley. Finally they expressed their approval of a grand remonstrance drawn up by Morris in the name of the assembly that recited the province's main complaints against Cornbury. Morris was subsequently directed to send all three documents and the evidence about the "blind tax" to Harley. At first it might seem strange that the assembly chose to entrust these to Harley, a moderate Tory who had no jurisdiction over colonial affairs as secretary of state for the northern department, rather than the Earl of Sunderland, a zealous Whig who had direct responsibility for the colonies as secretary of state for the southern department. However, West Jersey Quakers, who made up the bulk of proprietary party strength in the assembly, undoubtedly preferred to deal with Harley because they knew he stood higher than Sunderland in the estimation of the queen, enjoyed cordial relations with William Penn, and was sympathetic to dissenters.[10]

Morris' remonstrance formed the centerpiece of the assembly's attack on Cornbury. In it Morris skillfully wove together the general complaints of the people of New Jersey with the particular grievances of the proprietary party to produce a strong indictment of the governor's administration. Thus he rebuked Cornbury for neglecting the interests of New Jersey by spending so little time there compared to what he spent in New York. Little wonder, then, he implied, that during his term two convicted murderesses had yet to receive their just punishment, or that people accused of but not indicted for crimes were still obliged to pay court fees. He also accused the governor of discriminating against East Jersey by locating the provincial secretary's office and the probate office only in Burlington, thus causing great inconvenience to East Jerseyites who had business to transact at either of them. Furthermore, Morris declared, the grant of exclusive carrying rights to Hugh Huddy violated a statute against monopolies passed by Parliament during the reign of James I, while the practice of regulating fees without the assembly's consent was contrary to Magna Carta and the queen's instructions. Moreover, he argued that Peter Sonmans was unqualified to keep the East Jersey proprietary records and charged that he had made them unavailable to the inhabitants of East Jersey, many of whom needed them to prove title to their estates.

Still, Morris gravely observed, as bad as these grievances were, "there were others of an higher nature, and attended with worse consequences. . . . the unkind effects of mistaken Power, to whom we owe our Miseries." Thus Cornbury's interference with the West Jersey Council of Proprietors was a flagrant violation of the rights to the soil retained by the proprietors after the royalization of the government. His refusal to admit three Quakers into the assembly for almost a year after the lower house had determined they were eligible to serve was an outrageous usurpation of the assembly's right to judge the qualifications of its members and consequently a serious blow to popular liberties. Worst of all, however, was Cornbury's acceptance of a bribe from the antiproprietary party to dissolve the assembly three years before. The people of New Jersey had looked forward to the advent of royal government with high hopes, Morris concluded, but instead they now "find by these new methods of Government our Liberties and Properties so much shaken, that no Man can say he is Master of either, but holds them as Tenant by Curtesie, and at Will, and may be stript of them at Pleasure."[11]

The assembly presented this remonstrance to Cornbury in person on May 8, with Speaker Jennings reading it aloud, "often stopping and staring my Lord in the face, in Such an Insulting manner as was odious to all men of common Modesty." Soon afterward Cornbury met privately with Morris, Jennings, and several other assemblymen in an effort to convince them their complaints were groundless. At one point he sought to clinch an argument by referring to his royal instructions—only to be brought up short by Morris' confident rejoinder that "the Queens order and Instructions did not concern or effect them any further than they were warranted by law." Cornbury was dismayed by Morris' remark, and later Robert Quary, one of the governor's firmest supporters, denounced it as subversive of royal government "for having thrown off all respect and obedience to the Queens orders and instructions, by what must they be Governed, for the Laws of England they will not allow of but when it suits their interests or to serve a turn." This incident indicates how much Morris had changed since the days when he had regarded the queen's instructions as one of the firmest guarantees of proprietary rights and power in New Jersey.[12]

After failing to assuage his critics privately, Cornbury lashed out at them publicly in a reply to Morris' remonstrance that he presented to the assembly on May 12. Realizing that the declining influence of his English patrons made it impolitic for him to admit the justice of any of the assembly's grievances, Cornbury steadfastly refused to concede that he had given the people of New Jersey just cause for complaint and attributed the lower house's dissatisfaction with him almost exclusively to the malign influence of Morris and Jennings, "two men notoriously known always to have been Disturbers of the quiet and peace of this Province, Men always possest with passionate Heats and transports of most vindictive Tempers, but never capable of such serious Resentments as would become a House of Representatives." Of the two he evidently considered Morris the more dangerous adversary because he went out of his way to single him out as "the chief promoter of these unreasonable and frivolous Complaints at this time."

Having chosen such a simplistic explanation for the political crisis facing him in New Jersey, Cornbury proceeded to defend himself with consummate ineptitude against the specific charges of Morris' remonstrance. He denied he had sacrificed the interests of New Jersey to those of New York, but admitted he spent no more than three months a year in New Jersey. He vigorously defended the practice of compelling men to pay court fees who were accused of but not indicted for crimes by appealing to English precedent and insisted that regulating fees was no business of the assembly. The probate office, he assured a no doubt incredulous assembly, was "wherever the Governour is, and consequently not at Burlington only," and the grant to Hugh Huddy was no monopoly as "in all parts of Europe the having publick Carriages for Goods, has always been esteemed of absolute necessity," as if an appeal to European precedent was a sufficient reply to Morris' objection.

In regard to the grievances most directly affecting the proprietary party, Cornbury was especially adamant. He insisted that Sonmans was properly qualified to maintain the East Jersey proprietary records, though he well knew that the queen had denied Sonmans' claim to the five and one-quarter proprieties upon which in the last analysis the validity of his commission as proprietary agent and receiver general rested. He maintained that the West Jersey Council of Proprietors lacked any authority to dispose of land, which was certainly a revelation to the numerous West Jersey freeholders who had received their land from the Council. He stated that he had been justified in excluding the three Quaker representatives for so long because of their failure to show him evidence of their eligibility to serve in the assembly, which was equivalent to admitting he had indeed usurped the assembly's right to determine the qualifications of its members. Finally he flatly denied he had ever taken a bribe, though here the weight of the evidence seems to be against him, and warned the assembly that he would use his influence with his royal cousin to obtain "ample satisfaction for the great and Extravagant Injuries you have done me."[13]

Unimpressed by Cornbury's arguments or threats, Morris and Jennings next turned their attention to examining the accounts of public money kept by Receiver General Peter Fauconnier, doubtless in quest of still another "needful Certificat." Cornbury reluctantly allowed the assembly to examine these records only after it threatened otherwise to refuse to consider raising a new revenue for the government. However, he became alarmed when Morris, suspecting that Fauconnier's accounts concealed some financial irregularities, inspired the assembly to demand to see the vouchers on which they were based, and consequently he adjourned the assembly on May 16, before they could be produced. It was a measure of Cornbury's desperation that he ended this session without receiving as much as a one-year appropriation of money for his administration, much less the twenty-one year grant he had been instructed to obtain.

Morris continued to work for Cornbury's removal from office after the adjournment of the assembly. By now Morris and his family were living permanently on their Morrisania estate in New York, in part because of his fear that Cornbury might try to prosecute him for his opposition activities in New Jersey if he set foot there when the assembly was out of session and he was unable to claim legislative immunity. Nevertheless, during the interval between assemblies in New Jersey, Morris sent Secretary of State Harley the assembly's petition to the queen, the speaker's letter to the secretary of state, the assembly's remonstrance to Cornbury, and a collection of evidence about the "blind tax." This particular batch of documents failed to reach Harley because the ship which was supposed to bring it to England was apparently either lost at sea or taken by the French. Ironically, however, in January 1708 the Board of Trade received a copy of the remonstrance drafted by Morris enclosed in a letter from Cornbury vigorously impugning its veracity. Unfortunately for the governor, Board members were more impressed by the proprietary leader's complaints than by the noble lord's rebuttals. Morris also sent the West Jersey Society copies of the documents he had dispatched to Harley, though evidently by way of a different ship. It is not known precisely how the Society's officers put these to use, but it seems almost inconceivable that they did not bring them to the attention of their Whig connections, especially since the Society's interests in West Jersey were so adversely affected by Cornbury's support of Daniel Coxe.[14]

In the meantime Morris and the proprietary party dramatically intensified their opposition to Cornbury in New Jersey. When the assembly met again in October 1707 it pointedly ignored Cornbury's renewed request for a twenty-one year Support Act and formed itself into a committee of the whole to consider a reply to the governor's answer to its May remonstrance that Morris had written even before the opening of the current legislative session. In this reply, which the lower house approved on October 24, Morris reiterated at great length—one is tempted to say *ad infinitum*—the same points he had made in his earlier remonstrance and sarcastically observed that if the governor was correct in arguing that the assembly's complaints against him were groundless, "Then have we been the most mistaken men in the world, and have had the falsest notion of things; calling that cruelty, oppression and injustice, which are their direct opposites, and those things slavery, imprisonment and hardships, which are freedom, liberty and ease; and must henceforth take France, Denmark, and Muscovien, Ottoman and Eastern empires, to be the best models of a gentle and happy government." The only new element in Morris' reply was a rather unconvincing argument that no act of government performed by the governor when in New York was binding in New Jersey. This curious constitutional principle was later firmly repudiated by the imperial administration, and there is no indication that Morris himself adhered to it after the end of Cornbury's administration.

But during this session Morris did not confine himself to rhetoric. He also moved that the assembly should refuse to provide a revenue to the provincial government until Cornbury had redressed all the province's grievances and that even then it should only appropriate £1,500 for one year, both of which motions were promptly approved by his colleagues in the lower house. If Leonard Labaree is correct, this was one of only four occasions when a colonial assembly openly refused to provide a royal governor with a revenue. In this way Morris placed Cornbury in a seemingly insoluble dilemma. If the governor redressed all the complaints of the assembly, he would stand condemned by his own admission as an arbitrary ruler and receive support for only one year instead of for the twenty-one his instructions demanded. Yet if he continued to insist that these complaints were unfounded, he would get no money at all. Cornbury responded by adjourning the assembly, which was a virtual admission of the justice of its criticisms as otherwise he surely would have dissolved it and taken a chance on new elections. It would be difficult to imagine a more telling sign to the imperial administration that his effectiveness in New Jersey was at an end.[15]

After the adjournment of the assembly Morris turned again to England for a resolution of the political impasse in New Jersey. To begin with, he sought to enlist the support of the SPG against Cornbury. In doing this he was moved by a genuine concern for the welfare of the Anglican church as well as by an awareness that any opposition to the governor from the Venerable Society was bound to have a significant impact on that most devout of churchwomen, the queen. Thus late in 1707 or early in 1708 Morris wrote an elaborate memorial to the SPG in which he reviewed the progress of Anglicanism in New Jersey and New York and concluded that in both of them Cornbury was now "the greatest obstacle . . . to the growth of the church." In each colony, he noted, churchmen and dissenters alike were appalled by the noble lord's heavy indebtedness to "shopkeepers, Bakers, butchers &c" and scandalized by his fondness for feminine apparel. Dissenters in particular were aroused by his prosecution of Francis Makemie, an itinerant Presbyterian minister, for preaching without a license in New York. By this act the governor threatened to impede the spread of Anglicanism among dissenters, for in order to win these people over to the national church, Morris argued, "all the soft endearing measures should be used with gentleness . . . and not things but even words and arguments should be stript of all acerbity." But, he warned, the removal of Cornbury from office would only be the first step in the resumption of Anglican expansion in New Jersey and New York. Here as in other colonies the church also suffered from the lack of a bishop and the excessive dependence of Anglican ministers on lay officials. Therefore Morris urged the Venerable Society to strive for the creation of an American episcopate, to further clerical independence, and to win for itself the right to recommend royal governors to the crown in order to facilitate cooperation between the church and royal officials in America.[16]

Morris followed up his memorial to the SPG with an urgent appeal to Robert Harley for the appointment of a new governor of New Jersey. Writing to the secretary of state on February 9, 1708, Morris recited the familiar litany of proprietary party complaints against Cornbury and warned that it was unrealistic of the imperial administration to expect the New Jersey Assembly to make any long-term grants of revenue to the provincial government as "it is in my opinion impracticable to persuade an Assembly in this part of America to trust a Governor after my Lord Cornbury." Alas, Morris lamented, the noble lord's arbitrary methods of government were only too typical of those employed by many other royal governors in America, bringing the queen's government into disrepute and leading to an exodus of settlers from crown to chartered colonies, where the people could at least call errant executive officials to account "without the uncertain and tedious success of application to courts." For, Morris bluntly informed Harley, as if to anticipate the objection that it was colonial assemblies which were recklessly undermining royal authority in America, "its the impudent conduct of the Governours, to call it no worse, that has been the great prejudice of her Majesties service in America; the various kinds of injustice and oppression, the sordid and mercenary measures they have taken, the mean things they have stoopt to, the trash of mankind that has been their favorites and tools and by them raised to posts of honr and proffit as rewards for accomplishing the worst ends, has stunted the growth of these otherwise thriving plantations, and you may easily judge what effects are the unavoidable consequences of such causes, except mankind can be brought to love such things as by the principalls of human nature they must necessarily hate." Consequently Morris welcomed a report that Sir Gilbert Heathcote, a wealthy English merchant who represented London in Parliament and was a director of the Bank of England, was working for the appointment of his brother Caleb as Cornbury's successor and warmly recommended Heathcote's appointment to Harley, thereby abandoning the hitherto fruitless candidacy of Major Douglas. In Caleb Heathcote, a neighbor of his in Westchester who served on the New York Council and also belonged to the SPG, Morris thought he had found an ideal replacement for Cornbury, but unfortunately his proposed appointment was never approved in England.[17]

Lord Cornbury was finally dismissed as governor of New Jersey and New York owing to a combination of domestic political changes in England and the complaints of his opponents in America. By the end of 1707 the Duke of Marlborough and Lord Treasurer Godolphin, the principal intermediaries between the throne and Parliament, had concluded that it would be impossible to continue to wage war against France effectively as long as their ministry rested upon an increasingly precarious parliamentary coalition of Whigs and Harleyite Tories. Since the Whigs were more unflagging in support of the war against France than the Tories, Marlborough and Godolphin abandoned their alliance with Harley in February 1708 and formed a predominantly Whig ministry. This change would have boded ill for a High Tory official like Cornbury in any case, but it had an especially deleterious effect on his position because of the awareness among key English officials of his great unpopularity in America. At this time the Board of Trade was impressed by the criticisms of Cornbury's rule in New Jersey contained in the May 1707 remonstrance drawn up by Morris, while Lord Somers and the Earl of Sunderland, two members of the famed Whig Junto, were also familiar with complaints about his "arbitrary proceedings" in New York. Hence it was no surprise that in March 1708, even before Morris' appeals to Harley and the Venerable Society had arrived in England, John Lord Lovelace, a financially distressed English army officer with impeccable Whig credentials, was chosen to replace Cornbury as governor in both provinces.[18]

A month before his dismissal Cornbury made a final effort to retain his office by inducing Lieutenant Governor Richard Ingoldesby and six members of the New Jersey Council to sign an address to the queen sharply criticizing Morris and the proprietary party. In this address they claimed that the assembly's criticisms of the governor were entirely unfounded and attributable mainly to "the Turbulent, Factious, uneasy and Disloyal Principles of . . . Mr. Lewis Morris and Mr. Samuel Jennings . . . men notoriously known to be uneasy under all Governments, men never known to be consistent with themselves, men to whom all the Factions and Confusions in the Government of New Jersey and Pennsylvania for many years are wholly owing." As to Morris' and Jennings' motives in so villainously opposing a governor allegedly as free from fault as Cornbury, they were, the address ludicrously charged, nothing less than to encourage first New Jersey and then all of British America to overthrow royal authority and establish an independent empire. Without being aware of this address at the time, Morris in effect repudiated its fantastic allegations during the summer of 1708 in a poem in which he portrayed himself as nothing more than an opponent of arbitrary rule and popular licentiousness alike, which was certainly a more plausible role for him than that of precursor to the Founding Fathers:

> The Just, the righteous man is brave
> Nor to himselfe nor none a slave.
> The giddy mob his Soull disdaines
> The frownes of tyrants he contemns
> Firme to his purpose bravely stands
> Unmovd by their unjust commands.

When angry Auster moves the main
An unmov'd Courage he'll retaine
And in those stormes that move the deep
A firme unshaken mind he'll keep
Nor is it in natures power to shake.
Nay Jove himselfe should he descend
In thunder cannot make him bend
From his Just purpose. No let all
Thats made to Instant ruine fall
He'd sing at natures funerall.[19]

Cornbury's removal from office, though naturally pleasing to Morris and the proprietary party, still left several key issues unresolved in New Jersey. The Anglican wing of the antiproprietary party continued to dominate the provincial council, threatening to create a deadlock with any assembly controlled by the proprietary party. Peter Sonmans was still in charge of the sale of proprietary lands and the collection of proprietary quitrents in East Jersey, functions which the Scottish proprietors were anxious to reassume themselves. And a number of Anglican councilors continued to favor the exclusion of Quakers from public office, which was a constant threat to the very survival of the political alliance between West Jersey Quakers and Scottish proprietors. Since it was no longer practicable to safeguard proprietary interests in New Jersey by relying on the settlement between the proprietors and the imperial administration which he had helped to negotiate during his London mission, Morris now sought to achieve this goal by making the council a bastion of proprietary strength, by reinvesting the Scottish proprietors with sole authority over proprietary affairs in East Jersey, and by establishing the political rights of Quakers on a firm foundation.

Lord Lovelace's appointment as governor of New Jersey seemed to provide Morris with an excellent opportunity for accomplishing these objectives. For Lovelace arrived in America in December 1708 with a marked preference for Morris and the proprietary party. Before leaving England Lovelace had come under the influence of the West Jersey Society whose principal officers were Whigs like himself. In conjunction with the Society, the new governor had requested the Board of Trade to dismiss the leading Anglican members of the New Jersey Council—Daniel Coxe, Daniel Leeds, Robert Quary, Thomas Revell, and Peter Sonmans. At the time the Board saw no need for making such a sweeping change in the council, though it did agree to the removal of Leeds and Revell, who had made themselves particularly obnoxious to the proprietary party by inspiring Cornbury to refuse to admit the three Quaker representatives into the assembly in 1704. In addition Lovelace had been instrumental in persuading the imperial administration to restore Morris himself to his place on the council. As a result, Morris became the senior member of that body in point of service and as such was entitled to administer the provincial government in case of the death or absence of the governor and lieutenant governor.[20]

Morris welcomed the arrival of Lovelace, seeing in him a fit instrument for achieving his goals in New Jersey. Hence Morris resumed his seat on the council in December 1708 and no doubt looked forward with anticipation to the pleasant prospect of enjoying the new governor's support and favor for a long time to come. As if to accentuate the commanding position he expected to enjoy under the new dispensation, he did not join his fellow councilors in greeting Lovelace when the governor came to Perth Amboy to meet with the assembly in March 1709 but instead waited on him privately to present a fulsome address hailing his administration as the dawn of a new day in New Jersey and warning him to beware of those who would try to convince him that "the most Arbitrary Acts were an asserting of the Queen's Prerogative Royall" — an obvious reference to Cornbury's conciliar supporters. So excessively adulatory did Morris' address seem to some of these councilors that they circulated lampoons of it throughout Perth Amboy, one of which read:

As Jack-puddings on Stages have different waies
From the rest of the Actors to meritt the Bayes,
So Tall-Lewis-Morris o'retops all the rest
And by playing the fool Shows his Character best;
He addresses alone, because tis his Part
To differ from the Councill in Manner and Heart;
What matter though it never was heard of before,
He has more inconsistencies still in his Store.
Which makes him as fit for Dark-Room, and Clean Straw
As any Dull Madman that ever you Saw.

Not to be outdone by his poetical tormentors, Morris soon replied in kind:

As Ravens and Night-owls their Voices betray,
So asses are certainly known when they bray.
And Spight of the Noise and bustle they've made
Mankind will believe that a Spade is a Spade.
That Bullies and Bankrupts, and men without Store

Dull wretches that have not one Virtue or more,
The Pests of the Country, whose Practise has been
To flatter the Governor, and Lie to the Queen,
Have right to no favour in a well-govern'd State
But to Swing in an Halter, or peep through a Grate.[21]

While the feeble muses fumed and fretted, the assembly, accurately reflecting Morris' unforgiving spirit, sought to convince Lovelace to agree to a drastic purge of the council. The members of the lower house began by demanding outright the dismissal from the council of Peter Sonmans, the great antagonist of the Scottish proprietors. Next they asked for and received from Lovelace a copy of the previous year's address to the queen from the lieutenant governor and council accusing the assembly of having been a party to Morris and Jennings' alleged plot to destroy royal authority and break up the British empire. Not only did the assemblymen vociferously deny the truth of this address, but they also strongly questioned the wisdom of allowing any of its signers to remain in office. Since the signers included Lieutenant Governor Ingoldesby as well as Councilors Daniel Coxe, Roger Mompesson, William Pinhorne, Robert Quary, William Sandford, and Richard Townley, their dismissal, together with that of Sonmans, would have ended the dominance of the council by the antiproprietary party's Anglican wing. Unfortunately for Morris and his supporters, Lovelace adjourned the assembly early in April without making any changes in the council and then died suddenly on May 6, 1709.[22]

Lovelace's unexpected demise threw New Jersey into turmoil, temporarily casting Morris into political limbo and preserving Anglican control of the council. Lieutenant Governor Ingoldesby promptly assumed control of the provincial government and aligned himself with the very councilors whose continuance in office had recently seemed so uncertain — but not without some serious opposition from Morris. Morris denied Ingoldesby's authority, incorrectly arguing that the revocation of Ingoldesby's commission as lieutenant governor of New York in 1706 also applied to his commission for New Jersey, and asserted that he himself was entitled to act as Lovelace's temporary successor in New Jersey by virtue of his position as senior councilor. At first Ingoldesby ignored Morris' claims and called for a meeting of the assembly to consider the question of New Jersey's participation in the "Glorious Enterprise," a projected Anglo-American invasion of Canada which subsequently failed to materialize because of the last-minute diversion to Portugal of the British troops who were supposed to have taken part in it. But so successful was Morris in implanting doubts in the minds of the assemblymen about the validity of Ingoldesby's authority that for a while they hesitated to act under it. Eventually Ingoldesby overcame their reluctance and got on with the business at hand, but in order to save himself from similar embarrassments in the future he suspended Morris from the council in June 1709, Morris' third suspension in five years.[23]

As in the past, Morris reacted by turning to England for vindication. Thus he wrote to John Chamberlayne, the secretary of the SPG, and the Earl of Sunderland, the secretary of state for the southern department, again recommending the appointment of his New York neighbor Caleb Heathcote as governor of New Jersey and lamenting the loss of Lovelace as one who would have restored the tattered prestige of royal government by demonstrating that "the Queens prerogative was not Inconsistent with the liberties of the people but absolutely necessary for the preservation of that and their properties." Morris also went to great lengths to convince Sunderland of the untruthfulness of the charge that he had conspired against royal authority during Cornbury's administration, well knowing that if this accusation gained credit with the imperial administration it would destroy his chances of receiving any further preferment from the crown. Hence he strongly reaffirmed his loyalty to the queen and movingly argued that he had given ample proof of it by his willingness to spend almost a year of his life and £1,000 of his fortune in England to hasten the royalization of New Jersey "wch. may with no great Improprietie of Speech be called an Enlarging her dominions." At present no colony in America wished to be independent of Great Britain, Morris assured Sunderland, but if a spirit of independence ever did arise among Americans he predicted that it would not be the fault of colonial leaders but rather of "that haughtie and Superb Demeanour and those arbitrary and Illegal Encroachments on their liberties and properties wch. the governours of plantations are but too Often guilty of, Endeavouring to make the world believe the unaccountable methods they take to gratifie their Avarice or resentments is for [the queen's] Service and perpetrate the worst of Villanies under a pretence of asserting her prerogative royall." Morris' plea for Heathcote's appointment fell on deaf ears in England for the second time, but his stirring defense of his fidelity to the crown undoubtedly enabled him to withstand a determined effort by William Dockwra to persuade Sunderland and the Board of Trade to remove him from the New Jersey Council permanently on the grounds that he was "the very Incendiary of the Province both in ye Proprietors' time & ever since."[24]

It was not until the administration of Robert Hunter that Morris was finally able to achieve the goals which had eluded him under Lovelace and Ingoldesby. Hunter, a Whig army officer who had been chosen to succeed Lovelace as governor of New Jersey and New York in September

1709, also came to America predisposed to favor Morris and the proprietary party, for before his departure from England he had joined the West Jersey Society and the London East Jersey proprietors in persuading the imperial administration to restore Morris as the senior member of the New Jersey Council and to add to that body Thomas Gardiner and Thomas Gordon, two proprietary party stalwarts. Hunter's inclination to favor Morris and his political allies developed into an open alliance with them within a matter of months after his arrival in America during the summer of 1710. Hunter was grateful for the political support he received from Morris in New York — of which more in the next chapter — and this enabled Morris to become one of his most trusted advisers in New Jersey. Furthermore, as a native of Scotland, Hunter had a natural affinity for the Scottish proprietors of East Jersey, and conversely he was repelled by the antiproprietary party's coarse English nativism, which was vividly expressed in Peter Sonmans' defiant boast: "We will not go to North Brittian for Justice." Accordingly, just before the elections for a new assembly scheduled to meet in December 1710, Hunter unmistakably revealed his preference for the proprietary party by making several key changes in the magistracy which helped the familiar coalition of Scottish proprietors and West Jersey Quakers to win a majority in the lower house of the legislature.[25]

Morris took advantage of the proprietary party's electoral victory to press for an end to Anglican domination of the provincial council. Although he himself was a councilor once again, Morris worked closely with his allies in the assembly to convince Hunter of the need for terminating a situation in which rival political factions controlled the two houses of the legislature. To this end Morris and his colleagues began by securing assembly approval of certain bills which they knew in advance the council's Anglican majority would feel bound to reject, including measures designed to enable Quakers to hold offices of trust and serve on juries, to lessen the prerogatives of provincial Secretary Jeremiah Basse, and to punish certain judicial irregularities allegedly committed by antiproprietary judges and sheriffs. The council defeated all these bills, as Morris and his supporters had anticipated, and thereby gave Hunter an inkling of the deadlocks which were bound to develop between the assembly and the council unless the latter's membership was drastically altered. In order to leave no room for doubt by Hunter as to how to avert such impasses, Morris then drew up for the assembly a grand remonstrance which the lower house approved and presented to the governor at the end of the legislative session early in February 1711. In this remonstrance Morris described the abuses of various antiproprietary officials and called for their dismissal from office. Since those whom Morris sought to proscribe included almost every remaining antiproprietary councilor—Daniel Coxe, William Hall, Hugh Huddy, Roger Mompesson, William Pinhorne, Peter Sonmans, and Richard Townley—as well as Secretary Basse, in effect he was asking for nothing less than the virtual extinction of this faction as an organized force in New Jersey politics.[26]

Apparently Hunter would have purged the council in accordance with Morris' wishes if news had not arrived from England during the same month of February of the coming to power of a Tory ministry headed by Robert Harley. Harley's return to office followed the fall from favor and influence of Hunter's Whig patrons, which made his own position in America vulnerable. It was also accompanied by the return to power of the Earl of Rochester, the uncle of former Governor Cornbury, who had become third Earl of Clarendon after his father's death in 1709. This was especially significant because all the officials Morris expected Hunter to dismiss had ties to the new Earl of Clarendon, whose political stock had risen with his uncle's. They were also Anglicans to a man, so that if Hunter dismissed them outright he would run the risk of being called to account by a Tory ministry whose resurgence had been due in part to its use of the hallowed cry: "The Church in danger." This was a risk Hunter could ill afford when his Whig protectors were no longer able to assist him in England.

Consequently Hunter acted cautiously in complying with the wishes of Morris and the proprietary party. He began by replacing most of the judges and sheriffs appointed by Cornbury and Ingoldesby with supporters of the Scottish proprietors and West Jersey Quakers. In addition to reducing the power of the antiproprietary party, this also made Peter Sonmans' position as proprietary agent and receiver general intolerable, as he could not function without the support of friendly public officials, and paved the way for the Scottish proprietors to resume control over the sale of land and the collection of quitrents in East Jersey. Hunter dealt more circumspectly with the council, but in the end the result was equally pleasing to Morris and his allies. In May 1711 the governor asked the Board of Trade to approve the removal of Coxe, Hall, Pinhorne, and Sonmans, arguing that this was necessary to restore good relations between the council and assembly. In place of these four councilors as well as two others recently deceased, Hunter recommended the appointment of six men who were either proprietors themselves or well disposed to the proprietary party.[27]

As the final decision in this matter was now in the hands of the imperial administration, both sides tried to use their English connections to incline imperial officials in their favor. Morris urged the West Jersey Society to support Hunter's proposals, while Coxe and Sonmans besought

William Dockwra and Clarendon to defend their interests in England and secure the appointment of a new governor. In this case, unlike six years before, Morris' appeal to the Society produced results. Dockwra, who was already stricken by the debilitating illness which led to his death in 1714, was unable to present the imperial administration with an effective defense of his beleaguered allies in New Jersey, and the same was true of Clarendon, whose political influence dropped sharply after Rochester's death in 1711. In contrast, the West Jersey Society and the London East Jersey proprietors vigorously pressed the imperial administration to approve Hunter's recommendations. Under their prodding, the Board of Trade advised the queen in August 1712 to approve the reorganization of the New Jersey Council suggested by Hunter, and Anne finally consented to this change in the following April. As a result, the council became a bulwark of the proprietary interest in New Jersey and remained so for the rest of the colonial period.[28]

With the ending of Anglican dominance in the council, Morris was able to complete the task of safeguarding proprietary interests. Early in 1714, during the first meeting of the assembly after this radical change, Morris shepherded through the council a bill authorizing Quakers to hold public office and serve on juries, which effectively dashed any remaining Anglican hopes of depriving Friends of these rights. He also arranged for the return to the Scottish proprietors of the records they had been obliged to hand over to Secretary Basse in 1705, thus completing the process whereby the Scots regained control over East Jersey proprietary affairs from Peter Sonmans. Finally during this period he prevailed on Hunter to establish a chancery court in New Jersey, so that if necessary the proprietors could avoid the uncertainties of trial by jury in legal disputes about their rights to the soil.[29]

While Morris was obtaining additional protection for proprietary political power and economic interests, the antiproprietary party was in the process of dissolution. The tenuous alliance between William Dockwra's English East Jersey proprietors and the Nicolls patentees had already been strained past the breaking point by Peter Sonmans' enforcement of proprietary rights to the soil in East Jersey, rights which the patentees refused to acknowledge. The English proprietors themselves lost their cohesion and ceased to function as an effective interest group after Dockwra's death in 1714. At the same time West Jersey Anglicans received a stunning blow from the death of Queen Anne and the subsequent demoralization of the Tories, for the triumphant Whigs were much less responsive than the Tories to Anglican complaints about Quakers. These political changes did not eliminate tensions between Anglicans and Quakers in West Jersey or reconcile Nicolls patentees to the claims of resident proprietors in East

Jersey, but as New Jersey entered the Hanoverian era its political life no longer revolved around the rivalry between the proprietary and antiproprietary parties which had begun over a decade before because by then the original antiproprietary coalition had passed out of existence.

However, long before the accession of George I, Morris' political career in New Jersey had begun to yield in importance to his participation in New York political life. Morris continued to take part in New Jersey affairs through his membership in the provincial council and his activities as the West Jersey Society's American business agent, but after 1710 his involvement in that colony became increasingly episodic as he became more and more absorbed in his new role as Governor Hunter's legislative manager in New York. As a result, it is now time to consider Morris' career in the province of his birth.

⊱ 6 ⊰

"The Governour's Perticular Favorit"

HE ADVENT OF ROBERT HUNTER AS GOVERNOR of New York and New Jersey in 1710 opened up a new chapter in Lewis Morris' political life. Hitherto involved exclusively in New Jersey affairs, Morris now became an active participant in New York politics for the first time in his career. Although Morris remained one of the foremost proprietary leaders in New Jersey under Hunter's administration, during this period he shifted the main focus of his attention to New York, where he served as the governor's legislative manager in the assembly and became one of the colony's few native-born chief justices of the supreme court. In his capacity as legislative manager, Morris brought temporary political stability to New York by creating a powerful court party in the assembly and by resolving some crucial constitutional conflicts between that body and the governor. As a result, when Hunter's administration came to an end in 1719, Morris was undoubtedly the most influential political leader in New York.

Of all the governors who served the crown in America before the Revolution, few were more able or distinguished than Robert Hunter. Before his arrival in America, Hunter, who was born in Scotland shortly after the Restoration, had risen to high rank in the British Army, become acquainted with some of England's most famous men of letters, and acquired influential patrons from among the ranks of the Whigs and the Tories. Selected by Henry Compton, the martial bishop of London, as a member of the special bodyguard which escorted Princess Anne from the capital city during the Glorious Revolution, Hunter came to the attention of the future queen and her two principal counselors, the Duke of Marlborough and the Earl of Godolphin, early in his career. The duke displayed his favor for Hunter by appointing him as his aide-de-camp during the War of the Spanish Succession and by acting as his patron, notwithstanding the fact that once in 1706 the ambitious Scot reportedly provoked him to anger by receiving the surrender of Antwerp himself after Marlborough had designated that honor for another officer. Hunter, who attained the rank of colonel while on duty with Marlborough, also became familiar through military service with the Earls of Stair and Orkney, two politically powerful Scottish lords; and it was through the influence of Marlborough and Orkney that Hunter became the latter's deputy governor in Virginia in 1707 — a colony in which he never served owing to his capture by a French privateer while *en route* to America in that year.

Hunter was as much at home in the coffee houses of London as on the fields of Blenheim and Ramillies. An able poet and essayist who contributed some anonymous pieces to the *Tatler,* Hunter was familiar with some of the leading literary figures in Augustan England. He was on good terms with Joseph Addison, with whom he seems to have kept up a regular correspondence, and Richard Steele, who was nothing more than a convivial drinking companion. Jonathan Swift, whose thirst for preferment he vainly hoped Hunter would quench by securing him a Virginia bishopric, affected to think so highly of the Scot's literary powers as to credit him with the authorship of Shaftesbury's *Letter on Enthusiasm.* Hunter was also on good terms with such lesser writers as Ambrose Philips, whose ludicrously delicate verse did not prevent the governor from later employing him as his agent in England, and John Arbuthnot, the witty satirist and court physician, in whose medical abilities Queen Anne placed the greatest confidence.

Although personally "a stanch Whig," Hunter had access to influential patrons in the Whig and Tory parties by virtue of his military career and interest in *belles lettres.* Marlborough, though nominally a Tory, generally stood above party as one of the select group of "managers" who acted as intermediaries between the queen and the politicians in Parliament contending for her favor. Yet Marlborough's power perceptibly declined after he compelled Anne to part with Robert Harley in 1708, and Hunter did not owe his appointment as governor of New York and New Jersey primarily to the duke's influence. Orkney and Stair, like Hunter himself, were members of the "Squadrone Volante," the tightly knit Scottish faction that vigorously supported the Union of 1707 with England and thereafter aligned itself with the Whigs. Hunter's literary friendships reinforced his ties with the Whigs and, in fact, before 1710 almost all the members of his literary circle were adherents of that party, including Swift. Addison in particular was a political connection of the Earl of Sunderland, Marlborough's son-in-law and a member of the fabled Whig Junto, and it was probably as much through his friendship with Addison as his military service with Marlborough that Hunter acquired the patronage of Sunderland and Lord Somers, another Junto lord. In any case, Hunter, Sunderland, and Somers were all involved in the ill-fated effort to raise naval stores in New York with the labor of Protestant refugees from the Rhenish Palatinate that plunged the governor deeply into debt and made him amenable to the informal constitutional compromises Morris subsequently arranged in order to obtain a long-term revenue for his administration from the New York Assembly.

Despite Hunter's primary loyalty to the Whigs, he also had influential patrons among the Tories—a factor of cardinal importance when one recalls that the first half of his administration in New York and New Jersey coincided with the Harley and Bolingbroke ministry in England. The Earl of Mar, a member of the Old Court Party in Scotland, the natural rival of the "Squadrone," maintained a cordial, though admittedly ambiguous, relationship with Hunter. Mar, appointed by Harley as third secretary of state in 1710, kept a watchful eye on Hunter's interests in England, and this was certainly no detriment to the governor at a time when his Whig patrons were out of office. Hunter was also able to rely upon the good offices of Swift—a great tribute to Hunter's amiability, inasmuch as his failure to support the quest of that irascible clergyman for a Virginia bishopric hastened the conversion of the future Dean of St. Patrick's to Toryism. For, as Hunter tantalizingly revealed to Addison shortly after the fall from power of the Tories: "I have suffered beyond the force of human Nature without haveing Received the least Answer to my Enumerable Complaints during the whole course of the last Administration. Tho' your old Acquaintance the Tale of a Tub [Swift] who it seems had Power with the ruin'd faction was pleased to Interpose in my favour as the Lord Marr informed me."[1]

However, Hunter's most important Tory connection was John Arbuthnot, the clever satirist of Marlborough's military strategy, "Queen Anne's favorite physician," and Hunter's "most intimate and useful friend tho' he and the doctor differed greatly in their political sentiments." After his release by the French, Hunter returned to England in 1709 to find Marlborough and the Whigs nominally in power yet actually out of favor with the queen. In this extremity, Arbuthnot, disregarding his political differences with Hunter, asked the queen to appoint the newly freed Scot as governor of Jamaica, and Anne—as much, one suspects, to spite her ministers as to oblige a favorite—agreed to this appointment without consulting Marlborough or Sunderland, the principal dispensers of colonial patronage at the time. But Marlborough and Sunderland had already designated another man to fill the Jamaica vacancy, so that Hunter, being reluctant to offend those worthies, wisely declined this appointment. Shortly afterward news of Lord Lovelace's death arrived in England, whereupon Hunter, after first having obtained the approval of Marlborough, Sunderland, and Somers, asked Arbuthnot "to inform the Queen that he would rather have the government of New York than Jamaica and it was accordingly granted him."[2] Hence in September 1709 Hunter became governor of New York and New Jersey by the sanction of Queen Anne, through the influence of her "favorite physician," and with the support of Marlborough and some of the Junto lords. Arbuthnot continued to attend the queen until her death in 1714, and although there is no direct evidence that Hunter remained in contact with him during the final years of the reign of the last Stuart, it is not implausible to suggest that the doctor remained mindful of the governor's interests at court until he was dismissed as a royal physician in 1714 by the first Hanoverian.

Hunter arrived in New York in June 1710 and within a few months he and Morris were bound together by the ties of personal friendship as well as by the exigencies of provincial politics. By the fall of 1710 Morris was Hunter's acknowledged spokesman in the New York Assembly. Three years later he named his youngest son after the governor—Robert Hunter Morris. And three years after that Hunter readily admitted that Morris was "the Governours perticular favorit."[3] Since Morris' relationship with Hunter marked such an important turning point in his political career, the speed with which they became fast friends and close political allies requires some explanation.

Morris first came to Hunter's attention shortly after the Scot's appointment as governor in the fall of 1709. At that time William Dockwra was engaged in a strenuous effort to persuade the imperial administration to remove Morris from the New Jersey Council forever, while the West Jersey Society and the London East Jersey proprietors were working just as hard to restore him to that body after his suspension by Lieutenant Governor Ingoldesby. Hunter supported the efforts of the Society and the proprietors and was instrumental in convincing the Board of Trade to agree to Morris' restoration. Thus even before Hunter left England in March 1710, he seems to have been favorably inclined toward Morris.[4]

If Hunter came to America well-disposed toward Morris, then Morris, who was keenly aware of the need to obtain Hunter's support in order to realize his political goals in New Jersey, must have assiduously cultivated the new governor after his arrival in New York. In his old age, Cadwallader Colden, who had known Morris and Hunter well, remembered the governor fondly as a man who "wrote some elegant little pieces in poetry which never appeared in his name. . . . had an exceeding pretty and entertaining manner of telling a Tale . . . was a most agreable companion with his intimate friends . . . [and] was fond of men of learning and encouraged them whenever he had opportunity." It was probably this delight in "men of learning" that first drew Morris and Hunter together, for although Morris had had little formal education, he was an erudite country gentleman who read widely, wrote poetry, dabbled in natural science, and hungered for the company of men with similar interests. Since for the cosmopolitan Hunter New York and New Jersey were dreary cultural wastelands, it is not difficult to understand how he was attracted to a kindred spirit like Morris, in collaboration with whom he later created the first play written and printed in British North America.[5]

Hunter's friendship with Morris soon led to a political partnership between them in New York. Hunter, like every newly arrived governor in the colony, needed the assistance of a trusted legislative manager to guide him safely through the treacherous shoals of local factionalism and to facilitate cooperation between him and the assembly. Morris was admirably suited for this role. He had already demonstrated a capacity for mobilizing popular support and managing an assembly in New Jersey. Furthermore he was familiar with existing political alignments in New York but, owing to his absorption in New Jersey affairs for the past eighteen years, not involved in them. Consequently Hunter could reasonably expect Morris to organize support for him in the New York Assembly without undue regard for the interests of any particular faction, and therefore he apparently decided to rely upon Morris to act as his legislative manager even before his first meeting with the assembly in September 1710.

Morris welcomed the opportunity to work with Hunter in this capacity. Since moving back to his Morrisania estate in Westchester, Morris had never been able to exercise the political power in New York to which he felt his wealth and social standing entitled him. For Morris, the quintessential political animal who reveled in the rough and tumble of colonial politics, this was a severe deprivation. William Smith the historian captured the essence of this feature of Morris' character in a wonderfully perceptive sentence: "Tho' [Morris] was indolent in the management of his private affairs, yet thro' the love of power, he was always busy in matters of a political nature, and no man in the colony equaled him in the knowledge of the law and the arts of intrigue." Morris' mastery of the subtleties of Anglo-American jurisprudence may not have been as prodigious in 1710 as Smith suggests, but by that time he had undeniably demonstrated an exuberant lust for political life. Given the chance to act as Hunter's legislative manager in New York, Morris, fully alive to the need for winning the governor's support for the proprietary party in New Jersey and eager to display his talents in the colony where he now resided, readily grasped it. In colonial America a legislative manager was somewhat analogous to a prime minister in Hanoverian England. Whereas in England the prime minister's power rested upon the support of the king and his ability to transact the king's business in the House of Commons, in America the legislative manager's power depended upon the confidence reposed in him by the governor and his ability to organize support for the governor in the assembly. Having won Hunter's trust, Morris now had to gain control over the assembly in order to transact the governor's business, which then consisted mainly of securing an adequate revenue for his administration.[6]

Morris became Hunter's legislative manager when the central political question in New York turned upon who was to exercise effective control over the colony's government — the crown or the assembly? Under the first British empire the imperial administration sought to keep the colonies subordinate to the mother country by making royally appointed governors, councilors, and officials as independent as possible of popularly elected assemblies. Although the assemblies raised most of the money with which provincial governments were run, imperial administrators tried in a variety of ways to lessen the impact of this power on royal officials in America. Accordingly royal governors were instructed to secure long-term grants of revenue from their assemblies that were to be lodged in the hands of royal receivers general, dispensed through gubernatorial warrants issued with the advice and consent of provincial councils, and inspected periodically by royal auditors. Councils were encouraged to exercise their right to amend money bills passed by assemblies, and the crown sought to determine the salaries of royal governors, while authorizing governors and councils to regulate the pay of other royal officials in the colonies. Through these means the imperial administration attempted to enable the crown's servants in America to carry out imperial policies without undue regard for the wishes of the local assemblies which provided the money for their salaries as well as for most of the other costs of government.

But in reaction to the blatant misapplication of public money by Lord Cornbury and the resulting increase in the colony's public debt during a period of economic distress, the New York Assembly revolted against these features of imperial rule and sought to gain for itself stricter control over the provincial financial system. During Cornbury's administration the assembly, led by Speaker William Nicoll, a Suffolk County lawyer, denied the council's right to amend money bills, tried to fix the salaries of royal officials, and demanded the right to place the money it raised for the government in the custody of its own treasurer rather than in the hands of the royal receiver. Queen Anne removed Cornbury from office and allowed the assembly to appoint a treasurer to handle the money it raised on extraordinary occasions, as opposed to the regular revenue for the government, but these actions did not mollify the members of the lower house. Under the administrations of Lovelace and Ingoldesby the assembly stepped up its efforts to extend its powers by passing annual rather than long-term support acts, by specifying how the money raised for the government should be spent instead of leaving this to the discretion of the governor and council, and by usurping the right of the governor and council to regulate fees. Since these measures threatened to make royal officials more dependent on the assembly than the crown, Morris did not greatly exaggerate when he subsequently declared, in a satirical description of the political situation in New York at the start of Hunter's term: "The Clods [assemblymen] like a Vicious horse that had throwne his rider and run away with the reins on his neck Seem'd to despise all manner of restraint and was for taking into their hands the Exercise of all the powers of the Steward [governor] and Lord [monarch] of the mannour [New York] too."[7]

In addition to a highly assertive assembly, Morris also had to contend with a sharp disagreement between New York's landed and merchant interests over the issue of how to raise a revenue for the provincial government. While a series of lavish land grants to a small group of gubernatorial favorites had led to the development of a class of landed magnates who derived their incomes primarily from their great estates, New York City's commercial growth and Albany's central role in the northern fur trade had brought forth a class of substantial merchants who made their living mainly through overseas trade. In consequence New York was the only early eighteenth-century British colony with a landed and merchant aristocracy of roughly equal political power. Whereas great landholders like Morris and Robert Livingston wanted to provide the government with a revenue from trade duties and excise taxes, New York City merchants like Adolph Philipse and Stephen DeLancey and Albany fur traders like Peter Schuyler felt that the burden of supporting the government should be placed on property taxes. But neither the landed nor the merchant aristocracy was in itself strong enough to win control of the assembly and carry out its economic policy. Each was obliged to solicit the support of country farmers and urban artisans and craftsmen, who made up the bulk of the colony's electorate. Since New York was in the grip of a commercial depression at the beginning of Hunter's administration, however, the merchants were temporarily able to make their fiscal views prevail by cogently arguing that at such a time it would be the height of folly to burden trade with taxes in order to support the government.[8]

Morris' role as legislative manager was further complicated by the lingering hostility between the Leislerian and anti-Leislerian parties in New York. The revolt of Jacob Leisler against the government of the Dominion of New England in 1689 and the execution two years later of Leisler and his chief lieutenant, Jacob Milborne, had precipitated a bitter factional strife that was only beginning to recede at the time of Morris' entrance into New York political life. For almost two decades after 1691 supporters and opponents of the "martyred" rebel leaders had tried to accomplish each other's political destruction, aided and abetted by a series of shortsighted royal governors. Although constitutional and economic issues had moved to the forefront of New York politics by 1710, Morris still had to reckon with the remaining antagonisms between Leislerians and anti-Leislerians as he went about the business of organizing support for Hunter in the assembly. At that time the conflict between these two groups was largely confined to New York City, where Leislerian sentiment was especially strong among the predominant Dutch population, so that if Morris could somehow harness this force to the governor's cause he might win for the court party the four seats which had been allotted to the city in the colony's twenty-two member assembly.[9]

Morris first became aware of the magnitude of his task during Hunter's initial meeting with the New York Assembly between September 1 and November 25, 1710. Following the custom of his predecessors, Hunter dissolved the existing assembly shortly after his arrival and held elections for a new one. The ensuing electoral results cannot have been much to his liking. Morris was chosen to represent the borough of Westchester — whence he was returned to the assembly at every election but one during the next eighteen years — but otherwise the composition of the new assembly was generally unfavorable to the governor's interest. Fifteen of the twenty-two elected representatives were veterans of the assemblies that had begun the struggle for more popular control of the provincial financial system under Cornbury, and their selection of William Nicoll as speaker indicated that they were no more ready to trust in Hunter's discretion than they had been in that of his last three predecessors. For, in addition to having led the fight to limit the royal prerogative in New York, Nicoll also opposed the imposition of duties on trade, bluntly declaring that "The Custom-house at New York has contributed more to the upbuilding of Philadelphia than Mr. Penn's interest and artifice, which is not a little."[10]

Despite Hunter's opening entreaty on September 1 "to provide a suitable Support for her Majesty's Government," the assemblymen, their

memories of Cornbury's maladministration still fresh, ignored this request and resumed the more congenial work of circumscribing the queen's
prerogative. Thus they spent the next two months preparing various bills
to raise revenues for the provincial government, stipulating in each case
that the money so raised should be handled by their own treasurer rather
than the royal receiver. They also sought to prevent further gubernatorial
misuse of public funds by extending their control over the expenditure of
ordinary government revenues. Accordingly on November 4 they brought
in a one-year support bill which Hunter regarded as highly objectionable.
In addition to offering the governor only two-thirds of the salary he was
entitled to receive and his government only half of the money it needed to
meet its normal operating expenses, this measure also violated basic imperial policies by specifying the salaries government officials could be
paid and by directing the assembly treasurer to pay them.[11]

At this point Morris dramatically emerged from the obscurity in
which he had hitherto labored as a new assemblyman and forcefully
pleaded with his colleagues to pass a more liberal support bill. In a speech
delivered to the assembly on November 8, Morris justified his plea by citing the benefits which had accrued to New York under royal government
and as a result of Hunter's own actions. Since a regular form of royal government had been instituted in New York in 1691, Morris estimated, the
crown had spent £7,200 a year on the four companies of British regulars
which defended the colony's northern frontier and £22,500 a year on the
two guard ships which protected her trade. In addition, Morris pointed
out, Hunter himself had been personally responsible for the recent introduction of 2,500 Palatine refugees to produce naval stores in New York,
which, he calculated, was worth another £12,000 a year to the province.
In light of these vast expenditures and this significant increase in the colony's population, he told his auditors, it would be no exaggeration to conclude: "It is then to the bounty of the Crown solely, that we owe our being
rich or safe."

Yet in comparison to the liberality of the crown, Morris exclaimed,
how niggardly was the assembly! In return for the great sums it was ex-
pending to defend New York's frontiers and protect her trade, all the
crown expected from the assembly was a moderate support for the
queen's government. Instead the assembly was only offering Hunter an
annual salary of £1,000, which was £560 less than what his instructions
entitled him to, and it was being equally illiberal about making adequate
provision for the other costs of government. It was also guilty of repre-
hensible efforts to obstruct the introduction of motions merely to reconsider the issue of support, for in order "to prevent the Success of such a
motion," Morris sarcastically observed, "Sometimes discourses have been

raised, by three or four together to Overcome it with noise, at other times subjects altogether forreign to the matter Introduc't, to divert it, and gain time, Sometimes an Adjournmt. prayd, at other times Bills have been read to keep it off; and all these methods have prov'd Effectuall."

Having thus excoriated his fellow representatives, Morris then came to the heart of his proposal for increased government funding. In a bold attempt to win the landed interest for the governor's cause, he insisted that although New York was presently "poor and much in Debt," it was still possible to provide a more handsome support for Hunter's adminis- tration at relatively little direct cost to the people of the colony by "laying a Moderate Impost on Goods and liquors Imported." In this way, he argued, the assembly could raise the additional revenue needed by the government without resort to direct taxation of the inhabitants of the province, placing the burden instead on local merchants and such con- sumers as chose to purchase the goods the merchants imported:

> I appeal to you and to all the world, whether if an Easie duty had been laid on Cacao, if what was lately Imported would not have gone a great way to- wards supporting the Government, and without being felt by the Country. Wee may Expect such accidents, and there are many Strangers drop now and then in, which will by this method, be made to contribute, but if no such thing should happen, there will not be less Chocolate, Wine, or Rum drank, or less cloath wore, because these things will be a penny a pound, a quart, or a yard dearer than usuall. Trading men lay this tax on us every day, and ad- vance upon their Comodities as they are in demand, making the people pay for those necessitys, when the reall worth of the Comodities nor their charge on them, is no more than before such an advance. Since things are so, lett us take the most certain and Easie way of supporting the Government, and de- fraying our own Expences.

Morris concluded by sternly warning the assembly that unless it granted a more adequate revenue to Hunter the imperial administration would probably visit some unpleasant consequences on the colony. The four companies of British regulars might be withdrawn and the two guard ships removed. If so, the assembly would then have to increase drastically its own expenditures for provincial defense, which would lead in turn to an exodus of settlers from New York to neighboring colonies where the tax burden was lighter. So to avoid such harsh eventualities Morris for- mally moved that the assembly reconsider the question of support.[12]

The assembly's reaction to Morris' speech was scarcely what he had expected. Stung by his strong criticism of their behavior, the members of that body expelled him the day after he spoke on the grounds that he had "falsely and scandalously vilified the Integrity and Honesty of this House." Yet although Morris' speech failed to sway the assembly, it did strengthen his alliance with Hunter and raise his standing with the imperial administration. Hunter, who was grateful for Morris' vigorous effort in his behalf, sent a copy of the speech to the Board of Trade, and Board members were so impressed by it that they favorably alluded to it in a representation to the queen. George Clarke, the deputy auditor general in New York, also sent a copy to William Blathwayt, once the imperial administration's most influential member but now in the twilight of his career as auditor general of plantation revenues. Nor was knowledge of Morris' address confined to the chambers of Whitehall. John Chamberlayne, the SPG secretary, congratulated his American correspondent for "the Noble stand you made last year in your General Assembly in Defense of the Governor, or rather of the Royal Prerogative, for which you have been *tantum non Martyr,* and certainly a Confessor."[13] But this comment overlooked a highly significant feature of Morris' speech. Morris had criticized the assembly for inadequately supporting the government, but he had not denounced it for seeking extended control over the provincial purse. Like his erstwhile colleagues in the assembly, he was well aware of the misapplication of public funds by Cornbury and the need to prevent similar abuses in the future. He did not expect Hunter to imitate the noble lord in this respect, but he recognized that not every governor would be as personally honest as Hunter. Consequently he sympathized with the assembly's wish for stricter controls over the money it raised, but, unlike the current legislature, he wished to achieve them while retaining the essentials of royal authority required for balanced government.

After Morris' expulsion relations between Hunter and the assembly steadily deteriorated. In an effort to allay fears of further gubernatorial peculation, Hunter offered to make the royal receiver jointly responsible to the assemblymen and the crown, provided they gave up the pretensions of their treasurer to exclusive custody of all public funds. The assembly rejected this offer and proceeded to pass the very support bill Morris had criticized. After the council refused to approve this measure, Hunter adjourned the assembly on November 25, without having obtained any revenue for his administration; and then, when it continued to act obstreperously, he dissolved it in the following April. But as a result of his failure to receive fiscal support from the assembly, he complained to the Board of Trade, "all the absolutely necessary parts of the support of Government are now, and have been ever since my arrival here defray'd by my poor purs or credit, which you'l easily be convinced can not hold out long."[14]

Morris and Hunter's first encounter with the assembly left them with differing perceptions of how to deal with it. Hunter concluded that

his only hope of protecting the royal prerogative against the encroachments of the assembly was in securing a revenue for his administration
from Parliament. Otherwise, he assured his superiors in England, he
could only get funding from the assembly by agreeing to "give up Her
Majesties prerogative of appointg her own officers, and rewarding their
services, divert the Channell through which the receipt of her money has
ever run, and by these means reserve nothing but the name of a Government." In response to Hunter's pleas, the Board of Trade presented Parliament with draft bills to grant a revenue to the government of New York
in 1711 and 1713, but in both cases Parliament adjourned without considering them. Nevertheless in the long run the mere prospect of a parliamentary revenue had a sobering effect on the New York Assembly.[15]

In contrast, Morris sought to stave off parliamentary intervention
in New York by building up a court party in the assembly centered on the
landed interest that would provide Hunter with an ample revenue and satisfy the assembly's wish for greater control over provincial finances. Although Morris did not deny Parliament's constitutional right to grant a
revenue to the colony's government, he rightly feared that this would
lessen the powers of the assembly. At the same time he was drawn to the
idea of uniting the governor and the landed aristocracy both by interest
and temperament. As one of New York's foremost landed aristocrats,
Morris believed that this class was entitled to a preeminent role in the colony's political life and wanted it to shift the burden of supporting the government on to the merchants. Conversely he deplored the strong political
influence of the rival merchant interest, not only because the fiscal views
of its members were contrary to his own economic interests, but also because he had nothing but contempt for their business ethics, which he denounced as little more than a sustained effort "to amuse and deceive in
order to make a profitt."[16]

At first, however, neither Morris' nor Hunter's strategy had any ap-
preciable effect on the assembly. Whereas the coming to power of the
Harley ministry and the fall from favor of Hunter's Whig patrons made
the governor's continuance in office uncertain, thereby weakening his position vis-à-vis the assembly, New York's continued commercial stagnation lessened the force of Morris' arguments in favor of providing the
government with an ample revenue derived from trade duties and excise
taxes. Consequently Hunter's second assembly, which met at various in-
tervals between July 1711 and March 1713, refused to pass a support bill
that he regarded as financially adequate or constitutionally acceptable
and proved to be even more zealous than its predecessor in its efforts to
curb the royal prerogative. At length Hunter grew weary of trying to deal
with this obstreperous group of legislators, who obviously wanted to

make the provincial government more dependent on popular consent than the queen's prerogative, and therefore he dissolved the assembly in March 1713, after again having failed to obtain a regular grant of support for his administration from it. But in taking this step Hunter had little hope that new elections would produce a more accommodating group of assemblymen and bitterly complained to his friend Swift: "I am used like a dog after having done all that is in the power of Man to deserve a better treatment, so that I am now quite jaded."[17]

An obstreperous assembly was only one of the serious problems Morris and Hunter faced during the first half of the governor's administration in New York. They also had to contend with opposition to Hunter on the part of a small segment of the Anglican clergy in the colony. This issue was potentially explosive because it came to the fore while a Tory ministry was in power in England. Since the Tories took great pride in their role as defenders of the Church of England, Hunter could ill afford to appear hostile or indifferent to the Anglican cause in America lest he be replaced by a more zealous churchman. As a result, countering clerical opposition was almost as crucial to Morris and Hunter's political future in New York as reaching an accommodation with the assembly.

Hunter's difficulties with the clergy stemmed from his bitter feud with William Vesey, the rector of Trinity Church in New York City and the senior Anglican minister in the colony. Vesey was a vigorous advocate of Anglican expansion in America who viewed the more liberal Anglican Hunter with suspicion from the outset of his administration and whose misgivings soon developed into outright hostility. Vesey resented Hunter for giving Trinity Church a temporary rather than a perpetual lease on a tract known as the Queen's Farm, whence the rector derived part of his salary. Hunter further offended Vesey by renovating the Anglican chapel in Fort Anne, which had the effect of drawing parishioners away from Trinity and led the rector to accuse the governor of fomenting a schism in the church. But Hunter's gravest fault in the eyes of the rector was the restraint he exercised in dealing with a dispute between churchmen and dissenters over control of a church in Jamaica on Long Island. There George McNish, a Presbyterian divine, refused to relinquish possession of a church into which Hunter had inducted a young SPG missionary named Thomas Poyer in July 1710. In a similar case involving the same church some years before, Lord Cornbury had forcibly ejected the Presbyterian incumbent and installed another Anglican missionary, who had since died and been succeeded by McNish. Unwilling to follow the noble lord's arbitrary example and thereby offend New York's predominantly dissenting population, Hunter instead urged the Reverend Poyer to bring suit against McNish in a local court and offered to finance his appeal. However, Poyer rejected this generous offer and decided to await instructions from his superiors in England before acting. Morris applauded Hunter's decision to resolve the Jamaica imbroglio through legal means, but what to Morris was praiseworthy moderation was to Vesey final proof of the governor's lack of devotion to the interests of the church. Consequently Vesey became convinced of the need to have Hunter replaced by a more forceful defender of Anglican rights, and fortunately for him there was one ready at hand—Francis Nicholson, a peripatetic colonial governor and zealous churchman who had conquered Nova Scotia in the fall of 1710 and whose ambition to be Hunter's successor was no secret.[18]

Vesey did his best to enable Nicholson to realize this ambition. In this effort he received the wholehearted support of Jacob Henderson, a hot-tempered SPG missionary who stopped off in New York near the end of 1711 on his way back to England after unsuccessful pastorates in New Jersey and Pennsylvania. Henderson quickly came to share Vesey's belief that Hunter was more favorable to dissenters than churchmen and joined with him in striving to secure the governor's replacement by a more fervent exponent of Anglicanism. Accordingly, late in 1711, Vesey and Henderson prepared a memorial to the Bishop of London, who exercised ecclesiastical jurisdiction over the Anglican church in the colonies, which severely criticized Hunter's handling of the Jamaica dispute. They then circulated this document among their ministerial colleagues and obtained the signatures of a number of them who were apparently unaware of Hunter's offers of assistance to Poyer. However, when the memorial was brought to Aeneas MacKenzie, an SPG missionary on Staten Island who was more familiar with the facts in the case, he refused to sign it on the grounds that it was unfair to Hunter and subsequently persuaded most of its signers to retract their signatures. Consequently Vesey and Henderson were forced to draw up a second memorial to the bishop which simply described the Jamaica controversy, asked for guidance in the matter, and specifically disclaimed any intention of criticizing Hunter. It was then signed by eight ministers and taken to England by Henderson, who sailed from New York about the end of February 1712.[19]

Morris and Hunter, fearful that clerical criticism would destroy the governor's credit with the Harley administration, reacted strongly to the threat they perceived from Vesey and Henderson. Morris asked the two ministers for permission to read their memorial so that he could acquaint Hunter with their grievances, but his request was ignored. Hunter thereupon met with a special convocation of the New York clergy in February

1712 to present his side of the case in the Jamaica controversy. In an effort to disabuse the clergy of the notion that he had been lax in defending the church's rights, Hunter recounted his offers to finance a legal suit by Poyer and forcefully argued that English law left him with no other alternative. The assembled ministers assured Hunter of their confidence in his solicitude for the welfare of the church, but asserted that it still would be prudent for Poyer to await instructions from England before suing the dissenters. They also informed Hunter that their memorial cast no aspersions on him, but since they refused to show him a copy of it, he remained somewhat skeptical of their assurances.[20]

Morris and Hunter also took care to protect the governor's flank in England. Hunter wrote to the Bishop of London and the SPG, describing his services to the Anglican cause in New York and New Jersey in general and defending his behavior in the Jamaica affair in particular. Morris also argued the governor's case in letters to John Chamberlayne, his SPG correspondent, insisting that Hunter's refusal forcibly to install Poyer in the Jamaica church and his determination to settle this dispute by law were the wisest policies to follow under the circumstances, for only by going to court could the young missionary make good his claims without mortally offending the very dissenters whose conversion to Anglicanism was the main end of his mission. Moreover, he sharply criticized those clergymen who had caballed against Hunter, noting that in their zeal to oppose the governor they frequently lost sight of the spiritual goals the Venerable Society had sent them to America to achieve: "I could wish these Gentmn that are concerned in this matter, who are missionaries of the Society could be prevailed on to believe that making representations, and forming parties in Government or joyning and encouraging those already formed is not the interest of their mission, nor can be no good effect of it, and that others concerned may be told, if their own experience have not already convinced them of it, how much the more difficult it is to reconcile men than to divide them, and how much more becoming Persons, whose proper business it is to preach the Gospel of Peace."[21]

Morris' and Hunter's letters to these English church officials achieved their purpose. When Henderson arrived in England with the clerical memorial about Jamaica the SPG responded by requesting the queen to facilitate Poyer's suit by removing all restrictions on legal appeals to the governor and council in cases involving the Anglican church. Anne not only agreed to this request, but in January 1713 she also approved an order eliminating the restrictions on appeals to the Privy Council in such cases. Yet in all this the SPG was careful to assure Hunter that it was making no reflections on him and to commend the New York clergy for refraining from any criticism of the governor in their memorial.[22]

Unfortunately for Morris and Hunter, Henderson did more than simply deliver the Jamaica memorial while he was in England. He also launched a vicious attack on them as traitors to the church in New York and New Jersey. In a representation drawn up for the Board of Trade in June 1712, Henderson accused Hunter of virtually inviting the Presbyterians to seize the Jamaica church by replacing some local Anglican magistrates with dissenters soon after his arrival in New York. He also criticized severely Hunter's proposals to reorganize the membership of the New Jersey Council, alleging that they were deliberately designed to destroy Anglican control of that body and make dissenters politically supreme in the colony. In this regard Henderson was sharply critical of Morris, whom he described as the political leader of New Jersey dissenters and castigated as "a profess'd Church man, but a man of noe manner of principles or credit, a man who calls the service of the Church of England Pageantry, who has joyned in endeavours to settle a conventicle in the City of New York and whose practice it is to intercept letters, and let such as pleases him pass, and those that doe not he destroys as can be fully proved."[23] Although the queen ultimately approved the changes in the New Jersey Council suggested by Hunter, it is possible that Henderson's representation was partially responsible for delaying this action until April 1713.

Morris and Hunter took steps to rebut Henderson's charges almost as soon as they learned of them. Thus in February 1713 Hunter summoned a convocation of Anglican clergymen from New York and New Jersey and again proclaimed his zeal for the church. Morris also gave the assembled clergy a copy of Henderson's representation, together with a refutation of it he had written. In the latter Morris accused Henderson of gross ignorance of New Jersey affairs and flatly denied the personal charges Henderson had made against him, though he did admit that once he had had a conversation with the fiery missionary in which he had assumed the role of a dissenter and rhetorically argued that one part of the rite used in consecrating Anglican bishops did indeed smack of "Pageantry." Through these means Morris and Hunter induced the clergy to reaffirm their confidence in the governor and to repudiate Henderson's attack on his nominees for the New Jersey Council. Hunter thereupon dispatched the proceedings of this convocation to England where they helped to maintain his standing with his Tory superiors.[24]

Henderson's mission to England was the high point of Anglican opposition to Hunter in New York. Thereafter Reverend Poyer finally decided to follow the governor's advice and take legal action against the dissenters. In consequence he won a decision in his favor from a supreme court presided over by Morris himself in 1715, although in practice this judgment proved to be difficult to enforce. Rector Vesey was not won over so easily. He continued to hope for Francis Nicholson's appointment as governor, and in 1714 he went to England to try to bring this about. Although this goal eluded him, he did secure an appointment for himself as commissary of the Bishop of London and returned to New York in 1715 to begin a reluctant reconciliation with Hunter. Yet despite the failure of Hunter's Anglican opponents to effect his removal, they did succeed in temporarily making his situation in New York more difficult by contributing to the popular impression that his days in office were numbered under Harley's administration.[25]

This whole episode marked the beginning of a momentous transformation in Morris' intellectual and spiritual life. Although for the rest of his life Morris formally remained a member of the Church of England, he stopped corresponding with the SPG after 1712 and eventually ceased to be a Christian in any meaningful sense of the term. The inner dynamics of this change are largely unknown — and it certainly would be rash to attribute it primarily to his disgust with Hunter's ministerial adversaries — but the outward signs are clear enough. Morris abandoned his faith in the divine inspiration of Scripture and the divinity of Christ. He became bitterly anticlerical and looked forward to the end of "those feares and horrid Phantoms wch terrify the Superstitious and the bigots, to whom we Owe the power of priests and all the mischiefs Consequentiall to it." In place of the triune God of Christianity, he came to believe in a sort of Unitarian deity whom he described as "a being whose character consists in everything thats lovely and Amiable, and has nothing terrible or frightfull in it; who having all power, cannot faile of giving his creatures happinesse (for wch as I said before they could only be created); who Loves mankind beter than parents can love children, or friends Each other." Instead of the sacred mysteries of the church to which he nominally belonged, he eventually professed his adherence to "A rationall faith to which most priests are intire Strangers" and sought to conduct himself "According to the Dictates of Nature and reason." With such beliefs as these it was only to be expected that when the Great Awakening swept through the colonies Morris greeted it with scorn and contemptuously referred to "the Enthusiastick reveries of Whitefield" and "Whitefields Deliriums."[26] In short, as Morris advanced in years he exhibited that curious blend of religious liberalism and political conservatism which was also a distinguishing characteristic of many other adherents of the early Enlightenment in America and Europe.

Morris' success in helping to fend off clerical opposition to Hunter was matched by his success in building up a strong court party in the assembly. This process began in earnest during the elections for a new assembly in the spring of 1713. At that time Morris and Hunter both made direct appeals to the voters of the colony to select a more cooperative representative body. Morris published an address "To the Inhabitants and Free-holders of Westchester County," which despite its title was distributed throughout the province. In this pamphlet Morris sought to win the support of New York's landed aristocracy, yeomen farmers, and urban artisans and craftsmen by urging that the government be provided with a revenue derived from duties on imported trade goods and excise taxes on retailed liquor. Morris admitted that merchants would pass the costs of trade duties on to consumers, but argued this would still affect far fewer people than a land tax, for "since *Money* must be rais'd by some means or other, for the Support of Government, it must appear to all reasonable men to be much more for our ease and advantage to be done by a Duty than by a land Tax, because it is not the sober, industrious, prudent or needy part of Mankind who will bear that Charge, but the rich, vain and extravagant; for those who can satisfie themselves with being clad in home-spun, and instead of Wine, Brandy and Rum, make use of Syder, Beer and such Spirits as we can distill from our own produce, will be intirely free'd from paying any thing towards the Support of Government."

Morris rejected the contention of merchants that indirect taxation of trade would drive commerce away from New York. He pointed out that the rates to be imposed would be as moderate as they had been in the past and reminded his readers "that if we allow that the Custom on Liquors and *European* Goods to be really refunded by those who purchase them from the Merchant, the burthen thereof will only lie on such who are best able to bear it, as Gentlemen of Estates in Towns and Cities, and the Rich Farmer in the Country. And can it be thought hard for a Gentleman whose Estate allows him to spend two or three hundred Pounds annually in housekeeping and other good living, to add forty Shillings or three Pounds more to it, for the Duty of those Liquors his plentiful Fortune allows him to consume? Or will it be too heavy for our most substantial Farmers upon the gathering in of their Crops, and on other Occasions, to pay 10s. or 12s. extraordinary in the Price of their Rum towards the Support of Government?" Moreover, in an obvious effort to woo New York City artisans and craftsmen, Morris proposed to encourage local shipbuilding and break the stranglehold of Bermudians on New York's carrying trade by following the example of Pennsylvania and laying a discriminatory duty on all incoming vessels that were not owned by inhabitants of the colony.

Morris did not restrict himself to economic arguments. He also warned that unless the new assembly raised an adequate revenue for

Hunter's administration, Parliament would intervene and provide one for it. Morris raised no constitutional objections to parliamentary taxation, but he did note that in at least two ways it would significantly diminish the political autonomy New Yorkers had come to enjoy: "The first is, That for want of the Assemblies having an opportunity to inspect and examine the Accounts, we shall not be able to prevent Mis-applications, and so, in a great measure, loose the benefit of saving the Country from being burthened with many Taxes, which the Revenue, under a fair management, would defray and answer. And 2dly, Our Governours being provided for without our assistance, will make it very difficult for us to obtain such Laws as we want, but what we must dearly purchase." Morris tried to allay fears of future gubernatorial misuse of public funds by urging acceptance of Hunter's proposal to make the royal receiver jointly responsible to the assembly and the crown. Yet, sensing that this expedient would be dismissed as inadequate by proponents of more stringent popular control of provincial finances, he conceded that it might become necessary to consider "incerting such Clauses in our Acts for settling the Revenue as may secure us against Frauds, Abuses and Mis-applications" — a pregnant thought, as will be seen. Although some of Morris' opponents responded to his pamphlet by dubbing him one of the "Retainers to the Gyant *Revenue*," subsequent events were soon to demonstrate that his arguments in favor of taxing trade had impressed those groups to which he had directed them.[27]

While Morris attempted to rally the landed interest and urban craftsmen for Hunter, the governor eloquently defended the rights of the crown against the encroachments of the assembly. In a crisply written pamphlet entitled *To All whom these Presents may Concern,* Hunter reviewed all the constitutional points at issue between himself and the assembly and in each instance upheld the prerogative point of view. He called upon the voters of the province to elect representatives to the assembly who, in accordance with the queen's instructions, would provide his government with a revenue that would be held by the royal receiver and dispensed by gubernatorial warrants issued with the advice and consent of the council. In order to make this palatable to New Yorkers, he repeated his earlier offers of joint responsibility for the receiver and ridiculed those who asserted that unless the assembly exercised stricter controls over the provincial purse, "*Revenue* and *Slavery* are Synonymous Terms, and mean the same thing." Most important of all, however, he reiterated Morris' prediction that Parliament would intervene if the assembly did not grant adequate support to the government and warned New Yorkers to "Settle a Revenue and that Speedily, Or . . . *It will be settled to your Hands.*"[28]

Despite the efforts of Morris and Hunter, at first it seemed that the new assembly would be no more cooperative than the old. "All the avow'd opposers of her Majesty's interest are chosen again, and avowedly for that end," the governor complained to the secretary of the Board of Trade in May 1713, "for men of the best sence and figure have been rejected for the bare supposition that they would be for supporting the Government." In this case, however, Hunter thoroughly misread the temper of the returning assemblymen. To be sure, only five new members were chosen during the spring elections, but for a variety of reasons most representatives were finally ready for an accommodation with the governor. To begin with, they were apprehensive at the thought of parliamentary intervention in New York and were therefore amenable to providing the government with at least a short-term revenue. They were also anxious to pay off the colony's substantial public debt and in order to win Hunter's consent to this they were willing to tone down their attacks on the prerogative. In addition there was an upswing in New York's commerce in 1713 which weakened the force of merchant objections to imposing duties on trade and convinced a majority of the assembly to accept Morris' arguments in favor of indirect taxation. This was graphically illustrated in the spring of 1713 by the assembly's use of this method to raise the revenue for an otherwise ungenerous one-year grant of support to Hunter's administration. But later in the year Hunter's credit with the assembly and Morris' ability to function as his legislative manager in it were further enhanced by the arrival of news of the queen's approval of the governor's proposed changes in the New Jersey Council. Hunter immediately recognized the impact this striking sign of favor from the imperial administration would have in New York, observing that it would "enable me to struggle chearfully with all other difficulties, for indeed the notion that a faction here had spread, that I was disregarded at home, and consequently speedily to be recall'd had gained so much credit, that the friends of the government cooled whilst the others triumphed." Since Morris' power in New York was always partly a function of Hunter's standing in England, the imperial administration's action enabled him to proceed with confidence in working out a settlement between the governor and the assembly.[29]

The instrument by which Morris planned to achieve this settlement was the payment of New York's public debt. By 1714 the governor and the assembly both agreed on the need for paying this off. At that time a wide variety of New Yorkers had a large assortment of financial claims on the provincial government dating back to the period before the Glorious Revolution. Among these claimants, to list only the more common categories, were public creditors who had loaned money to the government, workmen who had performed services for it, militiamen who had not been paid for their participation in the three Canadian expeditions since 1690, and government officials whose salaries were in arrears. Hunter himself had incurred debts of approximately £30,000 since coming to New York and was naturally eager to obtain some compensation for them. Of this sum, £22,144 had resulted from his expenditures on the unsuccessful scheme to produce naval stores with the labor of Palatine refugees, which had been abandoned by the Harley ministry and could only be reimbursed by the British government. But the remainder had been occasioned by his need to pay for many costs of the government on his personal credit during the period his administration had received no revenue from the assembly, and it was for this amount that he expected repayment from the assembly. Morris had no monetary claims of his own on the government, but he was fully aware of the desirability of attaching the various claimants to the governor's interest.[30]

From the outset of a lengthy legislative session beginning in March 1714 and lasting almost continuously until the following September, Morris took the lead in "drawing and contriving" a momentous Public Debt Act which laid the foundation for a lasting accommodation between Hunter and the assembly.[31] So great was Morris' influence on this law that when Robert Livingston, a powerful landed aristocrat whose political career sometimes seems like nothing more than an exercise in mendicancy, surveyed the opposition to his claims in the assembly, he took comfort in the thought that "Mr. Morris is my friend."[32] Although Livingston failed to receive satisfaction for all his claims, his remark is still illustrative of Morris' high standing in the assembly at this time, which was itself a direct result of the imperial administration's recent show of favor to the governor Morris served.

The Public Debt Act Morris drew up and guided through the assembly was an important step in the creation of a formidable court party in that body. It set the provincial debt at £27,680 and provided for its payment in bills of credit which were to be periodically sunk by the revenue from a twenty-year excise on retailed liquors. The total amount of the debt set by the act was no more important than those whose claims it recognized, for, as Livingston also observed, in the assembly "everything goes to favouritism."[33] Among the several hundred claimants whose demands were honored, Hunter received £4,950 to make up for his "arrears of Salary" and expenditures on "publick services" since 1710. Numerous public creditors were finally paid for the loans they had extended to various administrations over the last two decades, just as were many workmen for the chores they had performed for the government during that period. Militiamen obtained long overdue compensation for their service in the Canadian expeditions, while royal officials received some of their back salaries. Perhaps the most important payment of all, however, was that of £2,025 to Jacob Leisler, Jr., in consummation of "a Bargaine . . . between Morris and [the Leislerian] party."[34] By this act Morris gave symbolic recognition to the legitimacy of the elder Leisler's revolt and won for Hunter the support of the fallen leader's predominantly Dutch following, which was still a force to be reckoned with in New York City and the Hudson River Valley. Finally, to prevent the widely detested Lord Cornbury (since become third Earl of Clarendon) from asserting a claim to the salary the assembly had denied him during the last half of his administration in New York, Morris wrote into the Debt Act a ban on future claims against the government.[35]

Morris also used the Public Debt Act to satisfy the assembly's wish for stricter control over the ordinary revenue of government. Samuel Mulford, a Suffolk County representative and close ally of Speaker William Nicoll, raised this issue early in the session in a way Morris could not ignore. Addressing the assembly on April 2, Mulford vigorously denied the legitimacy of the claims for compensation then before it. Since many of the claimants were the victims of the financial irregularities of New York governors, he argued that "when there was Sufficient [money] put into their Majesties officers hands for the support of Governmt and the same is Imbezzled, it cannot in Justice be a Debt of the Country, neither are they liable to make it good." Instead of paying the existing debt, Mulford told his colleagues, they should concentrate on preventing further misapplications of public funds and increases in the debt by placing all the money they raised in the hands of their treasurer and itemizing how it could be spent.[36]

Although most assemblymen were unsympathetic to Mulford's opposition to paying the public debt, they were receptive to his call for stricter popular control of provincial finances. Morris shared this sentiment, despite his public endorsement of Hunter's proposal simply to make the royal receiver jointly accountable to the assembly and the crown. Therefore, to satisfy the assembly's scruples while avoiding open embarrassment to the governor, Morris adopted an ingenious expedient. He inserted a clause into the Debt Act stipulating that whereas in the future the assembly would dispose of the money it raised and lodged in the custody of its treasurer, the governor and council could freely expend the funds the assembly placed in the hands of the royal receiver. By the simple device of entrusting virtually all the money it raised to the care of its treasurer, the assembly was now in a position to reduce the receiver to a nullity, lessen the fiscal prerogatives of the governor and council, and enhance its own control over the provincial purse. Needless to say, this is precisely what occurred after the Debt Act went into effect. This stratagem was a perfect expression of Morris' method of unobtrusively increasing the assembly's power of the purse by "incerting such Clauses in our Acts for settling the Revenue as may secure us against Frauds, Abuses and Misapplications for the future."[37]

Whatever qualms Hunter had about the constitutional implications of the Public Debt Act were offset by the financial relief it offered him and by his belated recognition that parliamentary intervention in New York was unlikely. Thus he gave his consent to this measure on September 4, 1714. Since the act entailed the emission of paper money, however, it was considered prudent to obtain royal approval of it before it went into effect, and so it was sent to England with a suspending clause. There it encountered strong opposition from the Earl of Clarendon, who criticized its failure to recognize his claims and its token payment of £90 to Morris, his hated rival, "for drawing of it, a thing never before heard of in that Government." But after the accession of George I the imperial administration was less impressed by the complaints of the Tory Clarendon than the arguments of the Whig Hunter, who asserted that confirmation of the Debt Act was essential to strengthen his hand in dealing with the assembly and to relieve his financial distress. Accordingly the king approved it in June 1715.

Although for Morris the monetary rewards of the Public Debt Act were slight, the political benefits were great. In addition to winning for the court party the support of Leislerians and many other beneficiaries of the act, the passage of this law also brought Morris to the highest public office he had thus far held in his career. After the death in January 1715 of Roger Mompesson, the chief justice of the New York Supreme Court, Hunter commissioned Morris to serve as Mompesson's successor at the "will and pleasure" of the governor and the king. Hunter pointed out to his English superiors that no one was better suited for this office than Morris, "he having by his labours and industry in the Assemblies, deserved well of the Government and to that it is in a great measure we owe our present settlement." But not everyone shared the governor's generous estimate of his legislative manager. In England Morris' appointment was attacked by Charles Lodwick, a London merchant who acted as an unofficial agent for New York merchants. Lodwick protested to the Board of Trade that Morris was unqualified to serve as chief justice and charged that he owed his appointment strictly to the fact that he was "the Governours perticular favorit." Lodwick conveniently ignored Morris' six years of service on the East Jersey Court of Common Right, but in any case it is safe to assume that he was less concerned about Morris' alleged legal ignorance than about halting the rise of the foremost opponent of his merchant allies in New York. Despite Lodwick's opposition, the Board of Trade—on which Morris' old friend, Paul Docminique, now sat— reported in favor of Morris' retention as chief justice, cogently arguing "that it is for his Majesty's service that persons in the Plantations who shall distinguish themselves in His Majesty's intrest and for the good of the Government, be rewarded with such places as are in the disposal of the Governors there." Consequently George I confirmed Morris' appointment on September 30, 1715, so that for the next eighteen years Morris held one of the most important public offices in New York, from which he could be removed only by a governor or a king.[38]

Although the paucity of Morris' legal papers and the terseness of the supreme court records preclude an extended analysis of his tenure as chief justice, a few general observations may be made. As chief justice, Morris presided over a supreme court which had original jurisdiction over "all pleas and causes, civil, criminal and mixed . . . as fully and amply . . . as the Courts of King's Bench, Common Pleas and Exchequer" in England as well as appellate jurisdiction in all criminal cases and such civil cases as involved disputes about land titles or other forms of property worth at least £20. In addition to sitting in New York City, the justices also conducted business at circuit courts in the outlying counties of the province. James DeLancey, Morris' immediate successor as chief justice, took advantage of the opportunity of riding the circuits to ingratiate himself with the people and build up popular support for himself and his faction. In this respect there is no evidence that DeLancey was following in the footsteps of his predecessor, because, unlike the gregarious DeLancey, Morris had an austere demeanor which even one of his friends admitted was not "fitted to gain popularity." On the other hand, in an age when public criticism of the established authorities could still lead to prosecution for seditious libel, Morris' presence on the bench tended to have an intimidating effect on his political rivals, and, as will be seen, he himself was not above using his judicial powers to advance his political goals.[39]

As the fates of the Public Debt Act and Morris' appointment as chief justice suggest, the political power of Hunter and his legislative manager was measurably enhanced by the accession of George I in August 1714. The accompanying demoralization of the Tories and return to office of the Whigs—including several of Hunter's patrons—strengthened the governor's bargaining power with the assembly by removing the prospect of his imminent recall by an unfriendly ministry in England. In addition the appointment of the West Jersey Society's Paul Docminique to the Board of Trade in the fall of 1714 gave Morris a highly placed connection in the imperial administration, although this was less important to him in his capacity as legislative manager than the fact that the governor he served stood high in the estimation of the imperial administration. With their English flank now secure, Morris and Hunter were finally in a position to achieve a goal that had thus far eluded them — a long-term support for the governor's administration.

The automatic dissolution of the assembly upon the death of Queen Anne gave Morris and Hunter an excellent opportunity to bring this about. Thanks in part to the governor's creation of two new assembly seats in the Hudson River Valley, his judicious distribution of crown lands, and his promise to support a general naturalization law, supporters and opponents of a long-term revenue were evenly divided when the new assembly met for the first time in the summer of 1715. Morris and Hunter thereupon broke this deadlock through an intricate series of strategic maneuvers and constitutional compromises. Morris and his supporters managed to effect the expulsion of Samuel Mulford, one of the most vocal advocates of short-term grants, after Mulford had imprudently published his previous year's speech to the assembly without the assembly's permission. The royal attorney general then prosecuted Mulford in the supreme court for malicious libel because of some criticisms of Hunter in that address. Mulford objected to the prosecution on the grounds that it was contrary to the privileges of the assembly "to Appeach any Member of the same in any Court or Place but in the House," only to have Chief Justice Morris overrule his objection and order the case to proceed. Although the ultimate outcome of Mulford's case is unknown, it seems virtually certain that his prosecution had an inhibiting effect on other opponents of Hunter.[40]

With Morris and the court party now holding a slight edge over their opponents, the assembly proceeded to pass a five-year Support Act in return for Hunter's approval of a comprehensive Naturalization Act. The latter, by naturalizing all foreign-born Protestants in the province, gave security of tenure to New Yorkers of French and Dutch descent who had had doubts about the validity of their land titles and enabled them to evade the provision in the Navigation Acts forbidding aliens to act as merchants or factors in the colonies. On the other hand, the Support Act represented the triumph of Morris' efforts to build up a court party based upon the landed interest and dedicated to the principle of stricter popular control over provincial finances. As Morris had advocated ever since 1710, this act provided the government with a revenue from the indirect taxation of trade by levying duties on imported European goods, wines, slaves, and distilled liquors. It also laid duties on all incoming vessels except those owned by New Yorkers, those coming directly from Great Britain, or those arriving from nearby colonies, so as to foster local shipbuilding and benefit the colony's artisans and craftsmen — a policy which, in somewhat different form, Morris had advocated in 1713.[41]

However, the unwritten provisions of the 1715 Support Act were even more significant than the written ones. In order to persuade the assembly to make a five-year grant, Morris first had to induce Hunter to give his word of honor to the assemblymen that he would expend the money to be raised by this act "in such proportions and to such officers, and such other uses only as they should ascertain in their Journal." In the absence of any hope of parliamentary intervention in his behalf, Hunter consented to this arrangement to secure the long-term revenue for his government that he had been seeking since 1710. By convincing Hunter to agree privately to expend support funds as the assembly's resolves directed, Morris enabled the assembly to acquire effective control over the disbursement of the ordinary revenue of government without having recourse to the passage of a Support Act specifically listing how the governor could spend the money it appropriated. This was perfectly consistent with Morris' aim of expanding the assembly's power of the purse through indirection rather than by a frontal assault on the prerogative. Morris tried to soften the impact of this usurpation of the king's right to reward his servants by later claiming that the salaries of Hunter and all other royal officials were determined by mutual agreement between the governor and the assembly, but Hunter's own testimony to the Board of Trade clearly shows that the assembly had the final say in this matter.[42] Thus Morris played a key role in simultaneously securing a lengthy grant of revenue for Hunter and bringing about greater popular control of the provincial financial system — a somewhat paradoxical achievement for which he unwittingly provided this explanation some years later: "Why you must Know tho the Steward [governor] and the clods [assemblymen] Seeme to be the most Opposite of Anything that can be, yet they are really Embarkt in one interest and manage with one View, for the Steward allwaies wants money which the clods can Supply but will not do it without a Quid pro quo and that must be some of the lords [monarch's] prerogatives or Lands which is in the Stewards disposall."[43]

With the passage of the Public Debt Act of 1714 and the Support Act of 1715, Morris achieved his goal of establishing the ascendancy of the court party in the assembly. This coalition was composed of several disparate elements. At its core were the great landed aristocrats of the Hudson River Valley, who welcomed the opportunity to shift the burden of supporting the government on to the merchants. Hudson River Valley farmers and New York City artisans and craftsmen also adhered to the court party: the former because of their aversion to property taxes and the latter because of the benefits they anticipated from an upsurge in local shipbuilding. In both these areas of the colony Dutch settlers, grateful for Morris' symbolic recognition of Jacob Leisler as well as the 1715 Naturalization Act, were firm supporters of the governor's cause. Indeed, more than a decade later Morris acknowledged that ever since he had first entered the New York Assembly "the Support that the Government has from time to time received has been chiefly owing to the Interest of those Members in the House who were of Dutch extraction.[44] Lastly, cutting across class, ethnic, and sectional lines, was the support the court party received from many of the beneficiaries of the Debt Act.

The achievements of the court party under Morris' leadership were as impressive as the breadth of its support. For the first time in almost a decade the provincial government had a regular, long-term revenue, while the people of the province had firm guarantees against executive misuse of it. Numerous public creditors had received satisfaction for their claims, while the infusion of more than £27,000 of paper money into the local economy quickened commerce. Dutch and French settlers, their land titles once in doubt, now enjoyed security of tenure. Apparently all that remained for Morris and Hunter was to capitalize on these achievements in order to increase the number of administration supporters in the assembly.

Before proceeding to this step, Morris and Hunter took time near the end of 1715 to satirize the principal political adversaries they had encountered during the first half of the governor's administration in New York and New Jersey. They did this through the medium of *Androboros: A Biographical Farce in Three Acts,* the first play written and published in a British colony. This satire, which Hunter deserves the major share of the credit for writing, deals with an only partly imaginary plot by the New York Assembly, some New York clergy, and West Jersey Anglicans to replace Hunter with Lord Cornbury or Francis Nicholson — a plot that is naturally foiled at the last minute by the timely efforts of Hunter, Morris, and their supporters. Such a vehicle gave Morris and Hunter many opportunities to vent their spleen against their opponents, and they did not hesitate to use them. Thus they wittily parodied the New York Assembly's attack on the prerogative by magically transforming Daniel Coxe, Jr., into a New York assemblyman and having him declare to his new colleagues "that neither this House, or they whom we Represent are bound by any Laws, Rules or Customs, any Law, Rule or Custom to the Contrary notwithstanding." But this was tame stuff compared to their acidulous characterizations of some of their other adversaries. In a scene where Speaker William Nicoll, who spearheaded the antiprerogative forces, urges the assembly to adopt rules of procedure, a character observes of him: "Tis something strange that he who ever affirm'd, That Laws and Liberty were things Incompatible, should propose to proceed by Rules." William Vesey, Hunter's main clerical opponent, is depicted as an inveterate schemer whose brains are "so shallow that a Louse may suck 'em up without surfeiting," while Adolph Philipse, a leading merchant, is portrayed as a satyr with "a wonderful Energy in the two most Unruly Members of the Body, [who] has been follow'd of late by the Women and Boys." One character expresses misgivings about Cornbury "because a man who could never yet Govern himself, will make but a sorry Governour for others," and another dismisses Nicholson as a blowhard who "talks of nothing but Battles and Seiges, tho' he never saw one, and Conquests over Nations and Alliances with Princes who never had a being." Although the impact of political satire cannot be measured with statistical precision, Morris and Hunter's first and only joint venture in this genre does seem to have been successful, for many years later one of their friends asserted that in consequence of the publication of *Androboros* "The general (Nicholson), the clergy, and the Assembly were so humorously exposed that the laugh was turned upon them in all companies and from this laughing humour the people began to be in good humour with their Governor and to despise the idol of the clergy."[45]

Morris and Hunter's confidence in their ability to flay their opponents in print with impunity was fully justified. In 1716 Hunter created two more assembly seats in the Hudson River Valley and held new assembly elections in which perhaps as many as two-thirds of the representatives chosen by the voters were adherents of the court party. Hunter was especially gratified by the defeat of four New York City merchants who had opposed passage of a long-term revenue in the assembly. Morris took advantage of this striking accession of strength to help win assembly approval in the following year for a second major Public Debt Act, which repaid Hunter for still more personal expenditures on public business, reimbursed many Leislerians for their services during the Glorious Revolution, and recompensed assemblymen and councilors for their attendance at the session which passed the act. But the most dramatic sign of Morris' success in reconciling the "monarchical" and "democratical" branches of the provincial government came in 1718 when William Nicoll, the leader of the assembly's assault on the prerogative, stepped down as speaker and was succeeded by Robert Livingston, Hunter's ally and the most politically influential landed aristocrat in the colony after Morris. Little wonder that Hunter boasted to the secretary of the Board of Trade: "All is well in both Provinces and a perfect harmony reigning among all parties."[46]

The governor's optimism was premature. Morris' success in establishing a strong court party in the assembly based upon the landed interest inevitably aroused the opposition of the rival merchant interest. This first appeared in the form of a protest against the Public Debt Act of 1717. New York merchants denied the legitimacy of many of the claims on the government this act recognized. They also feared that its provision for the emission of another £16,607 in bills of credit would depress the value of those already in circulation and that its extension of the excise on retailed liquors for another five years would tempt the assembly to lay other taxes on trade. Accordingly in November 1717 a New York City grand jury dominated by local merchants petitioned Hunter while the Debt Act was still under consideration by the assembly and urged him not to let it pass without a suspending clause. Hunter, who at this time was in no mood to wait for royal approval of his claims, turned this petition over to the lower house, where it angered everyone, including Speaker Nicoll. Morris seized the occasion to have the hapless merchants brought before the assembly and browbeaten for supposedly petitioning the governor in contempt of the councilors and representatives of the province. The merchants denied the charge of contempt but admitted the impropriety of their petition and were allowed to go free. Morris thus succeeded in cowing his opposition and went on to help pass a Public Debt Act which issued over £16,000 in bills of credit without the approbation of the king.[47]

Morris only temporarily subdued the merchants by these rough tactics. The merchants still opposed the second Public Debt Act, and their anger rose to even greater heights in January 1718 when Hunter misinterpreted a royal ban on the entry of French ships into New York to include a prohibition on the sailing of local vessels to the French West Indies. This deprived the merchants of some of their most lucrative markets, a loss that was only aggravated later in the year by the closure of the Spanish West Indies as a consequence of the outbreak of a short-lived war between England and Spain over the enormously complicated "Italian problem." The loss of these markets plunged New York into a commercial depression which lasted until 1722 and caused the merchants to call upon their English correspondents to help them secure the disallowance of the Public Debt Act of 1717 and the opening of the French West Indies to New York shipping. Morris contemptuously referred to the alliance between the merchants of New York and their English factors as "the Guinea Company . . . A company dwelling or Sojourning for the time being in the Capitall city [London] of the Lord of the mannour" and consisting "of men, women, boys, and girls of all nations, religions, and conditions that can be prevail'd on to contribute a guinea towards Supporting the pretences of the Nicks [New York merchants] when they grow moody and out of humour at anything done here."[48]

Morris' disdain for the "Guinea Company" was tempered by a

healthy respect for its influence with the imperial administration. Although English merchants like Charles Lodwick, Samuel Baker, and Samuel Storke ultimately sought in vain to have the second Public Debt Act disallowed, they did succeed in having Hunter ordered to reopen the French West Indies to New York commerce. Yet even before they had been besieged by cries for help from their American correspondents, the English merchants trading with New York had threatened to undo the accommodation Morris had worked out between the governor and the court party in the provincial assembly. To help raise a revenue for the government of the colony Morris and the court party had placed a differential duty on imported wine in the Support Act of 1715, charging a lower rate on wines brought directly from the place of manufacture. And to encourage local shipbuilding they had passed a Tonnage Duty Act in 1716, exempting ships wholly owned by New Yorkers from the charges on incoming vessels and charging a lower duty on ships owned and built by New Yorkers that carried slaves to the colony directly from Africa. English merchants charged that all three measures discriminated against English commerce. The first required English merchants who shipped Madeira wine from England to New York, for example, to pay higher duties than other ships carrying the same cargo to the same destination directly from the place of manufacture. The second and the third, on the other hand, gave New York shippers an unfair advantage over their English competitors — or so the merchants claimed. The Board of Trade gave ear to these complaints and in February 1718 ordered Hunter to have the assembly revise both acts in accordance with the interests of English commerce, or suffer their disallowance by the king. Since the Support Act of 1715 represented the triumph of the landed interest in New York, its annulment would have been a heavy blow to Morris and the court party.[49]

Morris immediately recognized the gravity of this threat. As soon as the governor conveyed the Board's directions to a session of the assembly meeting in the fall of 1718, his legislative manager began to move his colleagues in the lower house to comply with the imperial administration's expectations. Morris personally prepared a representation in the assembly's behalf for Hunter to send back to England. In it he defended the efficacy of supporting the provincial government and paying the public debt with taxes on trade rather than property, arguing that it was only fair that merchants "who received an Advantage by our Trade, contribute their Mite to the Support of that Government, which protected them and us in it." He also pointed out that while English ships had so far had to pay only £200 under the Tonnage Duty Act of 1716, New Yorkers had imported no wine from England to cause mercantile complaints there about the differential duty on that commodity in the Support Act of 1715. Yet

Morris was well aware that he could not treat the Board of Trade as cavalierly as he had treated the merchant opponents of the recent Debt Act. Thus he announced that the assembly would revise the two acts in question by lowering the duties on all wines and liquors directly imported from England, charging ships owned by Englishmen bringing slaves directly from Africa the same rates paid by ships belonging to New Yorkers, and exempting English vessels from the 1716 tonnage duty. As a result of these prudent concessions to English mercantile opinion, Morris prevented the disallowance of the Support Act of 1715 and maintained the court party's control over the assembly.[50]

Morris had barely mastered this challenge to the court party when an even greater one arose. In July 1719 Hunter suddenly returned to England on a temporary leave of absence owing to ill health, his wish to obtain reimbursement from Parliament for the £22,144 he had expended on the unsuccessful Palatine project, and the need to secure imperial approval of the 1717 Public Debt Act. After the governor's departure Morris assumed command of the government of New Jersey by virtue of his position as that colony's senior councilor, while Peter Schuyler, an Albany merchant who opposed the Morrisites, did likewise in New York. However, Hunter's absence from these two provinces became permanent in April 1720 when he exchanged offices with the comptroller of customs in London, William Burnet, the intensely Whiggish son of the celebrated Whig bishop and historian Gilbert Burnet. This unexpected action by Hunter, who had grown weary of serving the crown in America, plunged the New York political scene into turmoil. Morris suddenly found himself without the governor upon whose confidence and support his effectiveness as a legislative manager depended. The court party knew not what attitude the new governor would take toward it, while the merchant interest looked forward to Burnet's arrival, anticipating the customary dissolution of the existing assembly and hoping to rout their opponents in the ensuing election. Which side would prevail now depended upon Governor Burnet.

⚹ 7 ⚹

"A Wise Man Sick of Publick Employs"

OVERNOR WILLIAM BURNET'S ARRIVAL IN NEW YORK on September 16, 1720, touched off a spirited contest between Morris and the merchant interest to win the new executive's support. The merchants, fused together into a coherent political faction in response to the passage of the Public Debt Act of 1717 and the commercial depression caused by Hunter's temporary interdiction of trade with the French and Spanish West Indies in the following year, were eager to end Morris and the landed interest's domination of the provincial assembly. Led by Adolph Philipse and Peter Schuyler and enjoying the support of half the membership of the provincial council, the merchants besieged Burnet with requests for the election of a new assembly. They claimed that New Yorkers were entitled as a matter of right to the dissolution of the present assembly, forcefully arguing that just as a new parliament had to be elected upon the accession of a new monarch, so also did a new assembly have to be chosen after the appointment of a new governor. Despite this lofty appeal to the rights of Englishmen, it seems safe to assume the merchants were motivated as much by a wish to lessen the duties on trade as by concern for the sanctity of constitutional principles.[1]

In contrast to the merchants, Morris was determined to keep in being the last assembly elected under Hunter. It had taken Morris and Hunter six years to build up a reliable court party in the assembly, and Morris, whose ability to manage that body was one of the principal sources of his political power in New York, did not want to subject his party to the hazards of an election during a period of commercial stagnation the merchants were bound to blame on his policy of taxing trade. Therefore Morris sought to stave off new elections by promising Burnet that the present assembly would provide him with a five-year Support Act for his administration. In order to convince the governor of the legality of meeting with this body, Morris prepared a legal opinion in his capacity as chief justice justifying the continuance of Hunter's last assembly. Whereas in England a parliament was summoned to meet with the person of the king and must therefore be dissolved when that person died, Morris advised Burnet, in America an assembly was called to meet with a governor acting as the representative of the king and did not have to be dissolved after the appointment of a new governor because that official was as much the king's representative as his predecessor. Morris scoffed at the tendency among New Yorkers "When any Question arises here concerning a Governour or Assembly . . . to ask what the King or Parliament of England does on a like Occasion, Vainly thinking that whatever is done by a King or Parliament is fit to be drawn into Example for this Place." New York, he reminded the governor, was a "Dependent Dominion" like Ireland or England's other American colonies, and in those places, he was quick to point out, new governors often met with assemblies — or, as in the case of Ireland, parliaments — chosen under their predecessors.[2]

Morris' efforts achieved their goal. Even before his departure from England Burnet had received a favorable account of Morris from former Governor Hunter. However, Burnet, who had suffered heavy financial losses in the celebrated South Sea Bubble, was even more impressed by Morris' promise to secure a long-term revenue for him — a goal it had taken Hunter five years to achieve. Accordingly Burnet decided within a week after his arrival in New York to align himself with Morris and the court party and to forego elections for a new assembly, thereby making himself only the second royal governor in the province's history not to dissolve the last representative body selected under his predecessor. After Burnet had thus signified his confidence in him, Morris undertook to act as his legislative manager, just as he had for Hunter. Backed by the governor and master of the assembly, Morris seemed to have established his political power on firm foundations. "And indeed," a merchant critic complained, "the assembly now establishes our Governor in Chiefe under the comand of Chief Justice M--ris."[3]

Morris' success drove Philipse and Schuyler into more desperate forms of opposition. They planned to join their supporters on the council in refusing to cooperate with the assembly when it met in October 1720, thus forcing Burnet to hold new elections. This scheme never went into effect, however, because at the last moment all the parties concerned drew back from such a blatant act of insubordination to the governor. Nevertheless Burnet dismissed Philipse and Schuyler from the council and replaced them with two supporters of Morris, Cadwallader Colden, the royal surveyor general of New York, and James Alexander, the proprietary surveyor general of New Jersey, who thus began long and distinguished political careers in New York. In the short run Philipse's ouster from the council was a triumph for Morris, but in the long run it worked to Philipse's advantage, because it enabled him to pose as the champion of frequent elections struck down by the hand of arbitary power. Philipse subsequently combined general constitutional principles with the specific grievances of the merchants and became the leader of a formidable opposition to Morris and Burnet, as James Alexander related some years later:

When Mr Burnet thought that Mr Philipse had not Interest Enough to get into any of the Elections he was not well Enough acquainted with this Country, for he who dares publickly cry out agt a Governour and tells the people they are oppressed and Sets up for a patriot and defender of the Liberties and priviledges [of the] Country will soon thereby make an Interest here and when he desists that he as soon Loses it.[4]

While Burnet faced a near revolt in the council, Morris had to quell a great deal of unrest in the assembly. Many assemblymen were impressed by the constitutional arguments of the merchants in favor of new elections, and Morris was obliged to act decisively to counter this sentiment. Assuring Burnet that "he wanted only power that he might take an Assemblyman by the arm and lead him in the house and make him doe what he pleased," Morris dealt summarily with representatives who were skeptical about the propriety of their proceedings. First he prevailed on the assembly "to Sit and act without entring into the debate of the legality" of the situation. Then he relented to the point of allowing "any Member of the house [who] Seemed to doubt of the legality of their meeting" to confer on the matter with Burnet—who obligingly showed all the doubters Morris' own opinion on the constitutionality of continuing Hunter's last assembly, as well as supporting opinions by Attorney General David Jamison and Andrew Hamilton, the noted Philadelphia lawyer who later became celebrated for his defense of John Peter Zenger. These opinions satisfied all members of the assembly except that perennial gadfly, Samuel Mulford. Mulford continued to insist the assembly was meeting illegally, whereupon he was expelled from that body and threatened by Morris with prosecution for seditious libel "if he soe much as declared his opinions to his neighbours" — a chilling example of how Morris was able to use his office as chief justice to intimidate political opponents.[5]

With the restoration of order in the council and the assembly, Morris was able to turn his attention to the transaction of the governor's business, which at this time consisted of the provision of support for the government and the introduction of a far-reaching program for regulating the fur trade. In fulfillment of his promise to Burnet, Morris persuaded the assembly to grant the governor a five-year Support Act, with the revenue to be derived principally from duties on trade. Moreover, in accordance with the system of informal constitutional compromises adopted in New York under Governor Hunter, Burnet agreed to expend this money as the assembly specified by resolutions in its journal. Thus although Burnet received a long-term revenue, the assembly virtually controlled its expenditure. Morris' standing in that body was strikingly revealed by the provision it made for his pay as chief justice. The assembly kept his salary at £300 a year but ordered it to be reduced by £100 if anyone else succeeded him in that office.[6]

But the most significant act passed by this assembly was the one forbidding New Yorkers to sell Indian trade goods — duffels, strouds, blankets, firearms, and gunpowder, for example — to the French for three years. Morris drafted this act and guided it through the assembly, but in doing so he was merely adopting the ideas of his political ally, Speaker Robert Livingston, and following the wishes of Burnet. The object of this act was to end the traffic in Indian trade goods between Albany and Montreal in order to encourage a direct trade in furs between New York and the Great Lakes Indians, the main suppliers of pelts. At this time the Dutch merchants of Albany, who legally monopolized the fur trade in New York, received most of their pelts from French traders in Montreal in exchange for Indian trade goods made in England. In turn, the French traders used these low cost goods to engross the fur trade with the Great Lakes tribes and draw them into the orbit of French influence, thereby adding one more link to the chain of encirclement the French were drawing around England's North American colonies. By depriving the French of the English trade goods their Indian allies favored, Livingston hoped to entice these tribes into beginning a direct trade with New York and thus extend English influence over them. Burnet, whose intense Whiggery was sometimes indistinguishable from Francophobia, readily approved a plan calculated to lessen French influence in America, and Morris, who had no personal interest in the fur trade, dutifully followed the governor's lead and translated the speaker's ideas into legislative reality.[7]

Although Morris did not originate the policy behind the Indian Trade Act of 1720, his role in securing its passage profoundly affected his political career. The attempt to stop the trade in Indian goods between Albany and Montreal, William Smith the historian observed, "became the source of an unreasonable opposition against [Burnet], which continued thro' his whole administration." This "unreasonable opposition" directed almost as much of its fury against Morris as against the governor he served. The Indian Trade Act adversely affected the economic interests of Albany fur traders like Peter Schuyler, who throve on the now illegal trade with Montreal; New York City merchants like Stephen DeLancey and Adolph Philipse, who provided the Albanians with the English goods the French coveted; and London merchants like Samuel Baker, who supplied their New York correspondents with these articles in the first instance. Schuyler, Philipse, and DeLancey became the leaders of the opposition to Morris and Burnet and sought to win control of the assembly in order to lower the duties on trade and reopen the prohibited traffic between Albany and Montreal. In pursuance of this end, the New York merchants called upon their English factors to persuade the imperial administration to disallow all the acts passed by the assembly in 1720 and to order Burnet to dissolve that body, alleging that they could have secured memorials from every county in the province in favor of the assembly's dissolution "were it not [for] the fear of being prosecuted by the Chiefe Justice, who being a member of this Assembly awes all with his threats." Although the merchants failed to achieve either of these goals, the extent to which they blamed Morris for their grievances is nonetheless revealing. "It is the General opinion," one of them declared, "that all these violent proceedings from whence our Calamities Issue is owing to the Councills of our present chiefe Justice, who being a Member of that house carryes every thing on wth a high hand."[8]

Despite the formation of a formidable country party composed of New York City merchants and Albany fur traders aided by their connections within London's powerful mercantile community, Morris' continued power in New York seemed assured when the provincial legislature adjourned in November 1720. Burnet gave Morris and his supporters in the assembly control over the patronage in their electoral constituencies, whereupon Morris promptly dismissed two justices of the peace in Westchester County appointed by Schuyler, "soe that," a critic complained, "all the Justices may be men after his own heart ready to execute wt ever he pleases."[9] The governor was equally generous to the chief justice's family. He appointed Lewis Morris, Jr., clerk of the circuit court in place of George Clarke, the provincial secretary, who had criticized the governor for agreeing to expend support funds in accordance with the wishes of the assembly. Moreover, after the death of Caleb Heathcote in February 1721, Burnet appointed Lewis, Jr., to take Heathcote's place on the provincial council. With the elevation of young Lewis to the rank of councilor, the political future of Morris' family in New York seemed as bright as his own.[10]

Yet soon after the younger Morris' appointment to the council, the governor and his legislative manager found themselves on opposite sides of a dispute involving the fiscal powers of the assembly. According to imperial policy, the revenue raised by a provincial assembly was supposed to be held by a royal receiver and inspected by the auditor general in England or one of his deputies in America. However, after the assembly treasurer had acquired custody of these funds in New York under Hunter's administration, Morris and his supporters in the assembly refused to allow George Clarke, Auditor General Horatio Walpole's deputy, to audit this money. Clarke brought the assembly's recalcitrance to the attention of Walpole, who informed the Lords of the Treasury in June 1720 that the assembly was resisting his deputy because its members were "apprehensive that the money they had raised for his Matys use should be accountable to his Maty and your Lordships." Alarmed by the assembly's "Arbitrary proceedings," the Treasury came to the auditor general's aid in August of that year by ordering Burnet and Abraham DePeyster, the assembly treasurer, to allow Walpole to audit the treasurer's accounts of the revenue and to pay him a fee for this service equal to 5 percent of the annual revenue of the government of New York. Instead of complying with this order, DePeyster submitted it to the assembly on May 24, 1721, thereby causing an uproar in that body. [11]

DePeyster's action placed Morris in a delicate situation. Burnet supported the auditor general's claims for fear of incurring the wrath of his brother, Sir Robert Walpole, then the most influential statesman in England after the Earl of Sunderland, but the assembly objected to them as potential threats to its control over the provincial financial system. Feeling against Walpole and Clarke ran so high among the assemblymen, in fact, that Morris could not safely disregard it. Accordingly, when ordered by the lower house on June 15 to prepare a representation to Burnet for transmittal to England "upon the Head of the Treasurer's accounting with the Auditor General," he endeavored to draw up a statement of the case which upheld the assembly's recently won fiscal prerogatives without antagonizing Burnet.

In a "humble representation" presented to Burnet on June 30, Morris produced a masterpiece of evasion. Although he explicitly denied that the assembly intended "his Majesty, or his Ministers, should be unacquainted with the State of the Revenue here," he maintained that lodging the revenue in the hands of the assembly treasurer was necessary to prevent its misapplication by colonial executives and the resultant creation of a new public debt. He estimated that the fee demanded by Walpole would amount to £150 sterling annually and inveighed against this charge as unwarrantable in itself and as an intolerable burden on the revenue that would render it "impossible to pay the Officers of the Government their Salaries." Moreover, he insisted, DePeyster had already provided Hunter with accurate accounts of the revenue raised in New York for the use of the Lords of the Treasury in England. Yet, he implied, Walpole still might audit the treasurer's accounts—provided he waived his claim to the 5 percent fee. This was equivalent to taking back with the left hand what the right hand had given, for it was well known that Walpole was entitled to profit from his office. In short, Morris convinced the assembly to allow Walpole to inspect DePeyster's records, but to do so under conditions the auditor general was bound to reject.[12]

Morris' representation met with a hostile reception in England. Auditor General Walpole denounced the allegation that his fee was excessive as "a meer pretence to prevent my Deputies auditing and Inspecting their Accots. and by that means to have the Collecting and Disposing of the Revenues of that Province entirely in their own power"—as indeed it was. The Lords of the Treasury—including the auditor general's powerful brother, Sir Robert Walpole, concurred in this analysis. They dismissed Morris' arguments and ordered Burnet to secure payment of the auditor general's fee and reinvest the royal receiver with custody over the revenue, observing "Wee are of Opinion that the Behavior of the Treasurer in not accounting according to his Majts. positive Instruction to you, And the Directions received from hence is a very Arbitrary and Unwarrantable proceeding, And a Contempt of his Mats. Authority, And that this Excuse relating to the Auditors ffees has no manner of Colour or Foundacon in it."[13]

Initially the Treasury's response to Morris' representation angered the assembly and threatened to make the situation worse. Under the influence of Livingston and Burnet, however, the assembly at length agreed in 1723 to pay Walpole £1,600 in salary arrears, though soon thereafter it refrained from paying his regular annual fee and made certain that its treasurer continued to take custody of the revenue. The auditor general was apparently satisfied by this outcome, despite his deputy's complaint to him that the assembly's refusal to pay for an annual audit proved "this Governmt. Submits to the Kings orders only till an opportunity presents of contesting your right again, and to let future Assemblys See by these refusals, delays and excuses that they never intended your authority should take place here."[14]

Although Morris and Burnet remained on good terms throughout this affair, the audit controversy subtly weakened the chief justice's power in New York. As had been the case during Hunter's administration, Morris' influence in the colony was still directly proportional to that of the governor he had chosen to serve. But by "doing . . . [his] duty in supporting the Auditor's demand," Burnet antagonized the assembly, thereby rendering it less susceptible to gubernatorial influence and hence making Morris' task as legislative manager more difficult. At the same time, the governor's support of Walpole also redounded to the benefit of the Philipse-DeLancey country party, which was determined to wrest control of the assembly from Morris and reverse the policies it considered injurious to the merchant interest. After May 1721, "No Audit" took its place alongside "Frequent Elections" as one of the principal rallying cries the country party used to good effect against Burnet and, at least indirectly, Morris, too.

Yet neither the dissatisfaction of the assembly with Burnet nor the agitation of Philipse and DeLancey against the governor and the chief justice was serious enough to impair Morris' ability to manage the lower house when he turned his attention to the regulation of the fur trade again in 1722. Although the Indian Trade Act of 1720 succeeded in drawing larger numbers of Western Indians to Albany than ever before, it failed to cut off the flow of Indian goods from Albany to Montreal. It was supposed to be enforced by the sheriff and municipal officials of Albany, but it was beyond the power of the sheriff and contrary to the economic interests of some Albany officials to prevent recalcitrant fur traders from evading the prohibition on the sale of trade goods to the French. As a result, Canada continued to receive these coveted goods and French influence among the Western Indians, though no longer unchallenged, was still supreme.

Burnet and Livingston were especially anxious to halt this illicit traffic between Albany and Montreal, and to this end Morris drafted a bill of almost draconian severity which the governor approved on July 8, 1722. Under the terms of this act, anyone even suspected of selling Indian goods to the French could be made to take an oath requiring him to swear not only that he had not been engaged in this commerce, but also that he knew of no one else who was involved in it either. Those who refused to take this oath were *ipso facto* adjudged guilty of having sold the forbidden trade goods to the French and made subject to confinement in jail without benefit of a judicial hearing, much less a trial by jury, until they paid a fine of £100. To enforce this measure, a host of local officials were empowered to administer the oath; and to ensure the diligence of these officials, the act provided a fine of £200 and the forfeiture for life of all offices of trust in New York for any officer who refused to administer the oath to suspected traders or warned them about it beforehand. Thus Morris meant to implement the governor's fur trade policy with an oath which was an open invitation to perjury or to self-incrimination and with the aid of a group of Albany officials, some of whom stood to lose their fortunes if they enforced the law or their offices if they did not.[15]

The passage of the Indian Trade Act of 1722 marked the high point of Morris' influence as Burnet's legislative manager. Within the next three years the chief justice's role in New York politics was radically altered by the gradual disintegration of the court party and the political ineptitude of Burnet, which together enabled Adolph Philipse and the country party to achieve control of the provincial assembly by September 1725. Even while the second Trade Act was under consideration by the assembly, Philipse took his place in the lower house as a representative for Westchester County and quickly emerged as the principal leader of the country opposition to Morris and Burnet. Yet this in itself would not have decisively affected Morris' position in New York had it not coincided with the decline of the court party he had helped to create during Hunter's administration. Eight members of the assembly elected in 1716 died between May 1721 and September 1725; and although not all of them had been followers of Morris and Burnet, most of their successors became supporters of Philipse. As court party ranks in the assembly were thinned by death, they were also weakened by disaffection with Burnet, so that ultimately the chief justice found it impossible to manage the lower house for the governor.

Although the details are obscure, the general outlines of the rise of the country party and the decline of the court party are reasonably clear. After New York City merchants and Albany fur traders united to form the country party in 1720, they criticized Burnet for violating the constitutional rights of New Yorkers by his refusal to hold new assembly elections and charged that he was endangering the assembly's financial prerogatives by his support of the auditor general's claims. They also accused Morris of stifling debate in the assembly and complained that he used his office as chief justice to cow his political opponents. Finally they attributed the commercial depression that gripped New York until 1722 to Morris' policy of supporting the government through taxes on trade and called for a reduction in those taxes in order to stimulate commerce. All of these themes seem to have had a telling impact upon voters during the eight by-elections held in New York between 1721 and 1725, eloquently attesting to the truth of James Alexander's dictum that "he who dares publickly cry out agt a Governour and tells the people they are oppressed and Sets up for a patriot . . . will soon thereby make an Interest here."[16]

While the country party increased its following by cleverly appealing to constitutional principle and economic self-interest, Burnet seriously weakened the court party by his political ineptness. Thus he antagonized elements of the landed interest by his fondness for financing his fur trade policy with property taxes as well as by his opposition to an act to facilitate the partition of land held in joint tenancy or common, a measure favored by land speculators. He also made a number of enemies by his zest for acting as sole judge in chancery court, which invariably offended many of those against whom he handed down adverse decrees. Lastly his absorption in theology, his single-minded effort to unravel the sacred mysteries of scriptural prophecies—especially those contained in the Book of Daniel—diverted his attention from public affairs for long periods of time, making him the despair of his friends and the butt of humor by his foes. In politics criticism may wound, but ridicule can kill, as Morris ruefully intimated in a retrospective survey of Burnet's administration: "[Burnet had] an odd mixture . . . that rendered him often Verry Absent from himselfe and when Seemingly return'd Act so by fits and Starts and with such a rapidity as prov'd inconvenient in a publick conduct; and this was Said to be owing to his deep Study and meditation on a Sacred booke of Dreames and Visions."[17]

As a result of these developments, court and country were about evenly matched in the assembly when that body came together on August 31, 1725 to consider how to provide a new revenue for Burnet's administration in view of the imminent expiration of the 1720 Support Act. At this time Adolph Philipse replaced the ailing Robert Livingston as Speaker, but Philipse's election did not necessarily herald a decisive shift of power to the country party because it took place while seven representatives were still absent. A more ominous development for Morris and Burnet, in light of country party successes in the last five by-elections, was the recent demise of three more assemblymen and the accompanying need to fill their vacant seats. Accordingly Burnet adjourned the assembly until the middle of September and issued writs for the holding of three special elections. The ensuing electoral results could scarcely have been more displeasing to the governor and his legislative manager. Stephen DeLancey, one of the foremost members of the merchant interest, was chosen to be one of the new representatives, and the other two, though less well known, were also reputed to be opponents of Burnet. Suddenly the country party was on the verge of assuming control of the assembly.

At this point Morris and Burnet committed a stupid blunder which irretrievably destroyed Morris' effectiveness as the governor's legislative manager. In a desperate effort to preserve the ascendancy of the court party, Burnet decided to block DeLancey's admission into the assembly. Consequently when DeLancey, a Huguenot immigrant who had lived in New York for more than forty years and served in a number of previous

assemblies, came before Burnet on September 13 to take the oath of office, the governor refused to administer it to him, alleging there was grave
doubt that DeLancey was "a Subject of the Crown." Burnet's action
threw the assembly into an uproar. Court and country party representatives alike denounced it as a violation of the assembly's right to determine
the qualifications of its members, and among assemblymen of Dutch and
French origin there was great fear that by calling into question DeLancey's citizenship Burnet was setting a dangerous precedent that "might be
extended to their real estates and inheritances."[18]

Burnet, aware of the enormity of his mistake, turned to Morris for
help. In search of a graceful way out of an awkward predicament, Burnet
asked Morris to examine the legal evidence of DeLancey's citizenship in
his capacity as chief justice, and Morris agreed. As Morris pondered the
evidence tensions rose in New York and DeLancey threatened "to go for
England if the Chief Justice gives his opinion that he is an allien." At
length Morris submitted his opinion to Burnet on September 19. In an effort to save face for the governor, Morris declared that although there
was still great doubt that DeLancey was a full-fledged subject of the king,
his previous legislative service made it expedient to admit him to his seat
in the present assembly. Although Morris' grudging opinion paved the
way for DeLancey's admission into the assembly and ended the immediate crisis, in every other respect it was politically disastrous. Most assemblymen felt that as chief justice Morris had had no right to judge the qualifications of one of their colleagues, and they also suspected that he had
advised Burnet to oppose DeLancey's admission in the first instance.[19]

Burnet's inept attempt to exclude one of his opponents from the assembly and Morris' suspected complicity in the effort made it impossible
for Morris to continue to manage the assembly for the governor. Henceforth Adolph Philipse and the country party controlled the assembly,
while Stephen DeLancey became Morris' implacable foe, resolved to have
him "removed from the office of Chief Justice, if by any means it could be
don." The implications of the transfer of power in the assembly from
Morris to Philipse were dramatically revealed in October 1725, when the
lower house resolved to provide the government with a revenue for only
two years and to reduce Morris' salary as chief justice from £300 to £200 a
year. Burnet responded by demanding a five-year support and the continuance of Morris' salary at the previous rate of £300 a year. The assembly
refused to comply with these demands and Burnet adjourned it, afraid to
run the risk of a general election.[20]

This deadlock between the governor and the assembly illustrated
Morris' predicament at the end of 1725. He could no longer function as
the governor's legislative manager; yet he still enjoyed Burnet's confi-

dence. His enemies controlled the assembly, so he could not retrieve his fortunes by placing himself at the head of a country opposition—a position Philipse already occupied in any case. Dependent upon Burnet for his continuance in office and discredited in the assembly by his part in the DeLancey affair, Morris had only one role left to play in New York politics: that of defender of the royal prerogative.

Morris assumed this role out of conviction as well as necessity. For he was convinced that the assembly was abusing its power and endangering royal authority by its effort to reduce his salary as chief justice without Burnet's consent. Later scholars might interpret the assembly's action as a logical outgrowth of Morris' own policy of persuading the governors of New York to agree privately to pay royal officials according to the assembly's wishes. In Morris' view, however, the assembly's unilateral attempt to determine the pay of these officials was contrary to the letter and the spirit of the informal constitutional compromises on the salary question he had helped to work out between the assembly and Governors Hunter and Burnet in 1715 and 1720. History is often a matter of nuances, and unless we recognize how seriously Morris took this distinction it is impossible to make any sense out of his political career in New York during the next few years. At the same time, it must be admitted that it was more than coincidental that Morris became sensitive to the assembly's encroachments on crown rights only after that body had passed under the control of his determined adversary, Adolph Philipse.

Morris first expressed his criticism of the assembly's new course during the legislative session which began in April 1726. At that time the assembly resolved to offer Burnet a three-year Support Act—with the revenue to be derived from higher taxes on property and lower duties on trade—and to regulate the salaries of the governor and all other royal officials. In contrast to the previous year, however, the assembly called for a reduction of only £50 in Morris' salary as chief justice. Morris took advantage of this call to inquire into the grounds for the proposed reduction in his judicial pay. In a speech delivered to the assembly on May 3, he melodramatically expressed apprehension that "such a Reduction, might be construed to proceed from Faults of the worst Kind in his Conduct, which might not only affect his own Character, but perhaps reflect on his hitherto innocent Children." Consequently he asked his colleagues in the lower house either to allow him to vindicate himself at a public trial against the imputation of judicial misconduct their resolution entailed or to declare in their journal that their wish to lower his salary as chief justice was not "owing to any Thing justly blameable in his Execution of that Office." The assembly wryly assured Morris that it wanted to reduce his pay, not because it suspected him of any wrong-doing on the supreme court, but simply because "he himself formerly, and all Chief Justices before him, had no greater Salary than *One Hundred* and *Thirty Pounds per Ann.* and . . . the present Circumstances of the Colony make them less able to allow excessive Salaries now, than they were then." Morris thereupon secured the publication of his speech and the assembly's reply —a rather daring act when one considers the fate which had befallen Samuel Mulford in a similar situation eleven years before. Nevertheless Morris' appeal to New York's political public failed to weaken the assembly's determination to lower his salary or to prevent Burnet from reluctantly accepting the three-year Support Act.[21]

Morris' May 3 protest was more than a quibble about £50 a year. It was also an implicit challenge to the sole power the assembly was assuming to regulate the pay of royal officials in New York. After recovering from a "Sickness" which laid him low for more than a month, Morris made this challenge explicit in a speech he gave to the assembly on June 17. In it he forcefully denied that the assembly had a right to lower his own pay or that of any other servant of the king without the governor's consent. He reminded his colleagues that "the King is the only Judge of the merits of his Servants" and noted that the crown had authorized only the governor and council to determine the salaries of its officials in New York. Parliament did not set the pay of crown officials in England, and if Parliament refrained from exercising this power, so should the assembly, for Parliament, Morris caustically observed, "understand liberty and what are their inherent rights, much better than any house of representatives, in the Brittish Dominions in America."

In addition to exceeding its rights, Morris also accused the assembly of weakening the ties that bound New York to Great Britain. The lower house's effort to dictate the salaries of royal officials, he charged, was designed to do nothing less than "render the governour, and all the other Officers of the Government, So far dependant on the house of Representatives, as to receive no other Sallaries, but such as they from time to time will think fit to allow them." Such a power would be inconsistent with the colony's subordination to the mother country, and therefore he urged his auditors to remember:

That we are Plants, in a manner but of Yesterdays growth; and as appears by the Sibboleth, So easily distinguishable in most of our Speech the greater number, transplanted from a foreign Soil; and here tenderly nurst up, at the vast expence of the brittish Crown; that we are, and ought to be, a Dependant Government; and have no inherent right to be an Assembly and to Sit and make laws but by virtue of the Kings letters patent; are things too evident and notorious to be deny'd; and yet, we have taken upon ourselves the exercise of a power, not Seemingly agreeable to that dependance: or warranted by those letters patent, which gave being to our political constitution.

Morris concluded his address by charging the assembly with endangering royal authority throughout America and not just in New York. Noting that the assembly had published its resolves on salaries and that they had been reprinted in a Boston newspaper, Morris claimed that the assembly's action was part of a deliberate design to spread a spirit of insubordination through the colonies. As the New Jersey Council had once accused him of plotting to break up the British empire, so Morris now charged the assembly with fomenting a spirit of independence in the land. "Where these things will end God only knows," he solemnly warned, "but what they mean, is not very difficult to guess. How mischievous in its consequences, Such an Example may be to the rest of his majesties Plantations, and of what dangerous tendency, to lessen, or Shake off their dependance on the brittish Government, will be humbly Submitted to his majesty and his Ministers of State to Judge of."[22]

Morris' speech was received coolly by the assembly. It did not convince that body to raise his salary to £300 a year again and its reference to a "Sibboleth" was interpreted as a personal slur by Dutch and French assemblymen. Morris denied he had intended to reflect adversely upon representatives who were not of English descent and conceded that Dutch representatives in particular had usually been staunch supporters of generous appropriations for Hunter and Burnet. Yet he could not refrain from wondering "what has prevailed upon [the Dutch] these two last Sessions to be so different in their Conduct from what they used to be."[23]

Morris did not inform George I or his ministers of the assembly's allegedly nefarious designs because Burnet soon gave him an opportunity to reassert the court party's control over the lower house of the provincial legislature. Dissatisfaction with the inadequacy of the 1726 Support Act and resentment at the country party's determination to make him abide by a drastically reduced schedule of salaries for provincial government officials led Burnet to dissolve the assembly on August 10, 1726, in the hope that the court party would triumph in the ensuing elections. But this proved to be a forlorn hope as Philipse and the country party emerged from the elections held in September of that year with an even stronger following in the assembly than before.[24]

The court party's repudiation at the polls led Morris to resume his role as defender of the royal prerogative. Burnet met with the assembly in

October 1726 and asked it to provide him with additional funding to make up for the deficits he anticipated under the latest Support Act. The assembly replied by claiming that the funds from this act would be sufficient for the government's needs—provided Burnet spent them exactly as the assembly specified in its resolutions. In short, the assembly was openly claiming the right to control the expenditure of the ordinary revenue of government—a right imperial policy reserved exclusively to the governor and council. In 1715 and 1720 Morris had been instrumental in persuading Hunter and Burnet to agree privately to expend this money as the assembly wished, thereby allowing those executives to have the shadow of power while transferring the substance to the assembly. Now the country party wanted shadow and substance alike.

Morris opposed the assembly's latest effort to extend its powers. When Burnet indicated to him that he was inclined to spend support funds as the assembly dictated in order to obtain money to build a fur trading post at Oswego on Lake Ontario, Morris warned that compliance with the assembly's demands would be a "thing . . . of an extraordinary nature" and urged him to avoid it. Morris' position was supported by members of the provincial council who advised Burnet that he could expend the money appropriated by the assembly for the support of government "without any restraint or Limitation What soever." Thus strengthened, Burnet decided to reject the assembly's bid to control expenditures. For the remainder of his administration he paid royal officials as he chose, so that Morris continued to receive his customary salary of £300 a year. In this way the informal constitutional compromise Morris had helped to arrange between the governors and the assembly of New York on the subject of control over provincial finances came to an end, repudiated by the country party and disowned by its chief author. Morris' metamorphosis from legislative manager to prerogative man was now complete —or rather as complete as any change could be in his vertiginous political career.[25]

After this episode Morris receded into the background of New York political life for the duration of Burnet's administration and began to reflect upon what he perceived to be the implications of the transfer of power in the colony from the court to the country party. The first fruit of his reflections was a "Dialogue on Trade," written near the end of 1726, in which he critically analyzed the pretensions of the most important element of the country party—New York's merchants. In this unpublished work Morris scornfully dismissed the complaints of merchants that his policy of taxing trade had unfairly placed the main burden of supporting the provincial government on their shoulders. On the contrary, Morris maintained, the merchants had invariably passed on to artisans and farmers, in the form of artificially high prices on imported goods, the trade duties they had been obliged to pay under the Support Acts of 1715 and 1720. Nor did they lower prices after trade duties were reduced by the Support Act of 1726. Therefore Morris insisted that in effect artisans and farmers had paid taxes for the merchants between 1715 and 1725 and that the reduction of trade duties in 1726 had relieved the merchants of a burden they had in fact never borne. Yet without revealing how he would prevent merchants from victimizing artisans and farmers in the same way again, Morris concluded that a return to his program of taxing trade would be the best guarantee of prosperity for all classes in New York.

Morris' distaste for New York merchants ran deeper than mere disgust at what he considered to be their misrepresentation of his economic policy. It also reflected an intense social prejudice on his part. As a landed aristocrat, Morris sought to conduct himself according to the norms of a country gentleman. According to Morris' aristocratic code, merchants were almost beneath contempt because in their frenzied pursuit of immoderate profits they followed a loose standard of commercial ethics to which no self-respecting gentleman could subscribe without suffering the loss of his personal honor. "Should A countryman or A Gentleman turn merchant," he claimed in his most vigorous denunciation of the mercantile ethic:

> its ods but A little time would convince him of the folly of his undertaking for want of A Sufficient Skill in what is calld the misteries of trade. Should either of these happen to have damaged or bad goods he would be weake enough to tell his customers the truth. On the contrary you would praise Such commodoties to the Skies because they really need it. Is there a more common practice in the world than for a merchant to Say his goods are Verry cheap and that he bought them deare and yet all the world knows if what he said was true he must starve. Dos any trading man mind an Oath in custome house? Dont they perjure themselves dayly without being the least concern'd for doing so? and to the honour of merchants is not a custome house oath become a proverb? What is all this done for, is it not to amuse and deceive in order to make a proffit?[26]

From the chicaneries of merchants, Morris next turned his attention to the dangers of political factionalism. He dealt with this issue in a charge he delivered as chief justice to the grand jury of New York City during the supreme court's March 1727 term. If only men were as good as they might be and followed the dictates of reason, he told the jurors, there would be little need for laws and even less for lawyers. Alas, humanity had yet to reach this blessed state because too often men allowed themselves to be ruled by their "Passions and Appetites." In consequence of human concupiscence, governments were instituted to "protect the Innocent and Obedient, in the quiet and peaceable Enjoyment of the Fruits of their Labour and Industry." And of all the forms of government devised by man, the wisest and most beneficent was the one under which New Yorkers lived—that of Great Britain. For "such is the admirable Constitution of the *British Government,*" Morris declared, "That, while it is preserved in that Condition our Laws intended it should be, neither Princes nor Priest can Tyranize; nor a Democracy prevail; where the Blocks of their own Carving are only worshipt, when the Best and Bravest, insulted by the Dreggs of Humane Species, too often fall Sacrifices to popular fury and ungovernable Madness." Yet, he warned, in an obvious reference to the tactics used by the country party in its rise to power, the greatest danger to the stability of constitutional government was political factionalism. Factionalism, which he equated with unwarranted opposition to the administration in power and irresponsible criticism of public officials, destroyed the confidence of the people in their rulers and threatened to sweep away the foundations of constitutional rule in a flood of popular licentiousness. "The speaking irreverently or disrespectfully of [magistrates]," Morris gravely concluded,

will create in the Minds of the People a Contempt of them, and by Degrees of that Authority with which they are cloathed; and when the People, by ill Acts, are rendred disaffected, they naturally become disobedient. The Histories of all Nations abound with melancholly Instances of the terrible Effects of Faction; which, when let loose, has been like an impetuous Torent, capable of overturning all that lay in its Way; and those of our own Country are not without flagrant Examples, what small Sparks seditious Arts have blown into a Flame, not easily to be extinguished, and not long since endangered the Constitution it self; therefore no Care or Caution can be too much, to check such Things in their first Appearance.[27]

Morris combined his forebodings about his merchant rivals and political factionalism in a remarkable unpublished work he composed during the winter of 1727–28 entitled "A Dialogue between a South and a North Countryman." Written in the form of a satirical political history of New York during the administrations of Hunter and Burnet, Morris' "Dialogue" was at once a diatribe against Adolph Philipse's factiousness and a prescription for restoring the balance he found wanting in the provincial government. Morris interpreted New York politics between 1710 and 1728 in terms of a recurrent conflict between a court and a country party, although admittedly he did not use this exact terminology.

Whereas the country party was led by merchants who were averse to taxes on trade and hostile to royal authority, the court party was made up of diverse social classes which were disposed to cooperate with royal governors in return for specific concessions like land grants or the payment of the public debt. After having dominated the political scene from 1715 to 1725, the court party lost control of the assembly to the country party — a development Morris found fateful for the future of royal government in New York because he thought it would destroy the delicate balance among the three main branches of the provincial governent: the governor, council, and assembly.

For, according to Morris, now that Philipse was the autocratic master of the lower house, contemptuous alike of popular liberties and regalian rights, he was determined to use the legislature's power of the purse "to render the Steward [governor] intirely depending on the Chamber [assembly] and in a little time Effectually Establish an Onocracy" — or rule by the assembly. Nor did Philipse, Morris contended, even have to reckon with the possibility of gubernatorial opposition to his sinister designs. For no matter how contrary the interests of the governor and the assembly seemed in theory, in practice they were remarkably alike. The governor needed money with which to run his administration and this induced him almost of necessity to relinquish royal rights and lands to the assembly in order to obtain financial support. Was there nothing, then, to protect the liberties of the subject and the rights of the king from a grasping assembly and a weak governor? Fortunately there was an institution at hand to perform this function: the provincial council. Let the council but reassert its powers, Morris argued, and balanced government in New York might yet be preserved from an assembly only too willing to destroy it and a governor simply too weak to save it:

> The Lord [monarch] of the Mannour [New York] had entrusted them [councilors] in their Stations as well as he had Entrusted the Steward in his and did expect a punctuall performance of their duty from them, that if they for the future resolv'd to give their voices according to what they thought reasonable, having an Eye to the interest of the Lord and the benefit of the tennants [people of New York], the Steward durst not quarrell with 'em nor maltreat them . . . on the contrary he would pay A court to them and it would be in their power to Keep the Steward and the chamber of Clods [assembly] within their propper bounds.[28]

Yet because the governor had the power to suspend its members, Morris doubted that the council would systematically perform this mediating role — a prophetic insight.

Under the administrations of Hunter and Burnet, Morris had always enjoyed the confidence of the governors of New York, but during the tenure of Burnet's successor, John Montgomerie, he lost even that. Montgomerie, who arrived in New York on April 15, 1728, was appointed to succeed Burnet through the favor of George II rather than because of any personal merit of his own. The new governor had served as George's groom of the bedchamber when that monarch was still Prince of Wales and had elected to lose his office rather than abandon the prince after the heir apparent quarreled with George I in 1717 and was banished from court for four years. In gratitude for this loyalty, George II rewarded Montgomerie with the governments of New York and New Jersey after his accession in 1727 — a singularly unfortunate act of royal benevolence. For Montgomerie, although personally amiable, "had given himself up to his pleasures," according to a critic, "especially to his bottle and had an aversion to business." He left England deeply in debt, and his principal motive in availing himself of his sovereign's generosity was simply "to recover his fortune by the profits of his government with as little trouble to himself as possible."[29] Such a man was unlikely to favor Morris' critical attitude toward the provincial assembly.

Morris soon realized that Montgomerie was not interested in using him as an adviser or legislative manager. On the day he arrived in New York, the new governor, perhaps in response to a suggestion by Auditor General Walpole, chose George Clarke as his chief counselor, telling the provincial secretary and deputy auditor "that he would absolutely trust to his advice." Morris and Clarke had both served Hunter, but Clarke affiliated himself with Philipse during Burnet's administration because of his resentment at Burnet for replacing him as clerk of the circuit court with Lewis Morris, Jr., and his anger at the elder Morris for opposing his efforts to audit the assembly's accounts. Equally alarming from Morris' standpoint was the favor Montgomerie showed to the chief justice's principal rivals in the assembly, Philipse and DeLancey. In May 1728 the governor nominated Stephen DeLancey's son, James, to fill a vacancy in the council, and at the same time James Alexander nervously informed Cadwallader Colden that "Mr. Montgomery carries it very Civil to Every body . . . but is closely attended by Mr. Clerk [Clarke], Phillipse &c."[30] Montgomerie's association with Philipse and DeLancey was not entirely fortuitous. Philipse's country party had won the last assembly election conducted under Burnet in March 1728, and since Montgomerie meant to profit from his office, it was only natural that he decided to cultivate the leaders of the rising country party and ignore the head of the declining court party. This decision seemed justified after the governor held an election for a new assembly in June 1728 and, perhaps because of popular opposition to his prerogative views, the voters of the borough of West-chester rejected Morris for the first time in his career. Yet for some time Morris was outwardly unconcerned about Montgomerie's alliance with his political rivals because he was convinced that in the long run the governor would realize that his interests were incompatible with those of the country party. "Let nature work is the best policie," Morris advised one of his allies on the provincial council in the fall of 1728, as if a split between Montgomerie and Philipse was inevitable.[31]

In fact Montgomerie did come to an abrupt parting of the ways with a prominent New York political leader, but that leader was Chief Justice Morris, not Speaker Philipse. Morris' quarrel with Montgomerie was over his salary as chief justice. In August 1728 the assembly made another effort to control the salaries of royal officials and in the process it again called for a lowering of Morris' pay to £250 a year. At first Montgomerie responded to the assembly's action by striving for a solution that would avoid giving offense to Morris or to Philipse. Therefore he offered to issue Morris' salary warrants without specifying the length of time for which they were drawn, so that meanwhile the chief justice could appeal to England for a ruling on the assembly's right to reduce his pay. James Alexander and Cadwallader Colden, two of Morris' closest supporters on the provincial council, thought that this would be the most prudent course for him to follow. Morris himself disagreed. He wanted Montgomerie to pay him at the usual rate of £300 a year, not only because he firmly believed the assembly had no right to reduce his salary, but also so that he could precipitate a break between Montgomerie and the country party and force the governor to rely on him instead. But Montgomerie had no intention of alienating Philipse, whose party controlled the assembly, and at length on June 12, 1729, having grown weary of Morris' failure to appeal his case to England, he signed a quarterly salary warrant for the chief justice of £62.10.5 — the exact amount and time prescribed by the assembly.[32]

Montgomerie's action elicited a spirited response from Lewis Morris, Jr. At a meeting of the governor and council held the following day, the chief justice's son read a sharply worded protest against the reduction in his father's salary. He rebuked Montgomerie for having taken this step without prior consultation with the council, claimed that it violated the council's right to participate in the expenditure of the revenue, and charged that it was calculated "to render the members of the councill Insignificant and as So many Cyphers in one of the most considerable branches of the trust reposed in them by his Majestie and the law." He also accused the governor of undermining royal authority in New York by paying his father as the assembly dictated because "the complying with the assembly in this case is making all the officers of the government dependent upon them which is against his Majesties Interest and Derogatory from his royall and Just prerogatives." This protest enraged the normally placid Montgomerie and offended the five other members of the council who were then present. The councilors rejected Morris' charges and told him he could not meet with them again unless he first asked the governor's pardon. Unwilling at this time to risk the loss of his place on the council, Morris reluctantly made his submission to Montgomerie.[33]

Morris' son did not remain subdued for long. Soon after this incident he conferred with his father at Morrisania, and together they agreed that the time was ripe for an open break with Montgomerie and an appeal to England on the salary question. They came to this conclusion shortly after the elder Morris received a letter from William Burnet, now serving as governor of Massachusetts, which enclosed an account of a recent hearing before the Board of Trade in which an imperial official had threatened to have Parliament intervene and force the Bay Colony's assembly to comply with a royal instruction ordering it to pass a permanent revenue for the government of that province. The chief justice mistakenly interpreted this as a sign that England was about to adopt a stricter attitude toward the colonies, and therefore he believed that the imperial administration was finally ready to listen to his complaints about the encroachments of the New York Assembly. Consequently the Morrises decided that it would be to their political advantage to force Montgomerie's hand on the salary issue, because even if in the short run this led to the younger Morris' removal from the council, they were convinced that in the long run they would obtain redress from the imperial administration. It is impossible to be completely precise about what the Morrises had in mind at this time, but apparently they expected imperial officials to support their prerogative views and to order Montgomerie to conduct himself in such a way as to compel him to rely on them for advice and support.[34]

Young Lewis quickly put this strategy into effect. He attended a meeting of the governor and council on June 26 and read a second written protest against the lowering of his father's salary that was even more pointed than the first. In the course of seven closely written folio pages, the chief justice's son strongly reiterated his previous contention that Montgomerie's action had infringed the just rights of the council and encouraged the unwarranted pretensions of the assembly, bluntly adding that such conduct "would prove in its Consequences, dangerous to your self, destructive to his Majestyes Prerogative and Interest, depreciating and in a manner rendering useless his Majestyes Councill here, and tending to encourage an Assembly to persist in their claims of Such things, as are inconsistent with their Dependance upon a Brittish Government." There could be only one certain outcome after such a tirade and it was not long in coming. On that very day an angry Montgomerie suspended Morris from the council because of his "many Scandalous, unjust and false Reflections."[35]

Morris and his son lost little time in striving to reassert their influence in New York by portraying themselves to the imperial administration as undaunted defenders of royal authority in America. With the aid of his father, the younger Morris cast himself in this role in letters he wrote in July 1729 to the Board of Trade and the Duke of Newcastle, the secretary of state for the southern department. Virtuously disclaiming any wish to be restored to his place on the council, he drew an alarming picture of the assembly's encroachments on royal authority in New York since the time of Hunter, laying special emphasis on that body's efforts to control the salaries of royal officials and its opposition to any governor's acting as sole judge in chancery. He artfully vindicated his conduct toward Montgomerie by arguing that the governor's decision to lower his father's salary as the assembly demanded would soon make the king's servants unduly dependent on that body and by claiming that his refusal to act as chancellor was an imprudent act of appeasement to the opponents of the chancery court in the lower house. In short, he contended, Montgomerie's conduct as governor gave the assembly "but too much reason to persist in the claiming and exercising of powers, directly contrary to the letter of his Majesty's patent and instructns and seemingly inconsistent with their dependance on a British Govert, and his Majties dominion over them; and which may possibly render it very difficult for himself or future Governours to restrain without the aid of a British Parliament." In order to reverse this trend, he advised the imperial administration to order the governor to "alter his measures" and to forbid him to sit with the council when it met in its legislative capacity. Only if the council was thus made more independent, he argued, echoing the thought expressed in his father's last unpublished "Dialogue," would it be in a position to prevent the governor from yielding crown rights to the assembly in exchange for appropriations of revenue.[36]

The fate of the younger Morris' appeals to England reflected the limitations of acting as a defender of the royal prerogative in the colonies during the era of salutary neglect. Newcastle laid his complaints before the king, who perfunctorily referred them to the Board of Trade. The Board, in turn, held a hearing on the subject on December 17, 1729. At this hearing the interests of Morris, Jr., were defended by Vincent Pearse, a Royal Navy captain who was married to young Lewis' sister, Mary; Matthew Norris, another navy captain and the husband-to-be of Lewis' sister, Euphemia; and Paul Docminique, the chief justice's old friend from the West Jersey Society and an octogenarian member of the Board itself. But these three were no match for Martin Bladen, the single most influential member of the Board of Trade at this time. Bladen actively "Espoused Collo. Montgomeries Interest" and laid great stress on the fact that the governor had suspended Morris with the council's consent. He was also instrumental in persuading the Board to accept Montgomerie's contention that he lowered the chief justice's salary because the assembly had failed to provide him with enough money to pay Morris £300 a year and not because it had resolved that the salary should be lessened. As a result, the Board decided to confirm the suspension of Morris, Jr., and to approve the appointment of the nominee Montgomerie had recommended in his place—Philip Courtlandt, a local merchant. Contrary to the expectations of both Morrises, no rebuke was issued to the governor for imperiling the rights of the crown. In the England of Sir Robert Walpole, where the guiding principle of domestic and colonial policy was *quieta non movere*—"Let sleeping dogs lie"—conciliar insubordination, even in the interests of royal authority, was apparently a greater offense than gubernatorial negligence.[37]

The failure of his son's appeal to England was a stunning blow to Chief Justice Morris. It called into question his whole strategy of acting as a defender of the royal prerogative in New York. If the imperial administration would not sustain him in this role, then who else would? Morris tried to console himself with the thought that his son's removal from the council would ultimately work to the young man's political advantage, but he failed to explain how and in the wake of this distressing event he seems to have despaired of his own political future in New York for the first time. "But this and 1000 things more," he observed of Lewis' removal, "ought to make a wise man Sick of publick Employs and to prefere a little mean condition that will afford food and raynment to the most Splendid of them wch are all of ym Executed with trouble and Kept with Envy."[38]

As Morris' political fortunes in New York reached their lowest ebb, his thoughts began to turn to an office which once, he erroneously believed, had almost been his—the governorship of New Jersey. Despite his absorption in New York politics under the administrations of Governors Burnet and Montgomerie, Morris had retained a keen interest in proprietary affairs in the Jerseys. He continued to function as the American agent of the West Jersey Society during this period, although the Society constantly criticized his repeated failures to render an account of the land he bought and sold for it. He also took the lead in reconstituting the East Jersey Board of Proprietors in 1725 and served as president of that organization for the first five years of its existence. Yet he never manifested a comparable interest in attending to his duties as a councilor, which gave rise to popular demands for his removal from the New Jersey Council when Montgomerie was governor.[39]

Despite his personal unpopularity in New Jersey, Morris was presented with an opportunity to become governor of the province the year after his son's suspension from the New York Council was confirmed. Sentiment for the appointment of a governor of New Jersey distinct from that of New York, nurtured by resentment at the failure of New York governors to pay more than passing attention to Jersey interests, had been steadily gathering force in the colony where Morris began his political career. Upon the death of Montgomerie on July 1, 1731, Morris, who thereupon became acting governor of New Jersey by virtue of his position as president of the New Jersey Council, attempted to utilize this sentiment to his own advantage. In the middle of that month Morris received a petition from the council in favor of a separate governor of New Jersey and promptly dispatched it to the Duke of Newcastle — as well he might have, since the petition virtually nominated Morris himself for the office. After this petition failed to elicit any response in England, Morris wrote a second letter to the duke in June 1732. In it he warned the secretary that "the rendring governors and all other officers intirely dependant on the people is the generall inclination and endeavour of all the plantations in America" and modestly intimated he was the man best qualified to deal with this problem in New Jersey.[40] But once again Newcastle failed to respond to Morris' overture. Instead the duke secured the appointment of Colonel William Cosby, a relation by marriage, to be Montgomerie's successor in New York and New Jersey. Unable to compensate for his declining political power in New York by obtaining the governorship of New Jersey, Morris was thus obliged to look forward to an unpromising political future in both provinces.

⚮ 8 ⚯

"An Interest for the Cause"

L̲EWIS MORRIS' POLITICAL DECLINE, which began under Burnet and was accentuated under Montgomerie, seemed destined to continue after the arrival of William Cosby in New York on August 1, 1732. Cosby, a veteran of the War of the Spanish Succession who had served as governor of Minorca from 1718 to 1728, became Montgomerie's successor in New York and New Jersey through the influence of his wife's brother, the Earl of Halifax, a privy councilor, and her cousin, the Duke of Newcastle, the secretary of state for the southern department, and one of the principal dispensers of colonial patronage during the reign of George II. While serving in Minorca, the new governor had become heavily indebted as a result of his attempt to defraud a Portuguese merchant named Bonaventura Capadevilla of a valuable cargo of snuff, so that, as a critic acidulously noted, his appointment as chief executive of New York and New Jersey "came seasonably in his way to repair his broken fortune."[1] Determined to extract the maximum profit from his new position, Cosby ignored the politically impotent Morris and instead selected George Clarke as his confidential adviser on New York affairs. He also decided to continue the assembly dominated by Adolph Philipse that had been elected in 1728; and Philipse, whose rise to power had been partly owing to his demands for more frequent assembly elections, readily accepted this decision. Cosby thereupon received a five-year Support Act from the assembly as well as an additional £1,000 for his putative services as a lobbyist against the Sugar Bill in Parliament, although his instructions specifically forbade him to accept such "gifts" from colonial assemblies. With a long-term revenue, a cooperative assembly, and the support of Clarke and Philipse, Cosby was seemingly in a position to enjoy a quiet administration in New York. Indeed, James Alexander, looking back upon the governor's early months in the province, observed, with some exaggeration, that "Our Party Differences seemed over and every thing Seem'd to promise an easier Admin. than any Govr. had ever met with in this place."[2] Yet within a month after the adjournment of the assembly on October 14, 1732, the calm which had descended over New York after Cosby's coming was shattered, thrusting Morris to the fore as the leader of a new country party which, in terms of ideology and tactics, was the boldest and most imaginative political opposition in New York before the era of the American Revolution.

The conflict between Morris and Cosby grew out of a dispute between the governor and Rip Van Dam. Van Dam, an elderly Dutch merchant with an uncertain command of English, had governed New York, as the senior member of the provincial council, after Montgomerie's death in July 1731. In the presence of the council on November 14, 1732, Cosby produced a special instruction from the king, requiring Van Dam to pay him half of his salary and emoluments as acting governor of New York for thirteen months—a sum equivalent to £988. Van Dam, who had drawn the full salary and emoluments with the advice and consent of every councilor except James DeLancey, stoutly refused to comply with this instruction. Cosby, equally determined to make good his claim to the contested money, decided to settle the matter in court. But in what court? If the governor proceeded according to common law, which required a trial by jury, it was virtually certain that a local jury would pronounce in favor of Van Dam. Yet he could not proceed in chancery according to equity law, which was juryless, because as chancellor he would have to act as sole judge in his own cause. Hence he decided early in December 1732 to ask the supreme court to act as a court of exchequer and to bring suit against Van Dam on its equity side. Cosby could thus avoid the hazards of a jury trial—since equitable proceedings were juryless—and have his case decided by three judges—Chief Justice Morris, Second Justice James De-Lancey, and Third Justice Frederick Philipse—whose deliberations might well be influenced by the fact that they held office at his pleasure. Although this procedure commended itself to Cosby as a satisfactory solution to a knotty problem, to others it appeared as an alarming portent that the governor made "Little Distinction betwixt power and right" in his determination to maximize the profits of his office.[3]

Cosby's action affronted Morris' convictions, threatened his material interests, and presented him with an opportunity to reverse the decline of his political power in New York. Morris had long believed that the right to trial by jury was one of the fundamental rights of Englishmen and had once expressed the hope "that wherever the *English* are settled, it will always be a distinguishing Mark of their Liberty, That their Lives or Estates are not to be taken from them, but by Judgment of their Peers . . . according to the good old Law." Therefore he could not but view with alarm Cosby's effort to deprive Van Dam of this right. Moreover, Morris was well aware that if he ruled in favor of Cosby this would set a precedent by which the governor could then claim half of the salary and emoluments he himself had received as acting chief executive of New Jersey after Montgomerie's death. Although Cosby could only have claimed about £316 from Morris, the chief justice was sufficiently exercised over the prospect of forfeiting such a sum to regard the governor's suit against Van Dam with misgivings from the start. Above all, however, this case gave Morris a tempting chance to enhance his standing among the people of New York. New Yorkers had frequently complained about the exercise of equity jurisdiction by royal governors acting as sole judges in chancery, and few of them were pleased with the way Cosby chose to share this jurisdiction with the supreme court, correctly perceiving, as Cadwallader Colden noted, that "as the Judges hold their Commissions at the Governors Pleasure they were absolutely under his Influence and consequently instead of avoiding the ill consequences from the Power of a bad governor, it rather increased them, for even a Wicked man would rather that another should act the Villany that was to serve his purpose than to do it himself." Attacks on equity courts had long been a favorite tactic among the "outs" in New York politics, and as the most prominent "out" in the colony at this time, Morris was unable to resist the temptation to increase his popular following by joining in the assault.[4]

With these thoughts in mind, Morris forsook his role as a defender of the royal prerogative and girded himself for a direct confrontation with Cosby. For seventeen years Morris had had no objection to serving as chief justice of a supreme court based strictly upon a gubernatorial ordinance and as late as the summer of 1732 he had been convinced that this court had the authority to hear equity cases in its exchequer branch. Nevertheless, Morris privately reviewed the history of the New York judicial system during the winter of 1732–33 and concluded that the supreme court did not possess equity jurisdiction and that the governor and council could not establish an exchequer court without legislative consent. These conclusions resulted as much from political calculation as intellectual inspiration. For Morris meant to revive his sagging political fortunes in New York with an attack on equity courts and to deter Cosby from bringing suit against him in New Jersey for half of the salary and emoluments he had received as acting governor of that colony. In order to make his protest more effective, he decided to coordinate his strategy with James Alexander and William Smith, Van Dam's defense counsel. Accordingly, even before Van Dam's case came up for a hearing in the supreme court, Morris sent a rough draft of his opinion denying the supreme court's equity jurisdiction to Alexander and Smith and encouraged them to defend their client by challenging the jurisdiction of the court rather than by pleading the merits of the case. It is almost needless to point out that the chief justice's touching solicitude for Van Dam's lawyers was a gross violation of judicial ethics.[5]

Morris finally hurled his challenge at Cosby on March 15, 1733. On that day the Cosby-Van Dam case came before the supreme court, with Chief Justice Morris, Justice James DeLancey, and Justice Frederick Philipse presiding. Ignoring his younger colleagues, who were known to favor the governor's cause, Morris began the proceedings by ordering counsel for both sides "to argue only that part of the plea, which struck at the Jurisdiction of the Court in the Equity side of the Exchequer." Attorney General Richard Bradley, who had planned to argue the merits of Cosby's case, was caught off guard by this command and forced to make a hastily prepared argument in favor of the court's jurisdiction, to which Alexander and Smith, who knew beforehand of the chief justice's intentions, read a carefully prepared list of objections. As soon as Alexander and Smith had finished their argument, Morris astounded his auditors by reading a written opinion denying the jurisdiction of the supreme court in equity cases. As Cosby sarcastically remarked, it was almost as if Morris, Alexander, and Smith "had wrote by inspiration"—as indeed they had.[6]

Morris' opinion about the supreme court's lack of equity jurisdiction was more a polemical than a legal masterpiece. Appealing to the widespread desire among colonial Americans for a full share of the rights and privileges of Englishmen, Morris noted that even if one conceded "that the King has Powers and Prerogatives in America that he has not in England," it was also true that he had commissioned the justices of the supreme court to conduct themselves according "to the Laws, Statutes and Customs of England." But since in England the king could not create courts of equity by his letters patent without the consent of Parliament, Morris argued that he could not have empowered his governor and council to create such courts in New York "exclusive of the General Assembly of this Province." Yet in fact the king had expressly granted to royal governors and provincial councils the authority to erect equity courts without legislative consent, although Morris unconvincingly tried to deny this.

As a result, Morris concluded, in New York "no less or other authority than that of the whole Legislature can erect a Court of Equity."[7] Thus not only did he deny the authority of Cosby and the provincial council to establish an exchequer court in the supreme court without the consent of the assembly, he also implicitly called into question the legality of the existing court of chancery, which also rested upon nothing more than an ordinance of a governor and council. In this way he placed himself among the ranks of the advocates of more popular control of equity courts—a favorite tactic of politicians out of power and anxious to improve their standing with the people of the province. Equity courts, juryless and used by governors to collect quitrents and annul dubious land titles, were generally unpopular with New Yorkers. Therefore in attacking them, Morris chose a peculiarly inviting target, as Cosby explained to Newcastle:

> [Morris] strikes at Courts of Equity to please the people of New York. There Representatives Severall times Voted the Court of Chancery against Law, there haveing been great arrears of Quit Rents in New York recovered in Chancery and all or most of the Lands being granted by Governours, the people are apprehensive of haveing the Validity of some of these Grants questioned.[8]

Cosby reacted to Morris' defiance with unconcealed fury. Although Justice DeLancey upheld the supreme court's equity jurisdiction, Justice Philipse refused to rule on this question until the next court term in April 1733, thereby bringing the governor's suit against Van Dam to a temporary halt. In the interim, Morris expressed a wish to meet with Cosby and discuss the subject of equity courts with him, but the governor responded by letting the chief justice know "he wou'd neither receive a visit or any message from him; that he could neither rely upon his integrity nor depend upon his judgement or opinion; that he thought him . . . not at all fit to be trusted with any concerns relating to the King . . . nor did he desire to see or hear any further from him."[9]

After this outburst Morris became convinced that his removal from office was only a matter of time and accordingly he stepped up his efforts to win popular support. Thus when Cosby asked him later in March for a copy of his opinion about equity courts, Morris replied by having his opinion published as a pamphlet and distributed throughout the province, together with an appended letter bluntly reminding the governor that "if Judges are to be intimidated so as not to dare to give any Opinion but what is pleasing to a Governour, and agreeable to his private Views, the People of this Province, who are very much concern'd, both with respect to their Lives and Fortunes, in the Freedom and Independence of those who are to Judge of them, may possibly not think themselves so secure in either of them as the Laws and his Majesty intends they should be." Then, when the supreme court reconvened again on April 17 to hear the Cosby-Van Dam case and Justice Philipse announced that he concurred in Justice DeLancey's opinion about the court's right to exercise equity jurisdiction, Morris denounced the legal arguments of his two junior colleagues as "mean, weak and futile," stormed out of the courtroom, and vowed never again to preside over the court while an equity case was before it. After Morris' dramatic withdrawal from the bench, for all practical purposes the governor's suit against Van Dam came to an end.[10]

By now Morris had provoked Cosby beyond endurance. "I must either displace Morris or Suffer my Self to be affronted," the angry governor exclaimed in a letter to Newcastle on April 20, "or what is still worse, see the King's Authority trampled on and disrespect and irreverence to it taught from the Bench to the people by him who by his oath and his office is obliged to support it." Fortunately for Morris, Cosby displayed his characteristic heavy-handedness in the process of removing him from office. Without consulting the provincial council (as his instructions from the king required) or explaining his action beforehand to anyone in New York (as prudence dictated), Cosby suddenly dismissed Morris as chief justice on August 21, 1733. Then, two days later, he appointed James DeLancey as chief justice and Frederick Philipse as second justice, temporarily leaving vacant the third seat on the supreme court. Cosby strengthened his ties with the politically powerful Philipse and DeLancey families by these moves, but at the same time he made a popular hero of Morris by creating the impression in the minds of many New Yorkers that he had dismissed the chief justice simply because that official had delivered an unpalatable legal opinion.[11]

Morris was not slow to capitalize on this sentiment. Two days after his dismissal a broadside appeared in New York City which declared that "Lewis Morris Esqr. Chief Justice of the province of New York was removed from his Office for daring to give his Opinion in a court of law Contrary to the Govers. private Views" and warned that "When vice prevails and Impious men bear Sway/the post of honr. is a private Station."[12] This was the first sign of the formation of a new country party by means of which Morris sought, among other things, to secure his restoration as chief justice and to bring about Cosby's removal as governor. The former judge's transformation from prerogative man to country party leader was complete.

In pursuit of his objectives, Morris adopted a two-pronged strategy. Whereas on the one hand he fused together various discontented elements in New York to form a country party designed to discredit Cosby's administration and reform the provincial government, on the other he appealed to the imperial administration to redress the grievances of which he and his supporters complained. Each part of this strategy was vital to the achievement of Morris' goals. Only the imperial administration had the authority to nullify his dismissal by Cosby and recall the governor to England. Yet imperial officials would only act as Morris wished if they perceived that Cosby was demonstrably incapable of maintaining order in New York. Therefore it was essential for Morris to attack the governor on two fronts simultaneously.

The obstacles facing Morris as he prepared to carry out this strategy were almost overwhelming. Despite the unpopularity he had incurred by abruptly dismissing Morris, Cosby was still politically strong. His alliance with the Philipse-DeLancey faction gave him a comfortable majority in the assembly, while the Support Act of 1732 and the accompanying "gift" of £1,000 made him financially independent of that body until 1737. As a result, the assembly seemed like an unlikely place in which to engender a serious opposition to the governor. Nor was Cosby unduly troubled by the fact that Morris could claim the support of five of the twelve provincial councilors—Rip Van Dam, James Alexander, Cadwallader Colden, Philip Livingston, and Abraham Van Horne—and hope for the benevolent neutrality of at least one more—Archibald Kennedy. Since but five councilors were required to form a quorum and three to carry a decision, Cosby simply summoned only his most trusted supporters to council meetings: George Clarke, James DeLancey, Francis Harison, Daniel Horsemanden, and Henry Lane. Finally the governor could rely upon a friendly press, as William Bradford, the printer of the colony's only newspaper, the *New York Gazette,* was a public employee who was unwilling to risk the displeasure of the governor and the assembly by allowing Morris' propaganda to appear in the columns of his paper. Under these conditions, Morris clearly required all his native ingenuity to carry on an effective opposition against Cosby in New York.[13]

On the English side the situation looked equally grim. Under any circumstances during the Hanoverian era, colonial complaints about royal governors were treated with reserve by the imperial administration. However, when the governor in question was an appointee of the Duke of Newcastle and the brother-in-law of the Earl of Halifax, reserve was apt to become rigidity. Newcastle was the single most important English official involved in colonial affairs at this time as well as one of the most powerful members of Sir Robert Walpole's ministry. Halifax, though less prominent, was still in a position to render valuable assistance to Cosby through his membership in the Privy Council. As long as Cosby retained the support of Newcastle and Halifax, it would be extremely difficult for Morris to turn the imperial administration against him. Yet Morris had to contend with more than just Cosby's English patrons. He also had to reckon on the opposition of James DeLancey's. DeLancey was as intent upon remaining chief justice as Morris was upon being restored to that office, and in pursuance of this ambition the younger man was able to call upon the services of an influential martial relation, Sir John Heathcote, who was a member of Parliament and a trusted political lieutenant of Robert Walpole. In contrast, Morris had no English political connections remotely comparable in influence to Newcastle, Halifax, or Heathcote. Without such connections, so necessary to influence the decisions of the imperial administration, the success of Morris' plan to appeal to England was in doubt from the start.[14]

But if Morris labored under serious political liabilities, so, to a lesser extent, did Cosby; and the former chief justice was quick to turn the governor's distress to his own advantage. To begin with, Cosby was personally obnoxious to many inhabitants of New York. He firmly believed that New Yorkers ranked one link below Englishmen in the Great Chain of Being and made no effort to conceal this conviction, prompting Cadwallader Colden, usually the last person in the colony to speak disrespectfully of a royal governor, to explode in indignation: "[Cosby] recv'd [New Yorkers] with all the affected Spanish Gravity which, it may be supposed, he had acquired and practiced at Port Mahon, for which reason people began to think that he intended to use the same kind of Government over the English here that he had over the conquer'd Spanyards there." Cosby's inflated sense of superiority was matched by his almost boundless rapacity. He raged at an assemblyman who informed him in 1732 that the assembly was only planning to give him a "gift" of £750 instead of the £1,000 he wanted, and even his closest supporters were appalled by his habit of demanding a one-third share of each land grant he made. Yet Cosby continued to give free rein to his pride and avarice in New York, secure in the belief that the patronage of Newcastle and Halifax would prevent any recriminations. "How, gentlemen, do you think I mind that," he is said to have exclaimed upon being informed that a certain doctrine he entertained was illegal, "alas! I have a great interest in England."[15]

Personally unpopular, Cosby had the misfortune to govern New York during a period of economic distress. Since 1728 the prices of New York's principal export commodities—wheat, flour, and livestock—had sharply declined, while the colony's trade with New England and the West Indies—whence it derived the hard money to purchase English manufactured goods—fell off by 50 percent and 20 percent respectively. During the same period the sale of English manufactures to New York actually increased, enriching a handful of merchants at the expense of a progressively unfavorable balance of trade for the province as a whole, an upsurge of indebtedness among farmers, and an alarming rise in the rate of interest. To aggravate the situation, Bermudians took over the bulk of New York's carrying trade after the repeal of a Tonnage Duty Act favoring local shippers in 1726. As a result, ship building declined in New York, to the detriment of the colony's shippers, artisans and craftsmen. Although Cosby could not fairly be held responsible for any of these developments, Morris and his associates naturally hoped that indebted farmers as well as idle artisans and craftsmen would be more responsive to propaganda blaming the governor's administration for their plight than to objective economic analyses of their situation.[16]

Cosby compounded his personal unpopularity and the colony's economic slump by alienating important segments of the provincial polity. Normally stolid Dutch burghers resented his treatment of Rip Van Dam. Long Islanders were aghast at the rumor that he planned to increase his fees by compelling them to turn in their old land titles and take out new ones. The municipal corporation of Albany was taken aback when he incited some Mohawk Indians in September 1733 to burn a deed entitling the city to 1,000 acres of the tribe's most valuable land. And the Oblong Patentees, a group of local land speculators including Morris, his son Lewis, James Alexander, Cadwallader Colden, and William Smith who laid claim to a choice tract of land that Connecticut had ceded to New York in 1725 to resolve a boundary dispute, were offended by Cosby's support of a rival group of prominent English speculators who claimed title to the same tract.[17]

For those who disliked Cosby's imperious manner, for those who were adversely affected by New York's economic decline, and for those who either resented Cosby's arbitrary methods of government or felt that he threatened their material interests, Morris served as a convenient rallying point. Hence the precipitate revival of factionalism in the colony after his removal from the supreme court in August 1733. And since the governor's political position in the province was so strong, the opposition party Morris fused together out of such discordant elements became ideologically and tactically more radical than any other political opposition in eighteenth-century New York before the onset of the American Revolution.

Morris first appeared at the head of a new country party in New York at a by-election for the assembly in the county of Westchester on October 29, 1733. Morris decided to run for the seat vacated by the death of the incumbent, William Willet, in order to dramatize his own popular support as well as to be in a position to assist his son, Lewis Morris, Jr., who represented the borough of Westchester, in organizing opposition to Cosby in the assembly. The governor and the Philipse-DeLancey faction — which now became the court party by reason of its support for the current administration — immediately grasped the significance of Morris' decision and resolved to thwart his bid for office by supporting the candidacy of William Forster, an SPG schoolmaster who was reported to have supported the Jacobite rebellion of 1715. As a result, the ensuing contest was widely perceived as a test of strength between the "Court and Country's Interest."

The election itself took place in the town of Eastchester. At sunrise on the morning of the 29th, Morris entered Eastchester at the head of a column of 180 supporters from upper Westchester. There he was met by seventy recently arrived followers, in addition to about another fifty he had dispatched to the town the previous day to make sure that the court party did not hold the election without him. Three hundred strong, Morris and his supporters formed themselves into a column and rode around the town green three times, preceded by two trumpeters, three violinists, and a freeholder bearing a banner inscribed "King George, Liberty and Law." This slogan signified Morris' desire to identify himself with the Pulteney-Bolingbroke Patriot Coalition in England. Just as the Patriots were struggling to preserve the English constitution against the ravages of Walpolean corruption, it implied, so also was Morris laboring to protect the rights and liberties of New Yorkers against Cosbyite tyranny.

Morris' opponent finally appeared in Eastchester about an hour before noon. At that time William Forster rode into town with a group of 170 freeholders led by James DeLancey and Frederick Philipse, Morris' erstwhile colleagues on the supreme court. As Forster and his supporters circled the green, they exchanged shouts with Morris' partisans, the former raising the pro-Walpole cry of "No Land Tax" and the latter roaring back the anti-Walpole slogan "No Excise." Politically conscious New Yorkers were clearly responsive to the Excise Crisis then raging in England.

Considering the obvious disparity in numbers between the supporters of Morris and Forster, the former chief justice and his followers expected him to be declared the winner without the formality of a vote. Instead Sheriff Nicholas Cooper, a Cosby appointee, first called for a poll and then sought to influence the outcome by disqualifying thirty-eight Quaker supporters of Morris for refusing to swear that they owned enough property to vote. After this outrage, the sheriff held a poll which lasted for nine hours and at the end of which Morris emerged victorious with 231 votes to Forster's 151. Forster thereupon congratulated Morris on his victory and stated that he hoped Morris would not hold his candidacy against him. Morris, still seething at the disqualification of his Quaker followers, tartly replied that he "believed [Forster] was put upon against his Inclination; but that he was highly blamable, and . . . did or should know better for putting the Sheriff . . . upon making so violent an Attempt upon the Liberty of the People." Morris' supporters loudly cheered their leader's verbal sally — whereupon the triumphant candidate, ever an elitist, reproved them for making such an unseemly display. He then proceeded to New York City, where he was received in triumph by the local population and admitted into the assembly on November 1. At this point Cosby, fearful that a spirit of insubordination was abroad in the land, promptly adjourned that body until April 1734.[18]

Cosby's fears were well grounded. Even before the Westchester election, the two Morrises, Alexander, and Smith, the country party's principal leaders, had been forging a formidable instrument to mobilize opposition to the governor within the province: the *New York Weekly Journal.* The *Journal,* the first edition of which appeared on November 5, 1733, was a truly radical innovation in New York politics: a newspaper exclusively devoted to propagating the views of a party avowedly hostile to the existing administration. In the past, political oppositions in New York had occasionally resorted to the press to turn out a pamphlet or a broadside critical of the government in power. Now Morris and his allies meant to keep up a running barrage of criticism against Cosby through the medium of a weekly newspaper. For although the *Journal* was printed by John Peter Zenger, a Palatine immigrant who had once been apprenticed to William Bradford, its editorial policy and subject matter were determined by the Morrises, Smith, and Alexander, especially Alexander. Nor did Morris and his associates make any pretenses about objective journalism. As Alexander informed Robert Hunter, now serving as governor of Jamaica, the function of the paper was "Chiefly to Expose [Cosby] and those ridiculous flatteries with which Mr. Harrison loads our other newspaper: Which our Governour Claims and has the priviledge of Suffering nothing to be in but what he and Mr. Harrison approve of."[19]

The *Journal* was indeed unsparing in its criticism of Cosby and the court party. The paper's main contributors, the two Morrises, Alexander, Smith, and Colden, wrote pseudonymously to avoid prosecution under the English law of seditious libel and with a flair for satire and invective never before equalled in New York. They inveighed at Cosby's proceedings against Van Dam and his suspension of Morris as irrefutable evidence of his fondness for arbitrary rule. They waxed indignant at the governor's role in the destruction of the Albany Deed as but the most flagrant example of his general disregard for the rights of property. And they exclaimed in righteous anger that Cosby was criminally negligent, and possibly even treasonous, for allowing the French sloop *Le Caesar* to purchase supplies in New York for the strategic fortress of Louisbourg late in 1733, when in Europe England and France were on the verge of being drawn into the War of the Polish Succession on opposing sides. Country party leaders did not always maintain such an exalted level of political discourse. They also personally lampooned the governor and his supporters, once likening Cosby to a monkey and Francis Harison, his chief defender, to a spaniel. But this was mild fare compared to their effort to discredit Harison by claiming that he had plotted to poison James Alexander and his family, not to mention their attempt to play upon one of the baser strains in the American mind by reporting that the daughter of a Cosby loyalist had been raped by a black man.[20]

The *Journal* did more than hurl barbed shafts at Governor Cosby and his supporters. It also set forth a well-conceived program of political and economic reform designed to attract wider support for the country party in New York. Politically, country writers in the *Journal* advocated a provincial government more responsive to the popular will and a judiciary sufficiently independent to safeguard the liberty and property of the subject. In practice, a responsible government would be one in which the powers of the assembly were expanded while those of the governor and council were contracted. Hence the *Journal* called upon the assembly to impeach the nefarious advisers—conveniently left unnamed—who had encouraged Cosby to rule arbitrarily, to pass a Triennial Act so that every governor would have to hold new assembly elections at least once every three years, to appoint a colonial agent in London responsible only to itself, and to exercise greater control over the selection of sheriffs by the governor. The *Journal* also sought to enhance the standing of the country party in New York City and Albany by urging that their municipal mayors and recorders be made popularly elected officials instead of gubernatorial appointees.[21]

Legally, the establishment of an independent judiciary would also restrict the powers of the governor and council. Whereas in the past governors and councils alone had created courts and judges had been commissioned to serve only at pleasure, the *Journal* now insisted that the entire judicial system, especially equity courts, be placed upon a statutory foundation and that judges be commissioned to serve during good behavior. In this respect, Morris and the country party expressed the deep-seated desire of politically aware New Yorkers to apply English legal precedents to their province, so that thereby they could share more fully in the rights and privileges of Englishmen.[22]

Economically, Morris and his supporters made a special appeal to the "industrious poor," hard hit by the commercial depression which had beset New York since 1728. Country writers in the *Journal* advocated the passage of a tonnage duty favoring local shipping to break up the monopoly of New York's carrying trade by the Bermudians and to provide employment for local seamen, artisans, and craftsmen. They lashed out at usurers, not only for victimizing the poor, but also for keeping money out of circulation which might otherwise have stimulated trade and economic recovery. Moreover, the *Journal* proposed an imaginative solution to New York's deteriorating balance of payments problems. Since the West Indies could not import enough foodstuffs from the province to provide New York with all the hard money needed to pay for the manufactured goods it received from England, the paper urged the assembly to encourage the production of hemp and iron as export commodities which the colony could ship directly to England in exchange for these products. Finally, country party scribes, echoing one of Morris' long-standing prejudices, regularly took advantage of discussions of economic issues to criticize merchants who grew wealthy while farmers, artisans, and craftsmen suffered.[23]

In addition to castigating the Cosby administration and offering an alternative program of their own, Morris and the country party also used the *Journal* to invest themselves with something approaching cosmic significance. In a hundred different ways the *Journal* emphasized the antimony between power and liberty, which Bernard Bailyn has identified as the salient characteristic of colonial political ideology. Power, active and aggressive, constantly encroached upon liberty, passive and fragile: this was one of the basic lessons colonial Americans derived from their study of history. Nor was the phenomenon of power locked in ceaseless struggle with liberty confined to the Old World. It was universal in scope, the inevitable result of man's concupiscent nature. And it was this spectacle of power ravishing liberty that Morris and his followers professed to discern in the acts of Governor Cosby. Power threatened liberty when Cosby "unlawfully" set up a court of exchequer to sue Van Dam, "arbitrarily" dismissed Morris from office, "wantonly" destroyed the Albany Deed, and "illegally" approved the summary disfranchisement of Morris' Quaker supporters. Consequently, Morris and the country party claimed, they were not just another spiteful, self-interested political faction. Rather their cause was the cause of liberty itself. Or, as a contributor to the *Journal* stated, in the process of refuting the charge that country party attacks on Cosby were nothing more than vicious libels: "*The People* of this City and Province think . . . that their Liberties and Properties are precarious, and that *Slavery* is like to be entailed on them if some past Things are not amended."[24]

Despite his victory in the Westchester election and the slashing attacks of the *Journal,* Morris made very little headway against Cosby in New York during the year after his admission into the assembly. For every charge against Cosby that was made in the *Journal,* there was a countercharge in the *Gazette* that Morris and his supporters were simply the latest in a long line of political opportunists who were out of power and envious of those who were in. Cosby continued to receive the support of the dominant Philipse-DeLancey party in the assembly, moreover, and he studiously ignored Morris' supporters in the council. Furthermore the governor and the court party took some of the sting out of Morris' propaganda by appropriating parts of the program his party advocated. Thus in April 1734 Cosby advised the assembly to pass legislation to encourage New York's shipping industry, and during the ensuing legislative session Stephen DeLancey steered a Triennial Bill through the lower house. To be sure, a country party slate swept the New York City municipal elections in September 1734, but this did not significantly alter the balance of political power in the colony and it was soon followed by what appeared to be the beginning of a general suppression of the country party. On November 17 the governor and council had John Peter Zenger, the printer of the *Journal,* arrested on a charge of seditious libel, and six days later they had four issues of the paper publicly burned. Having failed to turn the assembly or the council against Cosby and threatened with the loss of his most formidable instrument of propaganda, Morris' only remaining hope was to outmaneuver the governor in England.[25]

Yet so far Morris had fared no better in England than in New York. As soon as he was dismissed as chief justice, Morris recognized the need to appeal to the imperial administration for Cosby's removal as governor and his own reinstatement in office. Thus he dispatched a series of letters to the Board of Trade between August and December 1733 in which he sought to lay the groundwork for Cosby's dismissal by portraying him as an arbitrary governor who was insensitive to the rights of New Yorkers and contemptuous of his instructions from the crown. Morris accused Cosby of violating royal instructions by accepting "gifts" of money from the New York and New Jersey assemblies and by dismissing him as chief justice without consulting the council. He alleged that the governor made the impartial administration of justice difficult by removing him for giving an opinion on a matter of law and charged that he endangered security of property by bringing about the destruction of the Albany Deed for the benefit of a group of land speculators including members of his own family. Finally Morris argued that Cosby unwisely gave French officers an opportunity to inspect New York's defenses during the *Le Caesar* incident and asserted that he fraudulently diverted to his own use some of the funds the imperial administration had sent him to pay the British regulars in New York as well as some of the gifts it had dispatched to the Iroquois in the colony. These were serious allegations, and if Board members had accepted them as such, perhaps they might have taken some action against Cosby. Unfortunately for Morris' cause, however, they simply read his complaints and then quietly ignored them.[26]

Morris failed to stir the Board of Trade into action because his allies in England were politically weak and his own charges lacked convincing supporting evidence. Since Morris was not personally in England to prosecute his complaints against Cosby, he had to rely upon the assistance of an agent, Ferdinand John Paris, and a marital relation, Matthew Norris, neither of whom possessed the requisite political power to move the imperial bureaucracy to take action against an appointee of the Duke of Newcastle. Paris, who represented a varied colonial clientele and who had been asked by James Alexander, one of his many clients, to protect Morris' interests in England, was a skillful solicitor but hardly a force to be reckoned with in his own right. Norris, a high spirited naval captain who was married to Morris' daughter, Euphemia, had access to some important figures in English public life, but none of them was in a position to help his father-in-law. Although Norris' father, Admiral Sir John Norris, was the commander-in-chief of the British navy, he was also a notorious "grumbletonian" who had been out of favor with Walpole since 1730. The younger Norris heartily despised Walpole and Newcastle and was acquainted with Lord Carteret and Philip Gybbon, two noted anti-Walpolean orators in Parliament. But since Carteret and Gybbon were opponents of Walpole, they were also out of office, so that, as Norris regretfully informed Morris, "it is too true my Friends have not a power equal to their inclination to serve you."[27]

Even if his son-in-law's connections had had power equal to their willingness to serve, Morris still would have been hard put to convince the Board of Trade to take his charges seriously. The Board wanted incontrovertible proof of Cosby's maladministration in the form of properly authenticated testimony from relatively disinterested parties in New York. Instead Morris provided it with three letters whose allegations were open to question because of his known hostility to Cosby and supporting evidence such as issues of the *Journal* and country party pamphlets that was suspect for the same reason. In the absence of more compelling evidence than this, Board members were naturally more inclined to side with the governor than his critics. "Things of this nature," Matthew Norris sagely informed his father-in-law in regard to complaints to England about Cosby, "appear in their greatest Lustre, when no private Views can be deduced from them."[28]

Morris was also frustrated in his efforts to induce the imperial administration to restore him to the chief justiceship. Once again he relied upon Paris and Norris to solicit his business for him in England, although in this case with slightly more success. As soon as the news of Morris' suspension from the supreme court arrived in England late in November 1733, Paris petitioned the Privy Council to require Cosby to explain his reasons for this act and to restore Morris as chief justice. Morris won a partial victory on January 8, 1734, when the Privy Council ordered Cosby to provide the Board of Trade with an explanation of his dismissal of the former chief justice, but this victory proved to be insignificant.[29]

Cosby took advantage of the Council's order to relieve all his pent up frustrations with Morris, as well as further to undermine the credibility of the country party leader with the imperial authorities. Writing in a tone of indignation not unmixed with relish, Cosby justified his behavior toward Morris in a June 19, 1734 letter to the Board of Trade in which he cited examples of Morris' alleged "partiality in the administration of Justice," noted the inconsistency between the former chief justice's past espousal of the supreme court's right to exercise equity jurisdiction without legislative consent and his present rejection of it, and denounced the country leader's attempt to "ingratiate himself with the people of New York" by the publication of his opinion about equity courts. Wherefore, Cosby concluded, he had removed Morris from office because "I thought it my duty to support this Court, and to maintain his Majties prerogative to the utmost of my power." At the same time, the governor also wrote to the Duke of Newcastle and urged him to prevent the reinstallation of Morris as chief justice, alleging that New Yorkers were "very much from his own reports afraid of his being restor'd, being a very Tyrant when in that post."[30]

The Board of Trade was so satisfied with Cosby's explanation of Morris' dismissal that it refused to give Paris a copy of the governor's letter for the former chief justice to answer until it was ordered to do so by the Privy Council in November 1734. Yet this order may also have marked the limit of the imperial administration's responsiveness to Paris and Norris' efforts in behalf of Morris. For when Paris signified his intention in the following month to apply to the Privy Council for an order enabling Morris to gather suitably authenticated evidence of his complaints about Cosby, William Sharpe, the Council's secretary, warned Newcastle that the issuance of such an order would be unprecedented, and would "introduce great disturbance in the province, and . . . be putting the petitioner [Morris] in Some measure on an equality with the Governr. and be attended too with great trouble and expense."[31] And, in fact, Paris never did request the Privy Council to issue this order, perhaps because he recognized the reluctance of the imperial administration to administer such a stinging rebuke to one of Newcastle's clients.

The failure of Morris' appeals to England, when combined with the arrest of Zenger in New York, made the country party leader decide to embark on a personal mission to London. Morris and his fellow country party leaders feared that Zenger's imprisonment might be the prelude to their own incarceration, and since they had so far been unable to wrest control of the provincial government from Cosby, they realized that their last remaining hope was to outflank the governor in England. Accordingly on November 19, 1734, two days after Zenger's detainment, Morris slyly asked the assembly for permission "to go home, being indisposed." Morris' unsuspecting colleagues in the lower house, thinking that "home" meant Morrisania, readily granted his request. But Morris' indisposition was primarily political rather than physical and his definition of "home" far more capacious than most of his fellow assemblymen imagined. Instead of going to his Westchester estate, he proceeded to New Jersey, where he took ship for England on November 23, accompanied by his twenty-one year old son, Robert Hunter Morris, and, if we can accept the testimony of his daughter, Sarah, by the prayers of the people of New York and New Jersey as well.[32]

Shortly before Morris sailed for England James Alexander prepared a set of instructions for him in conjunction with William Smith and Lewis Morris, Jr., that clearly reveal the design of his mission. These instructions advised the former chief justice to take no action against Cosby in England until he had received "further proofs and materials" about the governor's misdeeds from New York. After arranging this evidence into a convincing indictment of Cosby's maladministration and presenting it to the Duke of Newcastle and Cosby's other patrons, he was to request them to remove the governor from office, and threaten to "apply to the King and Council or Parliament for redress and to the press to Expose him and his supporters to all Brittain" if they refused. If threats and pleas alike left Cosby's patrons unmoved, the instructions cautioned the naturally impetuous Morris, "then Consider well your own Strength before you adventure to break with them and See clearly the probability of speedy success." For if the country leader concluded that his strength was not equal to that of Cosby's supporters or that the effort to remove Cosby against their opposition would consume too much time, he should "then give Ear to a Compromise which we think . . . they'll soon offer to you."

The compromise Morris was "to insist upon" in the event Cosby remained in New York was nothing less than the implementation of the principal demands of the country party. Thus Morris should be restored to the chief justiceship during good behavior. The present assembly should be dissolved and a new one elected. Francis Harison and Daniel Horsemanden· should be replaced as provincial councilors by William Smith and Peter Schuyler, thereby giving the country party a majority on the council. Newcastle and Cosby's other English patrons should order the governor to cooperate with the newly reconstituted council and assembly in the passage of a radically Whig program of political reform, including frequent assembly elections, the establishment of the provincial judicial system on a statutory foundation, the regulation of the qualifications and appointment of sheriffs and coroners as well as of the choice and legislative procedure of assemblymen and councilors, and the preservation of assemblymen from corrupting executive influence. As if these concessions were not enough, Newcastle and the governor's other English supporters should also order Cosby to sit apart from the council when it met in its legislative capacity, to take no reprisals against members of the country party, and to grant new charters to New York City and Albany making their mayors and recorders popularly elected officials. Finally, Morris should obtain a written pledge from Cosby's English patrons that they would withdraw their support from the governor if he refused to comply with the conditions of this compromise.

And what did the country party offer in return? Simply a promise to uphold Cosby's authority and to place no obstacles in the way of his "receiving the usual salary, perquisites, and emoluments as other Govs. used to have before him."[33] The disparity between what Morris and his supporters expected to receive from Cosby's patrons and what they were willing to concede in return would have been ludicrous had it not been for the conviction of at least some country party leaders that "the Compromise proposed is in Substance what Englishmen here are entitled to by the original Constitution of their mother country and its but Securing that Constitution to us upon as firm a basis as our Legislature can give it."[34]

Morris reached London early in January 1735 and quickly concluded that the roseate expectations of his supporters in New York were incompatible with the harsh realities of English political life. Shortly after his arrival, Morris asked the Duke of Newcastle to meet with him to discuss country party grievances against Cosby, but Newcastle studiously avoided this request. Newcastle's studied aloofness convinced Morris that Cosby's English patrons would not willingly consent to the governor's removal from New York, much less approve the sweeping terms of the so-called compromise country leaders hoped to obtain if Cosby remained in the province. At the same time, Morris was intent upon being restored as chief justice and determined either to redress the major country party grievances or to bring about the dismissal of the man he held responsible for them. Hence he decided to brave the opposition of Cosby's English supporters by appealing to the Privy Council, first for his own restoration, then later for the governor's recall to England. "I have been abroad for ten dayes," the sturdy veteran of more than forty years of political conflict in New York and New Jersey confided to James Alexander on February 8, 1735, "and that has been Employed in making an interest for the Cause and by my Selfe and friends have and hope to make one more considerable than your governour unless the ministry Joine and resolve to Support him which I believe his friends have so ill an Opinion of him that they will not attempt it."[35]

"An interest for the Cause"—this was what Morris had to create if he was to prosecute his complaints against Governor Cosby successfully. In order to incline the Privy Council to his favor, Morris had to acquire English allies with sufficient political influence to offset the power of strategically situated Cosby supporters like Newcastle and Halifax and to overcome the reluctance of the imperial administration to weaken royal authority in America by crediting the charges of a mere colonial against one of the king's viceregents. Yet where could he find such allies? Apart from his marital relations, Matthew Norris and Vincent Pearse, there was no Morris family in England to protest against the former chief justice's removal from office, and Morris himself, a life-long landed aristocrat who heartily despised merchants, had no connections with London's influential mercantile community. Moreover, thirty-three years had elapsed since Morris' last mission to England and since then death had claimed all the acquaintances he had made at that time with the sole exception of the aged Paul Docminique, who passed away several months after Morris' arrival in London. During these years Morris had lost contact with the Society for the Propagation of the Gospel in Foreign Parts as he developed into a Deist and had become estranged from the West Jersey Society because of that organization's dissatisfaction with his performance as its business agent. Lacking any immediate familial, commercial, or institutional connections in England, well might Morris complain to Alexander: "It requires more time than you are aware of before a man can get into his geeres here and know which way to come at the great folkes and have any tolerable acquaintance with any of them and tho I have had more advantage that way than perhaps any body that could have come from America . . . I am as it were but walking in trammels yet and have not got my paces to perfection but come gayly on."[36]

In spite of his unfamiliarity with the current English political scene, Morris zestfully went about the business of persuading the Privy Council to restore him to the chief justiceship in New York. During the winter and spring of 1735 he prepared a statement of his case for the Privy Council in which he laboriously refuted each and every justification that Cosby had advanced for his removal as chief justice and portrayed himself as a faithful servant of the crown who had been instrumental in royalizing the colony of New Jersey and persuading the assembly of New York to support Governors Hunter and Burnet. To represent him when his case finally came before the council, Morris retained the services of Attorney General John Willes, Solicitor General Dudley Ryder, and an aspiring young lawyer named William Murray, who later became a celebrated English jurist under the title of Lord Mansfield. At the same time, Morris sought support from members of the Walpole ministry in order to check the opposition he anticipated from Newcastle and Halifax. Hence he called upon the Marquis of Lothian, a friend of Cadwallader Colden and the political ally of the Duke of Argyll, the most powerful Scottish politician in England; but although Lothian indicated his willingness to intercede for Colden if his fellow Scot was threatened with the loss of his offices by Cosby, he refused to help Morris. Morris also brought his case to the attention of sundry members of the Privy Council; and though the evidence is fragmentary, he seems to have convinced the Earl of Wilmington, the council's president, and Joseph Jekyll, the independent Master of the Rolls, of the injustice of his dismissal from office.[37]

However, Morris' most reliable supporters in England were his marital relations. Two of his daughters, Mary and Euphemia, were married to British naval captains, Vincent Pearse and Matthew Norris. The Pearses and the Norrises provided Morris with political assistance as well as personal hospitality. Vincent Pearse and his brother Thomas, a commissioner of the navy and "a minor protege of Robert Walpole's," placed themselves at Morris' disposal throughout his London mission. Although Matthew Norris was on station in New York while Morris was in England, and although Sir John Norris was reluctant to have the New Yorker become embroiled in an open clash with the ministry, the mere fact that the commander-in-chief of the British navy was known to be in sympathy with Morris gave the country leader's complaints against Cosby a certain legitimacy they would otherwise have lacked. Moreover, it was probably through his acquaintance with Sir John that Morris acquired his first and only active ally within the Walpole ministry: Sir Charles Wager. Wager — an admiral in the British navy, first lord of the admiralty, a privy councilor and a member of Parliament — was on good terms with King George II and Walpole. Morris met Wager sometime late in January or early in February 1735 and so impressed him with his accounts of the iniquity of Cosby's administration in New York that he never lost his support thereafter.[38]

Even as Morris was in the process of appealing to the Privy Council for his restoration to the New York Supreme Court, he brought a variety of pressures to bear on the Duke of Newcastle to induce him to appoint a new governor of New York. Morris openly met with prominent leaders of the opposition to Walpole's administration on various occasions between February and April 1735, and toyed with the idea of allowing them to bring his complaints about Cosby's destruction of the Albany Deed and his handling of the *Le Caesar* incident before the House of Commons. He consulted with such notables as Lord Carteret, one of the most eloquent opposition spokesmen in the House of Lords; Philip Gybbon, a friend of Captain Norris and a close ally of William Pulteney in the House of Commons; and Micajah Perry, a correspondent of James Alexander and Cadwallader Colden, who gave voice to the growing dissatisfaction among English merchants with Walpole's pacific foreign policy toward Spain. Carteret, Gybbon, and Perry, ever on the alert for an issue with which to embarrass Sir Robert, were particularly receptive to Morris, since the former chief justice represented the destruction of the Albany Deed as the first step in the disintegration of the strategic alliance between the Iroquois and the English in New York and the *Le Caesar* affair as the prelude to a French descent upon New York City. But Morris, who was misled by his contacts with the ministry's opponents into believing that Walpole's majority in the House of Commons was only sixteen when, in fact, it was seventy-five, convinced himself that the mere threat to have these two incidents disclosed by the opposition would be sufficient to panic the ministry into removing Cosby from New York. However, Newcastle, who was well aware of the ministry's true parliamentary, strength, was unmoved by Morris' open flirtation with the opposition.[39]

The New Yorker was equally unsuccessful in his other efforts to persuade the secretary of state to abandon Cosby. In February 1735 Morris conceived the idea of appealing from the Walpole ministry to the English political nation by employing Abel Boyer, the long-time editor of the yearly *Political State of Great Britain,* to print accounts of Cosby's misgovernment in New York for the English public. Nothing ever came of this particular project, however, either because Morris could not locate Boyer or because Boyer would not risk the wrath of the ministry by publishing material critical of a relative and appointee of Newcastle. Morris did have several hundred copies of an account of Cosby's attempt to swindle the Portuguese merchant Capadevilla printed in London in April 1735; but since it is not certain to whom he distributed these pamphlets, it is impossible to measure their impact.[40] In addition to these rudimentary attempts to mobilize English public opinion against the ministry, Morris sought to induce Newcastle to forsake the governor by encouraging several aspirants for colonial office to apply for the government of New

York. Unfortunately for the country leader, the desire for preferment of his putative successors to Cosby far exceeded their power to convince the secretary of state to appoint them to the position they sought. Consequently in August 1735 the New Yorker was reduced to the pitiable expedient of requesting Newcastle to transfer the governor from New York to the lusher clime of Barbados — only to have the duke ignore this request and reaffirm his support for Cosby.[41]

Morris' failure to secure Cosby's recall and the repeated delays he encountered in obtaining a hearing before the Privy Council made him bitterly disillusioned with English politics and society. "O Venalis Roma," he exclaimed of the land whose constitution he admired and was supposed to be defending in New York — "O corrupt Rome." From the first Morris had been appalled by the high cost of living in London, as well as by what he regarded as the extravagant fees charged by English lawyers. But as the New Yorker became frustrated in his efforts to achieve his political objectives in England, complaints about living expenses and legal fees gave way to harsh criticisms of the imperial system. "Tis not the injustice of the thing that all affects those concern'd in reccomending of [Cosby]," Morris told Alexander, referring to the difficulties he encountered in prosecuting country party complaints against the governor, "provided it can be kept a Secret and the people not clamour and when they do if they meet with relief it is not So much in Pitty to them as in fear of the reflection it will be upon themselves for advising the Sending Such a man the sole intent of which was to make a purse." And if a royal governor's English patrons could not be persuaded to abandon him, Morris believed, it was unrealistic to expect assistance from Parliament or the Walpole ministry, both of which evinced a terrifying lack of concern about the misbehavior of wayward colonial executives. "We have a Parliament and ministry who I am apt to believe some of them know that there are Plantations and governors but not quite so well as we do," he complained, "Like the froggs in the fable the mad pranks of a plantation Governour is Sport to them tho death to us, and [they] Seem lesse concern'd in our contests than we are at those of Crows and Kingbirds." Morris despaired of reforming the imperial administration and making it more responsive to colonial complaints about royal governors. Instead, he bitterly concluded, "I think the only effectuall way to remove a governour, is to let those who Sent him See plainly, that he can not answer the Ends he came for Viz fill his pocketts; and then You will have some body Elce to try a different way of management." Coming from a colonial American who had previously gloried in all things British, the sheer ferocity of these strictures was an ill omen for the long-term stability of the empire.[42]

Yet if Morris ever despaired of bringing about Cosby's removal through the imperial administration, he never openly expressed any doubt that the Privy Council would restore him to the chief justiceship. For a brief period, indeed, it seemed as if his despair was about to be dispelled and his hope rewarded. After yet another delay, the Privy Council finally set November 5, 1735 as the date for considering Morris' case. Then, on the day before his hearing, the New Yorker received an unexpected message from Newcastle, which was delivered by Francis Gashery, Sir Charles Wager's secretary. Gashery informed Morris that the duke, who was by nature a timid man, was willing to join with Sir Charles in asking the king to appoint Morris governor of New Jersey if he agreed to "Drop the Complaints Against Cosby and Put Off the Hearing that was appointed to be the next day." But Morris, who interpreted this proposal as a sign of weakness on Newcastle's part and who had no guarantee that the duke would live up to his part of the agreement, emphatically refused to forego his hearing before the Privy Council. He assured Gashery that "Mr Cosbies Government was Verry Oppressive to the People, that they Had Complained of it to the King and Committed the management of those Complaints to Him . . . [and] He Could not in Honour Give them up on any termes nor would not if they would give Him the Government of Ireland." However, Morris did tell Sir Charles' secretary that there was one way for Newcastle to make him abandon his complaints against Cosby — and that was by transferring him to another colony.[43]

Morris was not as adamant about Cosby's removal as he appeared to be in his conversation with Gashery. Later the same day the former chief justice met with Wager and informed him that he would be amenable to Cosby's continuance in New York if his English patrons approved the implementation of some key country party demands. Thus Morris wanted to secure the exclusion of the governor from the council when it met in its legislative capacity, the dissolution of the current assembly, the appointment of a London agent independent of the governor, the settling of the New York judicial system on a statutory foundation, the appointment of judges during good behavior, and the restoration of the Albany Deed. These terms were far less sweeping than those set forth in Morris' instructions, but this was because the New Yorker's expectations had been greatly sobered by almost a year of solicitation in England. Sir Charles approved these conditions and thought they would be "for the interest of the Crown to Grant." Evidently the admiral's opinion was not widely shared in imperial circles. Although in January 1736 the imperial administration approved an instruction forbidding the governor of New York to attend legislative sessions of the provincial council, it ignored the rest of Morris' terms.[44]

Morris' failure to include his own restoration to the supreme court as one of the conditions he outlined to Wager undoubtedly reflected his confidence in his ability to achieve this goal through his appeal to the Privy Council. This confidence did not seem out of place after Newcastle's last minute attempt to induce him to drop his appeal. The council gathered together on November 5 to consider the constitutionality of Morris' dismissal as chief justice with the Earl of Wilmington, Lord Chancellor Hardwicke, the Earl of Halifax, the Duke of Newcastle, Sir Joseph Jekyll, Sir Charles Wager, Lord Fitzwalter, Lord Ilay, Speaker of the Commons Arthur Onslow, and Paymaster of the Forces Henry Pelham in attendance. Most of these councilors were far from being impartial judges of the case before them. Wager was Morris' avowed patron; Wilmington and Jekyll had both been of assistance to the former chief justice in prosecuting his complaints against Cosby; and Onslow, a relative of Admiral Norris' wife, was also thought to be in sympathy with the New Yorker. On the other hand, Newcastle and Halifax were open supporters of Cosby; Pelham was the duke's brother; and Fitzwalter, the secretary of state's choice as president of the Board of Trade, was inclined to follow Newcastle's lead. Hardwicke was also a Newcastle friend and ally, but throughout the proceedings he manifested a greater concern for legal proprieties than for the protection of the duke's appointee.[45]

Morris' counsel started to open the hearing, "but were stoped by my Lord Hardwicke, who said they were inosent till Proved guilty and therefore it was not their Place to begin." Consequently Cosby's lawyers seized the initiative. After observing how difficult it was for "Governours to Prove Everything they Say'd," they expatiated upon the justifications for Morris' removal from office that Cosby had given to Newcastle and the Board of Trade. When they argued that Cosby was legally entitled to half of the salary and emoluments received by Van Dam after the death of Montgomerie, however, a quarrel broke out between Morris and Newcastle. Whereas Morris declared that the additional instruction enabling Cosby to make this claim on Van Dam was unprecedented, Newcastle responded that it differed in no way from the instruction ordinarily issued to royal governors on this subject. Unfortunately for the duke, a comparison of the ordinary instruction defining the governor's right to a share of the salary and emoluments received by the president of a colonial council and the additional instruction given to Cosby revealed that they were "as Different as the Different Circumstances required, the one makeing no Provision in the Case of Death and the other is Very Particular in reciting the Death of Montgomery."

This was not the only setback Cosby and his supporters received in the Privy Council. After the governor's counsel had rehearsed the familiar justifications for Morris' suspension, they offered to substantiate them by first introducing into evidence an affidavit from the sheriff of Richmond County in New York. But at this point Hardwicke, the council's foremost legal authority, intervened and rejected evidence of this sort "by Declaring that no Ex Party Evidence taken before a Private majestrate was Legall Evidence at that Board, and further that in his opinion governours were as much obliged to Prove what they asserted as other men." Since the only other evidence Cosby's counsel had at their disposal was also *ex parte,* they were therefore obliged to confine themselves to arguing that Morris' suspension was justified because the publication of his opinion about the need for legislative consent to the erection of equity courts was seditious.

After having heard the governor's defense, the members of the Privy Council conferred among themselves and decided to hear Morris' rebuttal two days later. The governor's justification for the suspension of Morris must have made a poor impression on his partisans, for when the council reconvened on November 7, only Wilmington, Halifax, Wager, Onslow, Jekyll, and the Earl of Scarborough, a new and neutral member, were present. Thus, with the exception of Halifax, the New Yorker's counsel did not have to face a hostile audience. Since Attorney General Willes was not in London at the time, Solicitor General Ryder opened the former chief justice's case by challenging each of the reasons Cosby had offered to justify his removal from the supreme court. Then William Murray went to special pains to deny that the printing of Morris' opinion about equity courts had been disrespectful of authority. After the completion of these arguments, the privy councilors deliberated among themselves for several hours before reaching a decision. All the attending councilors frowned upon the publication of Morris' legal opinion because they believed that it was "a very wrong Step to print against a Gov. in a Province where he resides," but a majority agreed that neither this, nor any of the other reasons adduced by Cosby, justified Morris' dismissal from the supreme court. On the other hand, these same councilors, no doubt reluctant to weaken royal authority in New York by rewarding the leader of the opposition to the governor of that colony, did not see fit to recommend Morris' restoration as chief justice. Thus the council's decision was devoid of any practical significance for the country party leader.[46]

November 7, 1735, marked the high point of Morris' London mission, although he did not realize this at the time. The evidence is fragmentary, but there is reason to believe that the ultimate fate of the New Yorker's mission was decided at Robert Walpole's country estate in Norfolk shortly after the Privy Council handed down its decision on the 7th. Here Walpole met with Newcastle and Sir John Heathcote, Chief Justice De-

Lancey's relative and patron, and received the news about the council's disposition of Morris' case a day or two later. Although no records of their conversations have survived, it seems likely that Newcastle decided to continue to support Cosby and that Heathcote reiterated his wish that DeLancey remain as chief justice. Walpole undoubtedly found himself in sympathy with the wishes of his two followers. An English nobleman had once told Morris, for instance, that Walpole might remove Cosby from office but not under pressure from the people of New York. Furthermore the great minister was apt to look askance at an American who came to England and openly consorted with the leaders of the opposition to his administration. All things considered, Morris was a standing affront to Walpole's favorite policy: *quieta non movere.*[47]

The subsequent course of Morris' mission bears out the supposition that a ministerial decision to yield no further to him was made at Norfolk. Buoyed up by the deceptive success of his appeal to the Privy Council, the New Yorker resumed his attempts to obtain his reinstallation to office as well as Cosby's removal from New York. The fate of each effort revealed the imperial administration's determination to make no substantive concessions to the country party leader. In December 1735, with Sir Charles Wager present, Morris gave Newcastle a petition to the king requesting his restoration to the supreme court. The secretary of state accepted this petition, but, instead of presenting it to the king, he attempted to consign it to the limbo of his office files. At length, wearied by these Fabian tactics, Morris wrote in desperation to the duke on March 21, 1736, pleading for his restoration as chief justice, but the duke simply ignored him. Although Newcastle himself never explained his indifference to the New Yorker's pleas, his motivation was probably similar to that of an anonymous imperial bureaucrat, who had argued almost two years earlier that "Mr. Morris's printed arguments and letter and declared enmity to the Governor are of themselves sufficient reasons to justify his removal and to prevent his being restored."[48]

Morris found the imperial administration equally adamant about the continuance of Cosby as governor of New York. In the hope of duplicating his earlier apparent success before the Privy Council, the New Yorker presented that body with a series of complaints about Cosby's alleged maladministration in New York. Since the destruction of the Albany Deed supposedly threatened the sanctity of property as well as the perpetuation of the Anglo-Iroquois alliance in New York, the former chief justice made this the subject of two petitions he submitted to the council in behalf of the freeholders of Albany, the first on November 26, 1735, and the second on February 5, 1736. In each instance, however, the council referred the petition in question to Cosby for comment, instead of recommending his immediate dismissal from office as the country party leader hoped. Although the king was reportedly indignant at the news of the destruction of the Albany Deed, some privy councilors wondered why it had taken the Albanians more than two years to inform them of such a heinous deed. Hence the council's cautious reaction to Morris' petitions.[49]

Morris met with a similar fate when, in the presence of Robert Walpole, he submitted an omnibus indictment of the Cosby administration to the Earl of Wilmington, the council's president, on February 5. Indeed, at first Wilmington was so reluctant to accept this document that Morris, perhaps sensing the hopelessness of the whole effort, burst into a tirade, saying that "he had done his duty in informing the King and ministry of the misconduct of their governour . . . that they might make what use of it they Pleased . . . that he should not be at the Expence and trouble of Prosecuting the Complaints, but [would] return and let his Countrymen Know what success they were like to meet with in any application here." Despite Morris' outburst of righteous indignation, the Privy Council considered the country party leader's formidable allegations against Cosby, wondered why they were not supported by a formal address from the New York Assembly, and accordingly referred them to the governor for comment. But the final blow to Morris' hopes for convincing the imperial administration to appoint a new governor of New York fell on April 21, 1736, when the council rejected three petitions from that province requesting the recognition of Morris as the colony's agent, so as to lend greater weight to his complaints. Ironically, by that time there was no longer any need for Morris to proceed against Cosby in England as the governor had already succumbed to tuberculosis in New York the month before.[50]

As Morris began to realize the futility of striving to achieve his primary political objectives in England, his thoughts centered more and more upon the offer of the government of New Jersey that he had received from Newcastle in November 1735. He was still skeptical of Newcastle's willingness to appoint him to this position as late as January 1736, but by the following month Sir Charles Wager had persuaded him that this appointment would be neither impossible to obtain nor dishonorable to accept. As a result, Morris authorized Wager to inform the secretary of state that he had "reason to beleive from [Morris], that if your Grace would please to recommend him to be Governor of New Jersey, it would make him easy." But his "Grace" displayed no immediate inclination to make such a difficult opponent "easy." Despite Wager's failure to elicit a positive response from Newcastle on this matter, he assured Morris that he would use all his influence with the Walpole ministry to make him governor of New Jersey. Morris was grateful for Wager's offer of assistance, but doubtful of his ability to translate his good intentions into reality. In this case, however, Morris' skepticism was unwarranted, for it was largely through Wager's efforts that his political career was saved from ruin two years later.[51]

Morris' inability to achieve his objectives in England deepened his disillusion with English political and social life. He raged at the indifference of the imperial administration to his charges against Cosby and attributed it to a general desire on the part of the English patrons of royal governors to avoid responsibility for the misdeeds their clients perpetrated in the colonies.

> Complaints, if just, are very shocking things
> and not encourag'd in the courts of Kings
> t' accuse your Chief, they'll construe to be meant
> A Side reflection on the Government
> and Senders mostly will defend the Sent.

But Morris' disenchantment with England extended well beyond the imperial administration. It also included the whole of English society, which, he came to believe, was irretrievably corrupt. In the same poem he dealt with English divines, lawyers, merchants, physicians, and political leaders and pronounced them all to be riddled with corruption. In Morris' view they all subordinated the rightful goals of their professions to an unholy lust for enrichment and advancement. "Our Luxury is grown to such a Pitch," he wrote in relation to England,

> that tis a Scandal to be deem'd not rich
> which makes us leave no likely means untry'd
> to gain wherewith to gratify our pride.
> Virtue and Conscience, here, are words of course
> that on mans conduct have but little force
> Place and preferment yield substantial joys
> these are obtained by parting with such toys.

Only one person escaped Morris' strictures—the king. Morris did not include him in his catalog of corrupt Englishmen and, adhering to a common eighteenth-century convention, absolved him of responsibility for the unresponsiveness of the imperial administration by claiming that he was kept in ignorance of colonial complaints by his advisers. Morris was thus able to prevent himself from losing all confidence in royal government. Yet if Morris' reactions to Hanoverian England were at all typical of those of other visiting Americans, then perhaps it was well for the empire that 3,000 miles of ocean separated the colonies and the mother country.[52]

Morris and his son finally left England on July 22, 1736. The timing of their departure was due as much to the elder Morris' difficulties with the West Jersey Society as to the failure of his mission. For the past two decades the Society had grown increasingly exasperated with Morris' services as its business agent. To begin with, the Society was disappointed with Morris' failure to arrange the sale of its American lands, which it had been trying to dispose of since the time of Governor Hunter's administration. Morris led the Society to believe several times that he was about to purchase this property, but he never did, and he was also highly negligent in not pursuing offers from other potential buyers in America. Morris also remitted little money to the Society on the land he did sell for it. Between 1703 and 1727, for example, he remitted money to the Society only four times and then sent it no more than a total of £770. Finally Morris was remarkably lax in providing the Society with accurate accounts of the land he bought and sold for it. Incredibly, not until 1730 — twenty-seven years after his appointment as agent — did he send the Society an account of the purchase and sale of land during his agency — and even then the Society was disappointed with the quality of his accounting. In fact the Society was so exasperated with Morris' lax business practices that in 1727 it forbade him to sell any more of its lands — an order he blithely ignored.[53]

Morris' troubles with the Society finally came to a head during his stay in England. At that time the Society demanded a full accounting of his stewardship in America. Morris responded by submitting an account of his income and expenditures since 1703 which claimed that the Society owed him £130. The Society rejected this claim, decided he owed it £1,668, and demanded payment in full. In order to avoid compliance with this demand, Morris left England without informing the Society, whereupon he was dismissed from its service, thereby ending a curious business relationship which evidently lasted as long as it did mainly because of the Society's respect for Morris' political power in New Jersey.[54]

Morris left England in a bitter mood. Apart from securing an instruction excluding the governor from legislative sessions of the provincial council, Morris had not accomplished any of the objectives which brought him to England. This was in striking contrast to the success he had enjoyed during his first London mission, so that it is instructive to compare these two trips. In 1701–1702 Morris enjoyed easy access to the Board of Trade, the SPG, and the West Jersey Society, played a significant role in transforming New Jersey from a proprietary to a crown colony, and returned to America with an important appointment from the imperial administration. More than thirty years later he experienced frustrating delays with the Privy Council, found most members of the Walpole ministry to be inaccessible, and failed to achieve any of his primary goals. Morris' failure was partly due to the increased rigidity and unresponsiveness of the imperial administration since his first trip to England and partly to the profound difference in nature between his first and second missions. In 1701–1702 Morris went to England in furtherance of a goal — the royalization of New Jersey — which was in harmony with a fundamental aim of the imperial administration at that time: the elimination of charter and proprietary governments in the empire. In 1735–36, however, he journeyed to the seat of empire to prosecute complaints against a royal governor who was a client of the most powerful English official in colonial affairs lacking the sanction of any officially constituted authority in New York. In the end he was unable to convince the imperial administration that it would not endanger royal authority in New York by redressing the complaints of an ordinary subject against the king's governor.

Morris himself had no doubt about the basic cause of the failure of his second London mission. He attributed his lack of success to the English patronage system whereby royal governors were appointed to office through the influence of patrons in England who, he believed, were loath to call them to account for fear of reflecting adversely on themselves. As Morris explained in indignant verse:

> Your chief with other Chiefs sent o're compare
> A griping Chief is each dominion's share
> do you complain of having Neighbour's share
> were it your only case, then some relief
> might be expected 'gainst a lawless Chief
> One noble Lord perhaps might him defend
> but Others would your righteous cause befriend
> would introduce you to the Princes Ear
> and what You say he graciously would hear
> but when the evil's epidemick grown,
> Each patron surely will protect his own
> in doing this, tis' needful that they join
> his case to day, may be to morrow mine
> The Chiefs abroad are known to pay large rent
> for what they hold, or They had neer been sent
> Tis' this protects them, therefore, to complain
> of what they do, is bootless sure and vain
> The evil's too deep rooted for your peace
> remove the cause and then the effect will cease;
> till that is done, tis' vain to hope for Ease
> from remedies much worse than the disease[55]

Morris' cause was not as righteous as his poetry implied, and his efforts in England were greatly handicapped by his lack of support from any public authority in New York. Nevertheless, it is also true that he made no headway against Cosby in England because the power of the governor's patrons was too great for him to overcome.

As Morris and his son sailed across the Atlantic, New York moved to the brink of civil war. In order to guarantee the orderly transfer of power to a court party leader in the event of his death, Cosby, who had been stricken by tuberculosis, suspended Rip Van Dam from the New York Council in November 1735. Consequently George Clarke, the governor's confidential adviser, became the eldest councilor and the next in line to succeed Cosby. Yet immediately after the governor's death in the following March, a succession crisis broke out between Clarke and Van Dam. After Clarke assumed the administration of the colony, Van Dam challenged his authority, arguing that his own suspension from office had lapsed with the demise of Cosby. As it was difficult to determine whether Clarke's or Van Dam's right to the office was stronger, there were soon two rival claimants to the presidency of the New York Council backed by two competing political factions. Whereas Clarke received the support of the Philipse-DeLancey court party, Van Dam was backed by the country party, led now by James Alexander, Lewis Morris, Jr., and William Smith. Throughout the summer of 1736 each side hurled charges of usurpation at the other and hopefully awaited news from England of the confirmation of its claims. No word from England having arrived by the end of September, Clarke and Van Dam both nominated rival slates of municipal officials for New York City. Since these officials had to be sworn in by the acting governor of the colony on October 14, both sides looked forward to that date as a crucial test of strength.[56]

In the meantime Morris and his son arrived in Boston on September 18, unaware of the passions that had been aroused in New York. Morris was aware that the imperial administration had decided to recognize Clarke's claim to the presidency of the council and apparently had reconciled himself to this decision. He and Robert Hunter Morris both revealed the news of the imperial administration's action to some acquaintances in the Bay Colony, one of whom happened to be Clarke's son. When word of this admission reached New York and was triumphantly printed in the pro-Clarke *Gazette,* Morris' fiery son-in-law, Matthew Norris, rushed posthaste to Boston to acquaint him with the current political realities in New York. After consulting Norris, Morris decided to stake his political future in New York on a desperate gamble. He resolved to suppress his knowledge of the fact that the English authorities were supporting Clarke and steeled himself to encourage the pretensions of Van Dam. If Van Dam gained control of the government of New York, Morris apparently assumed, the imperial administration would accept an accomplished fact and abandon Clarke to his own devices.[57]

Once Morris had made this decision he did not turn back. He entered New York City on October 8 and was greeted with acclaim by enthusiastic throngs of country party adherents. On that day he addressed a gathering of his supporters in the city and assured them that Van Dam was rightfully entitled to act as president of the council. He announced his willingness to serve as chief justice under the elderly Dutchman and, in a final burst of demagoguery, exhorted his followers to remember: "If you don't hang them, they will hang you." Four days later Morris fanned the flames of popular indignation even higher by trying to lead a mob of his followers into the assembly chamber in an effort to force the dissolution of that body. The assembly managed to keep this crowd outside its chamber and then listened noncommittally as Morris mendaciously informed it that the imperial administration had not recognized Clarke's claims. Meanwhile a worried Clarke withdrew to the safety of Fort George, where he pondered the merits of having some of the country party leaders sent to England to be tried for treason. Country party partisans openly boasted that they would forcibly remove James DeLancey from the supreme court bench and replace him with Morris, and DeLancey himself secretly prepared a group of his supporters to defend him against attack. As only two days remained before two rival slates of city officials were due to be sworn in, greater civil strife and even bloodshed appeared to be unavoidable.[58]

But violence was averted, and Morris' reputation shattered, by the sudden arrival on October 13 of a vessel from England that brought a royal instruction recognizing Clarke as the rightful president of the council. In a trice Morris' most fervent supporters, realizing he had misled them, turned against him. "Coll Morris in one day from being the most popular man at that time in the Province," Cadwallader Colden later noted, "became the most detested after the people cool'd and began to think in what dangers he had been hurrying them by false Intelligence."[59] Morris' swift fall from grace was quickly brought home to him. Immediately after the arrival of news of Clarke's confirmation in office, Morris asked the assembly for permission to return "home." Frederick Philipse, whose judicial reasoning Morris had once scorned, mockingly inquired "if he meant London again." Morris said not a word in reply.[60] He had gambled his political future in New York and lost. It was a sorry end to an otherwise creditable career in his native province.

Morris next went to New Jersey and promptly became embroiled in another succession controversy. At issue in this dispute was the question of which man was to administer the government of New Jersey after Cosby's death—Morris or John Hamilton? Morris claimed that as the senior member of the New Jersey Council he was entitled to head the government of the colony until a new governor was appointed. Hamilton, who had been serving as acting governor in Morris' absence, maintained that Morris had forfeited his seat on the council by failing to observe a royal instruction forbidding councilors to leave the province for more than a year without the governor's consent. They both referred their claims to the New Jersey Council, which decided on October 21, 1736, that Hamilton was in the right. Morris refused to accept this decision and proceeded to issue two proclamations to the people of New Jersey as executive head of the province. Hamilton retaliated by ordering Morris' arrest, and the country party leader just managed to avoid this ignominious fate by prudently retreating to his New York estate. Both men then appealed to the imperial administration, which ruled in January 1737 that Hamilton was acting governor of New Jersey and that Morris had forfeited his council seat by staying in England for over a year without Cosby's permission.[61]

The imperial administration's decision threatened to end Morris' political career in New Jersey and deepened his disillusionment with royal government—a feeling which had been strong even before he lost his dispute with Hamilton. During his ill-fated trip from Boston to New York in 1736, for instance, Morris discovered that some Rhode Islanders favored the royalization of their charter colony and afterward noted in amazement: "One would think that Rhode Islanders who Enjoy an excesse of libertie and put in practice twenty things that other people dare not think of Should be contented with their happy Scituation: but I find it otherwise; for a considerable body of them are fond of having the Kings Government and Speake in raptures concerning it. I could from my own Experience have been a Samuel to them—but of that Enough."[62]

Yet by a consummate stroke of irony, the very acts which brought discredit on Morris in New York and New Jersey also helped him to become New Jersey's first separate royal governor. After Morris returned to America, Sir Charles Wager, true to his word, labored assiduously to persuade the Walpole ministry to appoint the former chief justice as governor of New Jersey. At first Wager's efforts in Morris' behalf foundered on the adamantine opposition of Newcastle, who now saw no reason to honor his earlier pledge of support for the New Yorker's ambitions. As the secretary of state began to receive reports from America about Morris' disputes with Clarke and Hamilton, however, he gradually came to share the view that it was "im'ediately Necessary for the Peace of the Government of New York that Lewis Morris . . . be made Governor of New Jersey."[63]

Even before Newcastle's reluctant conversion, Wager had succeeded in winning Walpole's support for Morris. Wager informed Sir Robert of Morris' interest in serving as governor of New Jersey and at length in September 1737 the great minister gave his approval to Morris' appointment to that post. Neither Newcastle nor Walpole was moved by altruism for Morris. Both men wanted to stabilize the political situation in New York and, failing to perceive the precipitate decline of Morris' power there, they believed that the best way to accomplish this was by virtually bribing the country party leader with the government of New Jersey. As old Admiral Norris, who supported this appointment, later informed Morris through an intermediary: "He hoped you made a good hand of your Government, or at least You would be to blame not to make the most of it since it was given you for that intent."[64]

With the backing of Newcastle, Norris, Wager, and Walpole, Morris' appointment now became a matter of course. The West Jersey Society, aghast at the thought of its delinquent agent in the governor's chair, toyed with the idea of opposing Morris but decided against it because "the Interest of S John Norris and S Charles Wager was so great at Court that they overcame all the opposition that was made against his being Governor." In consequence the king approved Morris' commission and instructions as governor of New Jersey in February and July 1738. Morris himself, his faith in royal government miraculously restored, gratefully accepted his appointment and proclaimed his authority in New Jersey in August of that year. Thanks to the fidelity of Wager, as well as the misconceptions of Newcastle and Walpole, Morris' political career entered its final phase.[65]

≮ 9 ≯

"I Think I Have Acted Rightly"

EWIS MORRIS' ADMINISTRATION AS GOVERNOR of New Jersey was a stormy chapter in that colony's history. For Morris chose to act as the stubborn defender of the prerogative of the crown and the authority of Parliament at a time when British involvement in wars with Spain and France made the imperial administration even less inclined than usual to come to the aid of embattled royal governors in America. So stoutly did the former country party leader champion the royal prerogative, parliamentary supremacy, and the primacy of imperial over local interests that he provoked a continuing series of conflicts with the New Jersey Assembly which threatened to plunge the province into political chaos several times before his death in 1746. Although most of these disputes were still unresolved when Morris died, this stalemate eloquently testified to the almost insuperable obstacles confronting any royal governor who tried to restrain the quest for power of a colonial assembly without effective backing from imperial officials in England. Thus by upholding royal and parliamentary authority in all their vigor against the New Jersey Assembly, Morris unwittingly revealed one phase of the process by which the British Empire was slowly being transformed from an organic whole, each part of which was subordinate to the ultimate authority of the king in Parliament, into a federation of self-governing commonwealths, all bound together by loyalty to the crown and voluntary acceptance of parliamentary regulation of their economies.

181

Morris' swift reversion to the role of defender of the royal prerogative after becoming governor of New Jersey was the last great *volte-face* of his career, the most striking manifestation of that tactical opportunism and ideological flexibility which underlay so much of his political behavior. Shortly before his appointment to this office, Morris, still under the sway of the radical Whig beliefs he had imbibed during his opposition to Governor Cosby in New York, had been distrustful of the English court, disillusioned with Parliament, disdainful of the imperial administration, and doubtful of the desirability of royal government in general. Almost as soon as he entered the governor's office, however, Morris' attitudes underwent some remarkable changes. Distrust of the court gave way to gratitude to the courtiers who had made his appointment possible. Disillusion with Parliament turned into admiration, and admiration begot a determination to deny the analogy between that body and the New Jersey Assembly which local representatives frequently drew to justify extensions of their power. Disdain for the imperial administration gave way to dependence on its cooperation and support, and doubt as to the worth of the king's government in America was replaced by a firm resolve to preserve the crown's prerogative intact against the anticipated encroachments of the assembly. Above all Morris meant to retain the support of his superiors in England so as to keep the office in New Jersey he had coveted for so long. "I think I have acted rightly," he told an English correspondent after dissolving his first assembly, "but if my Masters think other ways I must endeavour to trim my sailes according to the wind."[1] Shrewd calculation gave birth to intellectual conviction, and together they made Morris, the quintessential "Trimmer," an outspoken prerogative man throughout his administration.

In all this, of course, Morris was not simply adopting a completely new set of beliefs to fit an occasion. Throughout his career he had alternated between a country ideology, which stressed the rights of the subject, the expansion of assembly powers, and the restriction of royal authority, and a court ideology, which emphasized the duties of the subject, limitation of assemblies, and respect for royal authority. As governor of New Jersey, he naturally chose to emphasize the second. Moreover, elements of both ideologies were curiously present in the two major reforms he introduced during his gubernatorial administration. In order to strengthen the council as a counterweight to the assembly, he voluntarily absented himself from legislative sessions of the upper house, and in keeping with one of the cardinal tenets of his country party days under Cosby, he commissioned the chief justice of the supreme court to serve during good behavior rather than at pleasure. Neither of these acts, however, was motivated entirely by ideological considerations. Robert Hunter Morris, the governor's youngest son, was a member of the council, so that through him the governor could monitor its proceedings and make his views known even when sitting apart from legislative meetings of that body. In addition, this same son, at the age of twenty-six, was also the recipient of the coveted commission to serve as chief justice during good behavior, wherefore in this case it is impossible to determine if the governor was moved more by principle or nepotism.[2]

Morris' first meeting with the New Jersey Assembly set the tone for his administration by precipitating the division of the province into court and country parties. Morris' accession to office in August 1738 was hailed by New Jerseyites as signaling the end of the neglect of their interests which had grown up while their province and New York were governed by the same man. Morris sought to take advantage of this sentiment by dissolving the existing assembly, which had been chosen in 1730 and had last sat in 1735, and ordering elections for a new one. This turned out to be a wise decision as it resulted in the election of a group of assemblymen who were initially well disposed toward the new governor and eager to reap the advantages they anticipated from his appointment.[3]

Morris opened his first assembly with an address on November 15, 1738, which served notice on the assembled representatives that the erstwhile country party leader intended to uphold the royal prerogative with all his vigor. He urged the assembly to provide substantial financial support for the provincial government as a sign of gratitude to the king for having answered New Jersey's petitions for a separate governor. He cautioned the assembly to distinguish between the office and the office holder and not to let dislike of the latter lead to a reduction in the salary of the former. He warned the representatives to abjure any thought that the provision of financial support for the government was contingent upon his prior approval of laws they deemed necessary for the commonweal. On the contrary, he asserted, assuming unto himself a discretionary power he had never allowed any other governor, these two should be totally unrelated, for allegedly it was as inconceivable that a governor would refuse to assent to "Good Laws" as it would be improper for an assembly not to support the government.

Having virtually asked the assembly to renounce much of its control over the power of the purse, Morris also revealed his intention to restore the balance among the "monarchical," "aristocratical," and "democratical" branches of the government. Henceforth, he announced, he would absent himself from the council when it met in its legislative capacity—a concession to conciliar pride he could well afford to make since his youngest son was a councilor. By this act Morris hoped to give the council at least a semblance of independence from executive influence, thus enabling it to act as a checkmate on the assembly and to perform its appointed task of preserving "His Majesty's Royal Prerogitive and the Just Liberties of the Inhabitants of this Province" against any "Bills that Seem . . . to have the least Tendency to distroy or Impair either." Then, in an ambiguous conclusion that was soon to become the source of considerable controversy, he alluded to the expenses he had incurred in obtaining a separate governor for New Jersey and seemingly insinuated that he deserved to be recompensed for them.[4]

Despite a generally favorable reply to Morris by the assembly, relations between them quickly deteriorated. While the support bill for the government was under consideration by the lower house, Morris' supporters in that body attempted to obtain special compensation for him for his expenditures in acquiring the governorship of New Jersey, only to be defeated by a vote of thirteen to ten on December 15, 1738.[5] After waiting a month and a half for the assembly to reverse this vote, Morris sent it a stinging message in which he denied that he had ever directly asked it for such compensation. This was literally correct, but it was also true that the assembly could just as easily have interpreted Morris' opening address as an indirect request for this recompense. Even in his message of denial, moreover, where he argued that what he had originally referred to was a liberal Support Act, not a special gift, Morris asserted that only a fool could believe he "would have put himself to the Charge of procuring Such a patent [for the governorship of New Jersey], and moving his family Among You, if he had in the least imagin'd it would have proved a hurt to his private fortune."[6] At any rate Morris' intervention, when combined with threats by his supporters of wholesale changes in the magistracy if his wishes were not met, led the assembly on February 3, 1739 to grant him an additional £500 for his services in obtaining a separate governor for New Jersey. Morris' instructions forebade him to accept special presents from the assembly, but in this case the new defender of the royal prerogative found his instructions inconvenient and ignored them.[7]

The restoration of harmony between Morris and the assembly was only temporary. The lower house passed a three-year support bill on February 15, which Morris found inadequate, even though it gave him a salary twice that of any of his predecessors—£1,000 per annum. This measure, he thought, was but another effort by the assembly to make the king's officers dependent upon it, an effort graphically described by an assemblyman who is said to have declared, "let us keep the dogs poore and we'll make them do what we please."[8] Although Morris considered the schedule of salaries for provincial officers in this act too meager, worse was yet to come. When the council requested a conference with the assembly on the support bill, the assembly agreed—but only on condition that the council agree beforehand not to try to alter the substance of the bill. In response the council claimed that since the revenue for the provincial government was derived entirely from the interest money on loan office certificates rather than through taxation of the people of the province, it was perfectly entitled to offer amendments to the support bill. The assembly remained adamant, however, and at length the council approved the support bill in its original form so that the government would not be deprived of a revenue.[9]

Morris was furious at the assembly for denying the council's right to amend a money bill and accordingly he dissolved that body on March 15. In a stern message to the assembly, which had just gone through the longest legislative session thus far in New Jersey history, Morris rebuked the assemblymen for having spent so much of their time to so little purpose. This was a curious charge in view of the fact that Morris and the council had blocked much of the important popular legislation passed by the assembly. He thanked his supporters in the lower house for obtaining passage of the Support Act, insinuated that opponents of this law were "Enemies" of the government, and, in another unfortunate phrase, said that he regarded the revenue from the act as but "an Earnest" of what a more friendly assembly would grant him. But Morris reserved his heaviest fire for the assembly's refusal to confer with the council about the Support Act, which he denounced as an action subversive of the provincial constitution. "The King's Letters Pattent," he told the assembly, measuring the distance he had traveled since his days as a country party leader, were "the only thing that Establishes the Constitution of Government here, and gives the Power of making Laws of any kind." These gave the council the right to alter any bill passed by the assembly, and the assembly's refusal to acknowledge this right, he announced, was sufficient reason to dissolve it.[10] After delivering this speech, Morris, in a final burst of petulance, ordered the colony treasurer to withold the wages to which assemblymen were entitled for their legislative service. Morris soon rescinded this order, but the memory of it rankled and served as a symbol of his arbitrary temper.[11]

Morris' dissolution of the assembly completed the division of the colony into court and country parties. At the beginning of Morris' first legislative session he had been able to count on the support of a majority in the assembly. By the end of it his followers had been reduced to a small minority, and never again was he to enjoy the luxury of majority support in the lower house. Morris' opponents were upset by his failure to approve popular legislation like a triennial bill for more frequent assembly elections, his open dissatisfaction with the revenue granted to his administration, and his effort to limit the assembly's fiscal prerogatives. More than anything else, however, they were outraged by Morris' extreme pre-rogative views. In contrast to the governor, most politically aware New Jerseyites believed that their constitutional rights were part of the inher-ent rights of Englishmen and that only the popularly elected assembly had the authority to dispose of the money of the people. "Letters Patent are not binding but as far as they are agreeable to Law," a country scribe noted, in a pointed rebuttal of the views advanced by Morris in his March 15 address, and he also denied the governor's contention that the council could amend money bills by citing "the unalterable inherent Privilege vested in the People, of being *taxed only by themselves,* which conse-quently implies a right of directing the Application of the Sum levied."[12]

At first Morris was confident of his ability to deal with the erosion of his support in New Jersey. "There is so much Insincerity and Ignorance among the people," he told Sir Charles Wager, his foremost English pa-tron, "and with so rooted a Jealousy of their Governours and so strong an Inclination in the meanest of the people (who are the majority and whose votes make the assembly) to have the sole direction of all the affairs of the government and to make the governour and other officers Intirely depen-dant on themselves, that it requires much more temper, skill and Con-stancy to overcome these difficulties than falls to every man's share."[13] Nevertheless Morris was satisfied that he could cope with this problem without any special assistance from England. In a letter to the Board of Trade written several months later, he discussed the idea of having Parlia-ment require colonial assemblies to pay fixed salaries to royal officials in America and concluded that the time was not yet ripe for such a drastic expedient to curb the powers of assemblies. Local assemblies would un-doubtedly refuse to comply with parliamentary legislation of this sort, he advised the Board, and as a result its passage would "prove Impracticable or worse than the present distemper complained of."[14] Despite his sage warnings about the untoward consequences of radical parliamentary in-tervention in colonial political affairs, Morris soon came to view English intervention as a vital necessity for upholding royal authority in America.

The outbreak of the War of Jenkins' Ear between England and Spain in October 1739 immensely complicated Morris' task as governor of New Jersey. After the start of hostilities, the imperial administration re-quested most colonial governors to raise volunteers for an expedition against the Spanish West Indies led by Admiral Vernon and Lord Cath-cart. Morris, outraged by the "Injuries and Losses which the Inhabitants of the British Colonies have suffer'd by the Violence and Depredations of the Spaniards," enthusiastically complied with this request and issued a proclamation for volunteers. Eventually three companies of 100 men each were raised in New Jersey, but in order to enable them to reach the West Indies Morris had to call upon the assembly to provide funds for supplies and transportation. In New Jersey this was a ticklish business because the colony had a sizable Quaker population, which usually produced a conflict between the imperatives of imperial war policy and the pacifism of Friends.[15]

Morris first met with the assembly for this purpose in April 1740. He admonished the new assembly not to repeat the mistakes of its predecessor and warned it against doing anything to weaken New Jersey's dependence on Great Britain. Hectoring aside, he then asked the assembly to strengthen New Jersey's defenses against a possible invasion and to support the West Indian expedition.[16]

The assembly was unimpressed by the danger of a Spanish attack and unenthusiastic about the proposed expedition. Owing to the reluctance of Quakers to compromise their religious principles and the political needs of their non-Quaker allies, the assembly took no action on Morris' requests for more than two months. At length, on June 26, he repeated his plea for the provision of "Victualls, Transports and all other Necessaries" for the men who were volunteering to serve in the West Indies — only to meet with a request for an adjournment by the assembly. Morris refused to grant this because he believed the assembly was only stalling for time in the hope that its counterparts in New York and Pennsylvania would refuse to support the expedition and thereby justify its own recalcitrance. As a result of Morris' persistence, however, the assembly finally approved a bill on July 4, emitting £2,000 in bills of credit for the victualing and transportation of the troops.[17]

This bill was a hollow victory for Morris. It stipulated that the £2,000 should be expended by trustees appointed by and accountable only to the assembly. Moreover, it raised these funds by diverting them from the proceeds on the interest money on government loans, which had been the principal source of revenue for the New Jersey government since 1724, instead of by levying new taxes. Morris tried to persuade the lower house to revise the victualing bill so as to make the trustees responsible to him as well as to it, but the assembly refused, as much, Morris believed, from a desire to force him to disapprove the bill as from concern for the safekeeping of the public money. Eventually Morris approved the victualing bill, though not without complaining that this measure was "such complication of Blunders, Incoherencies and low craft" that it went "almost as much against my grain to consent to it as it did against theirs to do what they have done."[18]

Morris craftily evaded the restrictions of the Victualing Act. He regularly corresponded with Andrew Johnston, the speaker of the assembly, offering helpful hints on the supply and transportation of the troops, and he appointed to the council Peter Baynton, a West Jersey merchant whom the assembly had chosen as a trustee of the Victualing Act.[19] Morris dealt with other problems arising out of the expedition as well. He decided that indentured servants could enlist as volunteers because "every subject is by his allegiance bound to serve the King in his warrs within the Kingdom, or without, by his Commandment," but to avoid giving offense to the many masters who depended upon their labor, he ordered recruiting officers to be cautious of enlisting servants so that in fact few of them served.[20] He raged against merchants who refused to accept government bills in payment for supplies, tartly observing that "the mercantile part of men are much alike every where, and the making advantages by the rise and fall of Commodities . . . is the art, craft, or mistery of their trade, and a knowledge they serve seven years to acquire; and those who have the best knack of deceiving are most masters of their craft." At length all these problems were overcome and the last troop transport sailed from New Jersey in October 1740. Whether in the end all this effort was worthwhile is an open question. In the following year the New Jersey volunteers took part in ill-starred Anglo-American assaults on Cartagena and St. Iago de Cuba that merely reinforced the conviction of many Jerseyites that "our expeditions to America have been generally not so strongly conciev'd, as to hinder their proving abortive."[21]

Morris' dissatisfaction with the Victualing Act passed by the assembly was matched by the assembly's disenchantment with his performance as governor. In addition to alienating the Quakers by his insistence that they support the English expedition against the Spanish West Indies, Morris also diminished the numbers of his supporters in the assembly by continuing to withhold his consent from popular legislation. Thus he did not approve a bill providing for the extinction of the estates of married women because a similar act had already been disallowed by the king. He opposed a bill to allow the recording of deeds in each county because he claimed that its main purpose was to reduce the secretary's office to insignificance, and he rejected another to restrict the jurisdiction of the supreme court to cases involving £15 or more because he considered it a direct assault upon the court's authority. Finally, he regarded a bill for the mandatory election of a new assembly at least once every seven years as an unwarrantable infringement of the king's prerogative. But by opposing these measures to please his superiors in England, Morris seemed to be depriving New Jerseyites of the benefits they had expected to receive from a separate governor.[22]

Morris' latest encounter with the assembly convinced him of the need for drastic English action to retrieve the situation in New Jersey. Like his old adversary, Lord Cornbury, Morris decided that Quaker pacifism was incompatible with the need for effective colonial defense and therefore he recommended the exclusion of Friends from the provincial assembly to the Duke of Newcastle. He was even more concerned with what he took to be the tendency of the assembly to exceed its just authority. "They will fancy themselves to have as much power as a British house of commons, and more," he warned the Board of Trade, "notwithstanding any thing your Lordships has said, or can say: and if any of them had halfe the reason of some of the medling members of that honble house, I should not be without hopes of being able to prevaile upon them to entertain Juster sentiments of their duty and their true Interest, than the weakness of the men and their unaccountable obstinacy will at present admit them to do, and if long suffred to pass unnotic'd, may one day require the aid of a British Parliament to Perswade them to."[23] Thus he suggested to the Board that Parliament authorize the king to issue paper money in America and use the interest therefrom to pay the salaries of royal governors, councils, and officials, thereby freeing them from financial dependence upon local assemblies. In this way, he argued, the king could simultaneously prevent the depreciation of paper money in America and "render the severall Governours, Councillrs and Officers of the Government independant of Assemblyes for their support and consequently prevent these meane condescentions that are too often made to obtain a scanty subsistence; prevent the Governours from bartering the King's prerogatives, or lands, for bread; give the Councills a greater weight or Influence than they at Present have, and be a means of keeping Assemblyes within their Just and propper limmits."[24] But neither Newcastle nor the Board of Trade responded to his proposals. Small wonder, then, that Morris sardonically endorsed a subsequent letter from the Board: "Commending my Zeale in opposition to the Assembly &c. Laudatur et alget [It is praised and grows cold]."[25]

Lack of effective backing from England, when combined with the approaching expiration of the 1739 Support Act, made Morris decide to adopt a conciliatory attitude toward the second session of his second assembly when it met at Perth Amboy in October 1741. Suppressing his penchant for constitutional theorizing, Morris confined himself to making a few specific requests in his opening address on October 3. In addition to a renewal of fiscal support for the provincial government, Morris also asked the assembled legislators to provide a single capital for both Jerseys, complete with a residence for the governor, a meeting chamber for the general assembly, and an office for the secretary and the colony's records. He reminded them again of the need to repair New Jersey's defenses as a precaution against a possible Spanish attack but did not press this point, concluding instead with a fervent plea for harmony among all three branches of the legislature.[26]

The assembly, far from heeding the governor's plea for concord, took advantage of his financial dependence upon it to repass a host of popular legislation. Completely ignoring Morris' request for a revamped defensive system and rejecting out of hand his call for one capital for East and West Jersey, the legislators busied themselves with bills Morris had disapproved in the past. Thus they passed bills to restrict the jurisdiction of the supreme court, to provide for the conversion of married women's property (the so-called Feme-Covert Act), to register deeds, and to limit the period of service for local sheriffs appointed by the governor. Then, to register their extreme dissatisfaction with Morris' administration, the assemblymen approved a Support Act for only one year.[27]

Fortunately for the peace of the province, Morris did not have to bear all the onus for rejecting the lower house's most prized measures. Under the leadership of Robert Hunter Morris, the council threw out the bills regulating the registration of deeds and the terms of sheriffs. Morris himself disapproved of the Feme-Covert Act for the same reasons as before but accepted the restrictions upon the supreme court because the assembly compensated his son for the fees he was expected to lose as a result of them. He also approved the one-year Support Act, though not with any great enthusiasm. Still, he did not lose hope that by having chosen "the softest way of treating them" he had disarmed "the demagogues amongst them" so that "our next meeting may be attended with more successe than the last."[28]

Morris' hopes were dealt a rude blow by Sir Robert Walpole's fall from power in February 1742. Soon after this event, Sir Charles Wager, Morris' most influential English patron, was dismissed as first lord of the admiralty. These developments deprived Morris of his most effective connections in England, for although the Duke of Newcastle and Sir John Norris remained in office, they were not nearly as helpful to him as Wager. When news of these ministerial changes reached New Jersey, Morris thought that they might be the prelude to his own removal from office. "Perhaps during this hurly burly the governments in America may not be thought of," he wrote to his daughter, Euphemia, "but if the ministry changes it is not unnaturall to suppose that those employ'd by the last may not be look'd on in the most favourable light by their successors, and amongst the rest such a reptile as my selfe (tho' now treading on the verge of life and far from being an advocate for arbitrary power) may be remov'd to make room for some new man that will think this government worth soliciting for."[29]

Euphemia Norris hastened to reassure her troubled father even before his letter reached her. This remarkable woman, who had elected to remain in England after the death in 1738 of her husband, Captain Matthew Norris, was personally acquainted with some of the leaders of the opposition to Walpole, including Lord Carteret and Philip Gybbon. Almost as soon as the great minister left office, she canvassed her political friends to ascertain her father's prospects. She consulted with Gybbon, whom her father had met during his last stay in London and who was a commissioner of the treasury in the new administration, as well as Lord George Clinton, another acquaintance Morris had made in London who was soon to be appointed governor of New York as a client of Newcastle. Both men assured her that Morris would remain in office, and Gybbon in particular asserted that the governor was "very safe, for your Conduct had given generall Satisfaction, and that he recommended your Continuing to keep that harmony that you had hitherto done, for as he Justly Said, should you have any difference you would find no redress from hence, since they would leave you to fight it out with them." Her father-in-law, Admiral Norris, confirmed this analysis: "He said . . . that your behavior had pleased the ministry and he believed your keeping things so quiet, would Secure you, as they did not love to be troubled with Complaints from america." Euphemia relayed these assurances to Morris and added some advice of her own: "It is the opinion of your friends here that you should get what you can early and avoid as much as you can differing with them [assemblymen]."[30]

Morris was gratified at the prospect of continuing in office but handicapped by the collapse of his English interest. His own popularity in New Jersey was already low, and now he had no patrons in England who would personally intercede with the imperial administration in his behalf. This was a loss his opponents in New Jersey were quick to recognize and use to their advantage. Thus although he was going to remain as governor, he would have to serve without effective assistance from England. His superiors expected him to conciliate the provincial assembly, but conciliation was foreign to his nature. For a man of Morris' temperament, the situation was bleak indeed.

Morris' diminished standing was reflected in the sudden obstreperousness of the assembly which gathered together at Burlington in October 1742. In accordance with the advice he received from his daughter in England, Morris began the session with an uncharacteristically brief address calling for the passage of a new Support Act and expressing a wish for cooperation among the members of the general assembly. But the legislators, now more than ever determined to secure the passage of laws the governor had consistently disapproved, were in no mood to cooperate on Morris' terms. Once again they passed bills limiting the terms of sheriffs, prescribing the method for converting or extinguishing the estate of a feme-covert, and providing for the acknowledgement of deeds. On this occasion, however, Robert Hunter Morris was not present in the council, and consequently his colleagues approved all but the first of these bills.[31]

Conciliar defections proved to be the least of Morris' worries. Buoyed up by the conviction that it could bend the governor to its will, the assembly tacked a bill regulating fees onto a one-year support bill. The regulation of fees was normally a prerogative of the governor and council, while tacking was a legislative device which reduced the discretionary power of the governor in assenting to laws. Moreover, Morris was personally convinced that the object of the fee bill was nothing less than to render the officers of the government contemptuous by reducing their salaries to insignificance. Hence he waged a long and successful struggle to have the assembly separate the fee and support bills, after which the council rejected the former while he accepted the latter.[32]

Morris was particularly incensed by the assembly's effort to pass a law emitting £40,000 in bills of credit. Since New Jersey lacked an adequate supply of gold and silver coins, paper money was absolutely necessary for the province as a medium of exchange. Morris was well aware of this, but he opposed the further emission of bills of credit at this time because American paper money issues were then under attack in Parliament by English merchants, and he was loathe to incur the displeasure of the imperial administration when his own political position was so precarious. He was also offended by the assembly's failure to set aside any of the £40,000 as revenue for the government, and therefore he refused to approve this measure, once again sacrificing local to imperial interests.[33]

By the end of the third session of his second assembly, Morris felt that he had been goaded beyond endurance by overly assertive assemblymen and let down by spineless councilors. He therefore gave his assent only to the one-year Support Act and dissolved the assembly on November 25, 1742. In doing so, he abandoned his policy of conciliation and reverted to the role of strict prerogative man regardless of the consequences. In his closing address he blasted the assembly for having passed unsuitable laws which it well knew neither he nor the king could approve. Above all, he was incensed by what he considered the assembly's dangerous tendency to expand its powers at the expense of those of the crown.[34]

As he had done before, Morris turned to England for support, and as in the past, he received none. "They are genlly so fond of the example of the parliament of 1641 and that of their neighbours in Pensilvania," he told the Board of Trade, "that until some measures are taken in England to reduce them to their propper limits I suspect they will not mend much."[35] But what should these "measures" be? Morris did not say. He had suggested the appointment of Robert Hunter Morris as lieutenant governor of New Jersey to succeed him in the event of his death. But this was obviously no more than a stop-gap measure, and it was ignored by imperial officials. He still wished to have all royal officials in America paid from the interest on paper money issued by the king, but since the Board had failed to respond to his previous proposal on this point he did not feel justified in repeating it again. Once again therefore the imperial administration, absorbed in the problems of combatting Spain and aware that war with France was not far off, overlooked Morris' warning about the need for decisive British intervention to shore up royal authority in America.[36]

Morris' dissolution of his second assembly in 1742 only led to the election of a more unfriendly body, which he first met in October 1743. The governor tried to win over the new assemblymen by promising to approve the beneficial laws they passed if they also provided a liberal revenue for the government. The newly elected legislators, mindful of the fate which had befallen the many bills passed by their predecessors just a year before, asked Morris to demonstrate his good faith by approving their favorite measures before they passed a Support Act. Morris sternly replied that financial support for the government should never be conditional upon his prior assent to bills approved by the assembly.[37]

Despite this rather unpromising start, Morris got along well with this assembly mainly because he actually did approve such popular acts as those for the registering of deeds in each county, the regulation of fees, and the extinction or conversion of a feme-covert's estate, before he obtained appropriations for the government. Moreover, with his son back in attendance on the council, he could afford to let that body take the responsibility for stopping some of the more objectionable assembly measures. Hence the council rejected the by now inevitable measure to emit £40,000 in bills of credit and stymied the perennial bill to limit the terms of sheriffs.

This idyll did not last. Near the end of the session the assembly adopted a resolution declaring that the table of fees it had inserted into the Fee Act should be considered binding upon the officers of the government, despite the fact that the act itself had a suspending clause. This action elicited an anguished howl from Morris, who had visions of himself approving a paper money act with the proper suspending clause only to have the assembly adopt a resolution making it operative before it had received royal approval. The assembly innocently replied that its resolution was only an expression of opinion, but Morris quite rightly thought other-wise. No doubt he was particularly angered by this action because he him-self was planning to write home and advocate the disallowance of the Fee Act. Nevertheless, he decided to keep this assembly in being after he ad-journed it in December 1743 because of his acceptable relations with it.[38]

War and social unrest dominated the final years of Morris' adminis-tration in New Jersey. In 1744 England entered the War of the Austrian Succession to thwart the continental ambitions of France. This lent greater urgency to the issue of colonial defense in New Jersey than had been the case in 1740. Then the thought of a Spanish assault upon New Jersey had appeared unreal; now a French descent upon the province was well within the realm of possibility. Or so it seemed in theory, considering the relative proximity of Canada to New Jersey as well as the unfortified state of the Jersey coast. Yet no one in New Jersey really thought the French would attack. Not Morris, because he believed that such a project was beyond the resources of France. Not the assembly, because New Jer-sey freeholders in general rightly denied that their colony was of any value to the French and Quaker freeholders in particular desperately wanted to believe that this was so. But although Morris thought a French invasion of New Jersey improbable, he could not dismiss it out of hand, especially since he had been specifically ordered by the Lords of the Regency "to employ the most effectual means for putting this Colony in the best pos-ture of defense." Neither could he afford to have New Jersey unready to assist in repelling a French assault upon New York or Pennsylvania. He therefore resolved to press the representatives of the freeholders of the colony to reform their militia and strengthen their defenses.[39]

Morris dwelt upon these two subjects in his opening address to the second session of his third assembly at Burlington on June 22, 1744. He argued that the outbreak of war between England and France necessi-tated the revision of the existing Militia Act, since under this law evasion of militia duty was widespread owing to the failure of militia officers to enforce the prescribed penalties against delinquents. He also urged the assembly to consider the construction of new fortifications in New Jersey. And then to justify his proposals he invoked the spectre of a French descent upon the colony, in which neither he nor most New Jerseyites believed.[40]

The assemblymen who heard Morris' address were unimpressed. They discounted the possibility of a French assault upon their province but were convinced they could cope with it in the unlikely event it actually happened. Accordingly on June 26, they decided that the existing Militia

Act was sufficient for all exigencies, and on the following day, after assuring Morris of their willingness to pay for any forces required to repel an invader or assist a neighboring colony under attack, asked to be adjourned.

But Morris was not to be so easily denied. He inspired his son, Robert Hunter Morris, to introduce into the council a stringent militia bill, which was passed by that body and sent down to the assembly. But this measure was far too strict to suit the tastes of the members of the lower house, Quakers and non-Quakers alike. It provided harsh penalties for men who refused militia duty as well as for those who refused to accept commissions in the militia. Most objectionable of all, from the point of view of the assembly, was a clause in the bill empowering the governor to require every one hundred men in the province to contribute £40 for the purchase of military equipment. Opponents of the bill, combining vivid imaginations with dubious mathematical calculations, argued that this would enable Morris to raise a sum of £44,000 independently of the assembly and thereby endow him with the "Power to influence Elections at Pleasure; the Consequences of which would be intollerable and perhaps endless." As a result, the assembly rejected the council's militia bill by the overwhelming margin of sixteen to six. Morris thereupon accused it of indifference to New Jersey's safety and dissolved it on July 2.[41]

Morris had no illusions that new elections would produce a more cooperative assembly. He blamed this situation upon the allegedly baneful influence of the Quakers, but this was at best a half-truth. True, Quakers were opposed to the radical revision of the existing Militia Act, but then so were most New Jerseyites. Moreover, the center of Quaker strength lay in West Jersey; yet Morris lacked effective support in East and West Jersey alike. What Morris could not—or would not—recognize was that he himself had alienated virtually every segment of the New Jersey polity by his refusal to approve popular measures such as the further emission of bills of credit, his advocacy of unpopular policies such as tightening up the militia system, and his tactless handling of his disputes with assemblymen as when he accused them of bad faith for their refusal to adopt a stricter Militia Act. In any case the pent up frustrations of New Jerseyites found vivid expression in Morris' fourth assembly, which met intermittently at Perth Amboy, Burlington, and Trenton between August and December 1744.

Morris was unable to play an active role in the proceedings of this assembly because of a urinary disorder—strangury—which bothered him with increasing severity as he grew older. Yet he was sufficiently alert to realize that the actions of the legislators amounted to a repudiation of his administration. Ignoring Morris' threat to withhold his consent from any other laws until they had adopted a more efficient Militia Act, the new assemblymen repassed the bill for the emission of £40,000 in bills of credit and attached a rider to it which provided funds for the purchase of new arms and munitions for the militia, thereby solving the colony's currency and defense problems at one stroke. They also approved new bills to limit the terms of sheriffs and to restrict the jurisdiction of the supreme court. Then, to register the full measure of their discontent with Morris' governance of New Jersey, they agreed to pass a one-year support bill, which reduced by half the salaries Morris and his subordinate officers had received since the start of his administration. The council rejected all these acts, but this simply left the government without a regular revenue for the rest of Morris' term in office.[42]

The assembly's failure to provide the government with a long-term revenue was bad enough. Worse yet, in Morris' view, was its apparent contempt for the authority of Parliament. In 1744 Parliament was considering a bill which would have restricted the use of paper money in America and given all royal instructions the force of law. To the New Jersey Assembly the latter part of this measure was subversive of colonial liberties, and it passed a resolution to this effect. To Morris the assembly's resolution was inconsistent with the imperial constitution. For, as he averred in a private letter to Richard Partridge, New Jersey's London agent, "a British Parliament . . . can if they think fit take away and abollish any Priviledges and Concessions that they think inconvenient."[43] The implications of parliamentary supremacy in the empire could not have been stated more nakedly. Small wonder, then, that Morris dissolved this group of assemblymen in December 1744.

Morris, unwilling to obtain fiscal support for the provincial government by approving laws his superiors might disapprove, again turned to England for aid. "Unless the Ministry interpose to reduce them to their duty," he reported to his daughter, Euphemia, the assembly would not pass a suitable Support Act before he approved an act for the emission of £40,000 in bills of credit — the very sort of legislation which was currently under fire in Parliament. "Such a proceeding of the Assembly," he told the Board of Trade, referring to the assembly's refusal to grant the provincial government a revenue without the prior approval of popular legislation by the governor and council, "tends to fix the whole power of Legislation in the populace, and Consequently the whole power of the Government, which it is much Easier to prevent their having than to take from them." So once more Morris proposed to make the governor and council financially independent of the assembly, this time suggesting "that all money rais'd, or to be rais'd, in any of the plantations, either for the support of the government or on any pretext whatsoever, be declared [by Parliament] to be given to his majestie and that for the support of government, to be apply'd by his majestie to that use in such manner as he shall think fit."[44] Unfortunately for Morris, though luckily for the peace of the empire, the imperial administration ignored his plan for virtually nullifying the power of the purse exercised by American assemblies.

Despite his failure to obtain more than moral support from imperial administrators, Morris remained uncompromising in his dealings with the New Jersey Assembly. New elections had not appreciably altered the complexion of the assembly; yet this did not deter the governor. In his opening address at Perth Amboy on April 5, 1745, to the members of the fifth assembly elected under his administration, he excoriated the behavior of the representatives with whom he had had to deal the year before. He strongly insinuated that those assemblymen—many of whom had been reelected in 1745—were "Ideots." He accused them of bad faith for their refusal to pass a stricter Militia Act, as well as of impudence for their attempt to obtain a new emission of bills of credit in New Jersey when colonial paper money was under attack in Parliament. He heaped scorn on the resolution opposing this particular parliamentary measure which the assembly had approved in 1744. Were not the assemblymen aware, he asked, that "a British Parliament can abolish any Constitution in the Plantations that they deem inconvenient or disadvantageous to the Trade of the Nation, or otherwise?" He criticized the last assembly's refusal to provide fiscal support for his government and repeated his pet theme that the provincial government deserved a generous revenue despite his failure to approve popular legislation. Finally, Morris ended his tirade by coupling a general plea for mutual cooperation with specific requests for legislation from the new assembly to strengthen New Jersey's defenses, to appropriate a revenue for the government, and to assist the current Massachusetts expedition against the French fortress of Louisbourg.[45]

If Morris had hoped to intimidate the assembly with his belligerent address, he miscalculated badly. The members of the lower house diverted £2,000 from the interest money on public loans, which was the main source of revenue for the New Jersey government, to aid the attack against Louisbourg, but in all other respects they refused to bend to the governor's will. In a reply to Morris' address, the representatives took him to task for his unseemly references to the previous assembly. They also declared that an act emitting £40,000 in bills of credit, with a suspending clause, was absolutely vital for the economic well-being of the colony, and claimed that the controversial resolution passed by their predecessors was directed against enforced obedience to royal instructions rather than parliamentary restrictions on colonial paper money. Most of all, however, the legislators expressed their disgust at the general tenor of Morris' administration. "We are the third Assembly your Excellency hath met with in these Ten months last past," they told the governor, "from which we have learnt rather to expect Dissolutions than Laws."[46] Surely it was not for this that they had bothered to obtain a separate governor.

The assembly's message left Morris unmoved, despite the fact that just one day before he received it, the members of the lower house had agreed to pass a one-year support bill similar to the one the council had rejected in 1744 because of its meager provisions for the salaries of government officials. The governor's first response to the assembly was a long-winded repetition of the major points of his opening address. The assemblymen, perhaps aghast at the prospect of being subjected to a third executive harangue, then indicated that they would provide the government with a liberal revenue if the governor would assent to acts for the emission of £40,000 in bills of credit, the limitation of the terms of local sheriffs, and the restriction of the jurisdiction of the provincial supreme court. But Morris was adamant. He refused to approve a new paper money act while paper money itself was still suspect in Parliament. He wanted a generous revenue from the assembly before he acted upon its favorite measures or he wanted none at all. Consequently he got none.[47]

Shortly after the adjournment of this assembly, Morris found himself face to face with a crisis of even greater severity than the obstreperousness of the legislature or the bankruptcy of the provincial government. In September 1745 the long-standing conflict between the East Jersey proprietors and the Nicolls patentees came to a head with the start of a decade of land riots by the latter. These riots were precipitated by the decision of the proprietors to establish title to the 750,000 acres of land claimed by the patentees by bringing a suit before the New Jersey Court of Chancery in which Morris acted as sole judge. There could be little doubt as to the outcome of this case. Morris had already ruled against the patentees as a judge on the East Jersey Court of Common Right in the case of *Fullerton* v. *Jones,* and in 1703 he had drawn up the celebrated "Long Bill," which had asserted proprietary title to the disputed lands. Moreover, the two main leaders of the proprietary assault on the patentees were Robert Hunter Morris, the governor's son, and James Alexander, his long-time political ally. It was no accident, then, that five months after Alexander filed a bill in chancery denying the patentees' claims, the patentees began the first in a series of land riots that disrupted New Jersey society and politics for the next ten years. But what to the patentees was nothing more than a legitimate protest against a prejudiced legal system, was to Morris nothing less than anarchy. In this case he found himself in hearty agreement with some lines of poetry his son wrote after the first outbreak of rioting: "No man is safe in property or fame / Where laws are broken or where laws are lame / Much less when force suspends all legal right / Making men wrongfully submitt to might."[48]

So it was with an added sense of urgency that Morris met the provincial assembly in the fall of 1745. Owing to his "weakness and ill state of health," he could not personally attend the session at Burlington. Nevertheless, he did send a relatively conciliatory address to the legislators in which he asked them to pass a generous Support Act for a government which had had none for almost a year, to revise the militia system, and to approve punitive measures against the land rioters in East Jersey. "If the Indians can be prevailed on to joyn in attempts of this kind," he warned, invoking an eighteenth-century equivalent of the Red Scare, "we may Soon have a War with them in Our own Bowels."[49]

The representatives were not moved. The governor wanted a Support Act before all else; they wanted his prior assent to acts emitting £40,000 in bills of credit, limiting the terms of sheriffs, and restricting the jurisdiction of the supreme court. Neither side displayed any disposition to placate the other. Consequently, Morris dissolved his fifth assembly on October 18, after another acrimonious session productive of naught but ill will among the various branches of the provincial government. Now more than ever did he look to England for a way out of his political conundrum in New Jersey. "The Confus'd and miserable Condition we are in here," he told the Board of Trade five days later, "seemes to make the aid of his Majestie and his Ministers necessary both to the Province and to my Lords, &c." Yet he did not specify what form English intervention should take, so that this, his last plea for help, also went unheeded by the imperial administration.[50]

The spread of rioting against the Scottish proprietors throughout East Jersey and the provincial government's crying need for revenue compelled Morris in February 1746 to meet still another assembly. Advancing sickness inclined him to conciliate the newly elected legislators. Hence, in an address remarkably free from rancor, he simply asked them to support the provincial government, suppress the rioters, and strengthen New Jersey's defenses.[51]

Although Morris' last assembly contained only three new members, it, too, was disposed toward conciliation, perhaps from weariness with the repeated dissolutions to which the governor had resorted. In any case the assembly made a favorable reply to the governor's address and indicated that it was ready to support the government, willing to put down the rioters, and eager for harmony among all branches of the provincial legislature. In this somewhat idyllic mood, the assembly prepared support and militia bills, as well as the familiar measures concerning paper money, sheriffs, and the supreme court; while the council, the bastion of proprietary influence in New Jersey, drew up an act for the punishment of rioters. Suddenly it seemed as if Morris' conciliatory approach might be successful.[52]

But this was not to be. In the midst of its deliberations, on April 30, 1746, the assembly received a letter from Richard Partridge, its London agent, which revealed that Morris' complaints were about to cause the disallowance of the 1743 Fee Act—the very act whose suspending clause the governor had striven so mightily to prevent the lower house from evading. All at once the assembly's good will toward Morris evaporated. On the 1st of May it rejected the anti-insurrection bill it had received from the council. Six days later it told Morris that he would have to approve several popular laws just to receive a rather ungenerous appropriation of revenue for his administration. Morris refused to approve any of these acts unless the assembly first promised to be more liberal about the amount of financial support it gave the government, but this was a remarkable concession for him to offer in view of his adamantine opposition to compromise on this issue in the past. Now, however, it was the turn of the members of the lower house to be stubborn. They absolutely refused to increase the appropriations for the government they had already decided upon; and when Morris learned of their decision, he remarked that "it was very well, he should not alter his Resolution."[53] So once again the vice-regent of the crown and the representatives of the freeholders of New Jersey had reached a deadlock—and this at a time when land riots were sweeping through East Jersey, the provincial government was in dire need of revenue, and the entire colony (or so it seemed to Morris) was crying out for more paper money.

This proved to be one impasse it was beyond Morris' power to resolve. He had been appointed governor of New Jersey when he had almost reached his allotted span of three score years and ten, and since then he had suffered from a variety of ailments, including gout and strangury. At length old age and illness finally took their toll. After May 8 Morris became too ill to meet with the assembly. He then entered into his final decline and died at Trenton on May 21. From Trenton the family transported his body to Perth Amboy and thence to Morrisania. There on the 27th he was laid to rest in the family crypt after the performance of a simple Anglican burial service. After many storm-tossed years in public life, peace had come to Lewis Morris.[54]

Yet not even death could erase the bitterness Morris' administration had engendered among the people of New Jersey. In 1749 the assembly received a request for the payment of Morris' salary arrears from his widow and two surviving sons. Invoking the example of Lord Cornbury, who had been denied a salary in the last years of his administration because of his arbitrary ways of governing, the assembly overwhelmingly rejected the Morris family's request for compensation, "it being a Subject So universally disliked in this Colony, that there is none, except those who are immediately Concerned in point of Interest, or particularly Influenced by those who are, will Say one word in its Favour." It would be difficult to imagine a more damning commentary on Morris' tenure as governor.[55]

Conclusion

EWIS MORRIS HAD ONE OF THE MOST REMARKABLE POLITICAL CA-
REERS in early American history. Born when the First British Empire was still in the process of formation, he rose to power in East Jersey during the last great wave of imperial centralization in the seventeenth century, was a key political figure in New York during the era of salutary neglect, and died as governor of New Jersey just a few years before the onset of a new surge of imperial reorganization for which he had pleaded in vain during his administration. The offices he held were no less impressive than the stages of Anglo-American history through which his life passed. Member of the East Jersey Council and Court of Common Right at twenty, president of the New Jersey Council at thirty-six, representative in the New York Assembly at thirty-nine, chief justice of the New York Supreme Court at forty-three, and royal governor of New Jersey at sixty-six—these were but the most outstanding official milestones in a career spanning more than half a century. Even more noteworthy was the multiformity of roles he assumed during his political life. He was, at different times in his career, both a critic of proprietary government in East Jersey and a leader of the proprietary party in New Jersey, an advocate of popular control of the provincial financial system in New York and a proponent of executive fiscal discretion there, a radical country party leader in New York under William Cosby's administration and a conservative prerogative man in New Jersey during his own tenure as the king's governor.

The list of paradoxes might be extended, but the main point is clear. For sheer longevity and variety, Morris had few equals and no superiors among colonial American political leaders.

Morris' career sheds some light on several of the vexing questions of early American historiography, starting with the issue of the general nature of colonial American politics. Throughout his life Morris stood for the political and social dominance of the landed interests of New York and New Jersey. The means by which he sought to achieve this varied, but the end in view was always the same. In New Jersey, Morris first tried to secure the dominance of the landed interest and to protect the economic privileges of the Scottish proprietors by reducing the political power of the colony's farmer majority through the imposition of artificially high property qualifications on voters and assemblymen. After the failure of this effort, Morris proved adept at mobilizing popular support for his faction during his struggle with Lord Cornbury, but in the end he chose to protect proprietary interests by relying on control of the royally appointed council and the cooperation of the king's governors. In New York, on the other hand, Morris pursued an entirely different set of tactics. There he strove to enable the landed interest to gain the upper hand over the merchant elite by forming a coalition of landed gentlemen, country farmers, and urban artisans that was dedicated to the taxation of trade and the expansion of the assembly's power of the purse. Thus whereas Morris' New Jersey career fits the model of aristocratic-democratic conflict developed by Progressive historians, his New York career corresponds to the paradigm of elite competition in a deferential society favored by many Neo-Whig scholars. This duality will only surprise those who believe that the complex political development of thirteen colonies with different forms of government, social structures, economic systems, and cultural and religious traditions can be explained in terms of a single, all-embracing synthesis, whether it be the struggle for self-government, sectionalism, class conflict, competition between rival elites, or the working out of the implications of radical Whig thought.

Morris' career also illustrates the danger of placing undue emphasis on the significance of English Opposition thought in early American history. This is not to deny the importance in colonial America of ideology in general or of Opposition ideology in particular. It is merely to note that colonial political leaders had at their disposal at least two systems of political beliefs — a court and a country ideology. Whereas court ideology emphasized the duties of subjects, the subordination of the colonies to England, and respect for royal authority, country ideology stressed the rights of Englishmen, the need for greater colonial self-government, and the limitation of royal authority. Both saw liberty being endangered by power, but each perceived the danger in a different source. Court ideology was wary of popular licentiousness and assertive assemblies, while country ideology was fearful of executive arbitrariness and ministerial corruption. Morris espoused court and country beliefs at different points in his career, and at times he displayed elements of both simultaneously. He was an exponent of country principles during his opposition to Lord Cornbury and Governor Cosby and of court principles during his political decline under Governor Burnet and throughout his own gubernatorial administration. As legislative manager for Governors Hunter and Burnet, on the other hand, Morris acted on court and country principles alike, as he simultaneously expanded the powers of the New York Assembly, emphasized the need for cooperation with royal governors, and refused to suffer opposition gladly.

If Morris had been unique in alternating between court and country ideologies, then this phenomenon could rightly be dismissed as a personal quirk of no general historical interest. But in reality there was nothing peculiar about his behavior in this respect, except perhaps its intensity. In this study we have seen how the Philipse-DeLancey party rose to power in New York partly on the strength of its demands for more frequent assembly elections and then abandoned this plank after its alignment with Governor Cosby. Furthermore the political careers of James DeLancey and Benjamin Franklin, to cite but two of the more striking examples, demonstrate that Morris was not alone in fluctuating between court and country principles. Ideological considerations bulked large in the conduct of colonial politics, but which ideology colonial leaders espoused often resulted as much from calculations of personal advantage as intellectual conviction. Eventually country ideology won the day in America, at least during the Revolution, but it is good to remember that before that convulsion court principles offered a real alternative to provincial political leaders, particularly those who held appointive offices from the king and were unpopular with local electorates.

Finally Morris' political career was Anglo-American in scope, influenced as much by developments in England as events in America. From at least the time of his first London mission in 1701-1702 Morris realized that the imperial administration played a central role in the colonial political system and that good relations with it were often decisive in determining which local leaders won or lost power in America. The imperial administration appointed and removed royal governors, reviewed colonial legislation, approved appointments to various provincial offices, and responded to complaints by English interest groups, especially merchants, about disadvantageous colonial actions or policies. Since colonial leaders were rarely able to be present in London to influence the deliberations of imperial officials, they had to rely on English connections to do this for them. During his first trip to the seat of empire, Morris acquired valuable English contacts among the officers of the Society for the Propagation of the Gospel and the West Jersey Society who inclined the imperial administration in his favor at crucial points in his struggle against Lord Cornbury as well as during his partnership with Governor Hunter. After this, Morris' first English interest passed out of existence as a result of the death of its members and changes in his religious beliefs, and its disappearance was a significant factor in the failure of his second London mission in 1735–36. Yet on that trip Morris formed another English interest made up of high-ranking naval officers like Sir Charles Wager and Sir John Norris who saved his political career from ruin by securing his appointment as governor of New Jersey. In short, Morris' adeptness in the arts of Anglo-American politics was a key ingredient of the political power he enjoyed for so long in New York and New Jersey.

Turning from the career to the man, the key to understanding Morris lies in his lifelong effort to uphold his pretensions as a landed aristocrat. Driven by a strong lust for power, Morris was convinced that membership in the landed aristocracy endowed him with the requisite economic power, social prestige, and wisdom to act as one of the natural leaders of society whose guidance the lower orders should accept and whose status royal officials should respect. He firmly believed that merchants were unqualified for a leadership role of this sort because they were too absorbed in the pursuit of private profit to consider the common good of society as a whole, and to him it was simply axiomatic that artisans, craftsmen, and farmers should follow the lead of those he considered their social superiors. The maintenance of an aristocratic station in life was Morris' principal ambition and the unifying theme of his career. To this end the naturally pugnacious Morris was willing to confront any challenges to his power, whether they emanated from a proprietary governor in East Jersey, a royal governor in New York, or a provincial assembly in New Jersey. He also exhibited a truly amazing ideological flexibility in the pursuit of his political goals, as when he suddenly became a critic of the New York Assembly's expanded powers after losing control of that body to Adolph Philipse or as when he quickly substituted traditional royalist for radical Whig views upon becoming governor of New Jersey. There were limits to Morris' expediency, to be sure. He never betrayed the interests of his class, and he always believed in the virtues of balanced government, though sometimes it seemed as if the only governments he considered unbalanced were those controlled by his adversaries. These exceptions aside, Morris was a consummate opportunist and an engaging trimmer who could be accused of many things but never of tactical consistency.

The often erratic course Morris steered throughout his political life was not just the result of his wish to realize his personal ambitions or his need to satisfy a strong will to power. It also reflected the tensions in the structure of colonial politics produced by the recurrent conflict between the American impulse toward greater self-government, which ultimately implied the federalization of the empire, and the English insistence on rigidly subordinating the colonies to the mother country, which assumed the continuance of a tightly integrated empire. Morris always acknowledged the dependence of the colonies on England, but in reaction to the arbitrariness of royal governors he also spurred the development of local autonomy in New York and New Jersey. He professed to find no incompatibility between these positions throughout most of his career, except for a brief time in New York during the late 1720s when he was on the decline and sought to curry favor with the imperial administration by criticizing the excesses of the provincial assembly. Only after he became governor of New Jersey did he unalterably conclude that the expanded powers of colonial assemblies were dangerous to royal authority in America and inconsistent with a due subordination to England. Yet by then the imperial administration was too absorbed in wars with Spain and France to pay heed to his calls for radical parliamentary intervention to shore up the royal prerogative in America. Hence Morris' dual significance in colonial American history. He played a key role in promoting the so-called "silent revolution," which greatly altered the nature of the British Empire in the first half of the eighteenth century by expanding the powers of provincial assemblies at the expense of royal authority, and then advanced some proposals for severely curtailing the powers of these assemblies through parliamentary action which, when put into effect in other forms after 1763, helped to precipitate the dissolution of the imperial structure he had hoped to save. It seems only fitting that a man whose political career was studded by so many contradictions should ultimately be able to lay claim to such a paradoxical significance in history.

Notes

1—"One Poor Blossom"

1. Robert Bolton, *A History of the County of Westchester from its First Settlement to the Present Time,* 2 vols. (New York, 1848), 2:285; Elizabeth Morris Lefferts, comp., *Descendants of Lewis Morris of Morrisania, b. 1671 d. 1746: First Governor of New Jersey as a Separate Province* (New York, 1907), chart A; Kathryn Morris Wilkinson, *A Morris Lineage: Descendants of Richard Morris and Sarah Pole of Morrisania* (Milwaukee, 1966), pp. 1–9.

2. Richard Morris, Description of a Comet, Jan. 9, 1665, Ashmolean MSS, 423, fol. 244, Bodleian Library, Oxford, Library of Congress transcript; Matthias Nicoll to Lewis Morris, Sr., Oct. 29, 1672, Bolton, *History of Westchester,* 2:287; Robert Hunter Morris to Valentine Morris, June 7, 1763, Morris Papers, Box 3, Rutgers University Library; Lewis Morris, Jr., "Acct. of the Morris Family," Morris-Popham Papers, Box 4, Library of Congress.

3. W. N. Sainsbury et al., eds., *Calendar of State Papers, Colonial Series, America and West Indies, 1574–1660* (London, 1860–), pp. 166, 295, 358–59, 383 (hereafter cited as *CSP*); Vincent T. Harlow, ed., "The Voyages of Captain William Jackson (1642–1645)," *Camden Miscellany* 13 (1923): 13n1, 25; *Calendar of State Papers, Domestic Series, 1651,* pp. 213, 217, 221–22, 258, 274; Nicholas Darnell Davis, *The Cavaliers and Roundheads of Barbados, 1650–1652* (Georgetown, British Guiana, 1887), pp. 223, 226–27.

4. Richard Morris, Description of a Comet, Jan. 9, 1665, Ashmolean MSS; William Penn to Unknown, April 29, 1701, William Penn Papers, Historical Society of Pennsylvania, microfilm; William Loddington, *Plantation Work the Work of this Generation* (London, 1682), pp. 17–18; John Talbot and Daniel Leeds, *The Great Mystery of Fox-Craft Discovered* (New York, 1705), pp. 3–5; *CSP, 1669–1674,* no. 1101.ii.

5. Lewis Morris, Sr., to Arlington, Sept. 30, 1671, *CSP 1669-1674,* no. 635.

6. Bolton, *History of Westchester,* 2:293-96.

7. Dean Freiday, "Tinton Manor: The Iron Works," New Jersey Historical Society, *Proceedings* 70 (1952): 250-61.

8. Lewis Morris, Sr., "Instructions for walter webley," April 25, 1676, Mrs. Lawrence M. C. Smith Collection, Germantown, Philadelphia, Pa.; Robert Hunter Morris to Valentine Morris, June 7, 1763, Morris Papers, Box 3; Lewis Morris' Will, 1746, William A. Whitehead, ed., "The Papers of Lewis Morris, Governor of the Province of New Jersey, from 1738 to 1746," New Jersey Historical Society, *Collections* 4 (1852): 326 (hereafter cited as *Lewis Morris Papers*).

9. William Smith, Jr., *The History of the Province of New-York,* ed. Michael Kammen, 2 vols. (Cambridge, 1972), 1:139n.

10. Lewis Morris, Sr.'s, Will, Feb. 7, 1691, Bolton, *History of Westchester,* 2:290; John Strassburger, "The Origins and Establishment of the Morris Family in the Society and Politics of New York and New Jersey, 1630-1746" (Ph.D. diss., Princeton University, 1976), p. 91.

11. New York Council Minutes, May 8, 1691, Mrs. Lawrence M. C. Smith Collection; *Lewis Morris Papers,* pp. 323-25; William W. Shaw, ed., *Encyclopedia of Quaker Genealogy,* 6 vols. (Ann Arbor, 1936-50), 3:224. See also the releases of claims to Morrisania by Thomas Williams, Oct. 10, 1698; by John Williams, Feb. 20, July 6, 1699, Oct. 6, 7, 1701; and by Benjamin Felton, June 22, 1699, all in the Mrs. Lawrence M. C. Smith Collection.

12. Lewis Morris, Account Book, 1690-98, Trent House; Inventory of Lewis Morris Sr.'s, Estate, Oct. 23, 1691, Bolton, *History of Westchester,* 2:294-300; Edward Randolph to William Blathwayt, Aug. 16, 1692, *Prince Society Publications* 31 (1909): 402.

13. Earl of Bellomont to John Locke, Sept. 7, 1699, Bellomont-Locke Papers, Bodleian Library, Oxford, microfilm; Smith, *History of New-York,* ed. Kammen, 1:140; Paul M. Hamlin and Charles E. Barker, eds., *Supreme Court of Judicature of the Province of New York, 1691-1704,* New-York Historical Society, *Collections* 80 (1959): 90-98.

14. Isabella Morris to Robert Hunter Morris, April 8, 1735, Morris Papers, Box 2; Lewis Morris' Will, 1746, *Lewis Morris Papers,* pp. 326, 329; William A. Whitehead et al., eds., *Documents Relating to the Colonial History of the State of New Jersey,* 1st ser., 43 vols. (Newark, 1880-1949), 19:146.

15. These eleven children were, in the order of their births: 1. Mary (d. 1747); 2. Sarah (d. 1736); 3. Lewis, Jr. (1698-1762); 4. Isabella (1705-1741); 5. Euphemia (1705?-1756); 6. Anne (1706-1781); 7. John (1707-1737); 8. Arabella (alive 1767); 9. Margaret (1711-84); 10. Elizabeth (1712-84); 11. Robert Hunter (1713-64). Lewis Morris, Jr., "Acct. of the Morris Family," Morris-Popham Papers, Box 4; Lefferts, *Descendants of Lewis Morris,* chart A. I have followed the order of births given by Lewis Morris, Jr.

16. Lewis Morris to John Morris, May 25, 1730, Morris Papers, Box 2; Anne Morris to Robert Hunter Morris, May 29, 1735, ibid.

17. Elizabeth Morris to Robert Hunter Morris, Jan. 22, 1735, ibid.; Leonard W. Labaree et al., eds., *The Autobiography of Benjamin Franklin* (New Haven and London, 1964), pp. 212-13.

18. Lewis Morris, Account Book, 1690–98, Trent House; Joseph Haviland to Lewis Morris, Nov. 12, 1707, Sept. 12, Nov. 18, 1709; Samuel Dennis to Same, July 9, 1708; Isabella Morris to Same, Dec. 28, 1713, Sept. 12, Dec. 20, 1715; Lewis Morris to James Fleming, Oct. 24, 1728; Same, Agreement with William Clark, Dec. 14, 1728, all in Morris Papers, Box 1.

19. Patent for Tinton Manor, Oct. 3, 1676, Indenture Collection, Rutgers University Library; George Carteret, Articles of Concession to Lewis Morris, Sr., May 1, 1677, Morris Papers, Box 1.

20. Morrisania's Charter, May 6, 1697, Jerrold Seymann, ed., *Colonial Charters, Patents and Grants to the Communities Comprising the City of New York* (Albany, 1939), pp. 365–71; "Some farther Observations," [1720], Jay Papers, Box 3, New York Historical Society.

21. Edgar J. McManus, *Black Bondage in the North* (Syracuse, 1973), p. 41. See also Inventory of Lewis Morris, Sr.'s, Estate, Oct. 23, 1691, Bolton, *History of Westchester,* 2: 300; "The Census of 1698 for Mamaroneck, Morrisania, and New Rochelle, Westchester County, New York," *New York Genealogical and Biographical Record* 59 (1928): 104–105; "A Schedule of Stock and Utensills belonging to Lewis Morris Esq.," Feb. 9, 1701, Mrs. Lawrence M. C. Smith Collection; Westchester County Census, 1712, E. B. O'Callaghan, ed., *Documentary History of the State of New York,* 4 vols. (Albany, 1849–51), 3:949; New York Slave Census, 1755, ibid., pp. 852–53.

22. Lewis Morris et al., "Certificate on behalf of Elias Neau," [ca. April 24, 1716], Records of the Society for the Propagation of the Gospel in Foreign Parts, Ser. A, 9:294–96, microfilm (hereafter cited as *RSPG*); Lewis Morris, "Observations on a printed Sheet," Miscellaneous Manuscripts-Henry Ludlow, New-York Historical Society; Same to John Morris, April 30, 1730, Morris Papers, Box 2; Sheldon S. Cohen, "Elias Neau, Instructor to New York's Slaves," *New-York Historical Society Quarterly* 55 (1971): 7–27.

23. Franklin B. Dexter, ed., *The Literary Diary of Ezra Stiles,* 3 vols. (New York, 1901), 3:366n.3; Lawrence A. Cremin, *American Education: The Colonial Experience, 1607–1783* (New York, 1970), pp. 58, 397.

24. The following discussion of Morris' reading is largely based upon these sources: Lewis Morris to William Beveridge, July 12, 1703, *RSPG,* Ser. A, 1, no. 110; Same to James Alexander, Aug. 25, 1735, Jan. 11, 1736, Rutherfurd Collection, 2:129, 171, New-York Historical Society; Same to John Clark, May 25, 1739, and to Euphemia Norris, Dec. 13, 1743, *Lewis Morris Papers,* pp. 47, 178; Beverly McAnear, ed., "An American in London, 1735–1736," *PMHB* 64 (1940): 356, 374; *Parke-Bernet Auction Catalogue,* Sale no. 134 (Oct. 25–26, 1939), item 248.

25. Lewis Morris to John Morris, Dec. 30, 1733, Morris Papers, Box 2.

26. Lewis Morris, "A Dialogue between a South and a North Countryman," [1727–28], ibid.; E. B. O'Callaghan and Berthold Fernow, eds., *Documents Relative to the Colonial History of the State of New York,* 15 vols. (Albany, 1856–87), 6:9.

27. Richard Cook, "Lewis Morris—New Jersey's Colonial Poet-Governor," *Journal of Rutgers University Library* 24 (1961): 105.

28. Lewis Morris, "The Dream and Riddle, A Poem," [1736], Morris Papers, Box 2.

29. Ibid.

30. Verses on a Seat of Government for New Jersey, nd, ibid.

31. Lewis Morris to John Chamberlayne, 1702, *RSPG*, Ser. A, 1, no. 48; John Chamberlayne to Lewis Morris, July 21, 1708, SPG Papers, 14:107, Lambeth Palace Library, microfilm; Lewis Morris to Peter Collinson, May 24, 1742, *Lewis Morris Papers*, pp. 146-47. For further evidence of Morris' scientific interests, see Edward P. Alexander, ed., *The Journal of John Fontane* (Williamsburg, Va., 1972), pp. 114-15; and McAnear, ed., "An American in London," pp. 195-96, 357.

32. William Penn to Unknown, April 29, 1701, William Penn Papers; John Chamberlayne to Lewis Morris, June 11, 1711, Morris Papers, Box 1; Smith, *History of New-York*, ed. Kammen, 1:139.

33. Edward Randolph to William Blathwayt, Aug. 16, 1692, *Prince Society Publications* 31 (1909): 402.

2 – "Morris's Inconsistencies"

1. For a discussion of the legal invalidity of the Duke of York's grants, see Charles M. Andrews, *The Colonial Period of American History*, 4 vols. (New Haven, 1934-38), 3: 138n1.

2. *A Bill in the Chancery of New Jersey* (New York, 1747), pp. 4-6, 16-17, 22-23; *An Answer to a Bill in Chancery of New Jersey* (New York, 1752), pp. 5-13, 25; George J. Miller, ed., *The Minutes of the Board of Proprietors of the Eastern Division of New Jersey*, 3 vols. (Perth Amboy, 1949-60), 1:passim; John E. Pomfret, *The Province of East New Jersey, 1609-1702: The Rebellious Proprietary* (Princeton, 1962), chaps. 2, 3.

3. John E. Pomfret, *The Province of West New Jersey, 1609-1702: A History of the Origins of an American Colony* (Princeton, 1956), pp. 173-89; Frederick R. Black, "The Last Lords Proprietors of West Jersey: The West Jersey Society, 1692-1702" (Ph.D. diss., Rutgers University, 1964), pp. 65-92.

4. Robert G. Albion, "New Jersey and the Port of New York," New Jersey Historical Society, *Proceedings* 58 (1940): 84-92.

5. Philip Haffenden, "The Crown and the Colonial Charters, 1675-1688," *WMQ*, 3d ser., 15 (1958): 452-66; Eugene R. Sheridan, "Daniel Coxe and the Restoration of Proprietary Government in East Jersey, 1690 – a Letter," *New Jersey History* 92 (1974): 103-109.

6. Lewis Morris to Elizabethtown, July 13, 1698, Sunderland Papers, New Jersey, 1698-1709, Henry E. Huntington Library, microfilm.

7. East Jersey Council Minutes, Oct. 5, 1694, July 30, 1695, *NJA*, 13:206-207, 219; Elizabethtown's Petition to the King, [June 1697?], ibid., 2:124-29; Preston W. Edsall, ed., *Journal of the Courts of Common Right and Chancery of East New Jersey, 1683-1702* (Philadelphia, 1937), pp. 96-101, 246-47, 256-57, 274; W. L. Grant and James Munro, eds., *Acts of the Privy Council, 1613-1783*, 6 vols. (Hereford and London, 1908-1912), 2:306-307.

8. *NJA*, 2:138-42, 155-71, 174-75, 177-78, 180-85, 200.

9. East Jersey Council Minutes, April 7, 8, 1698, ibid., 13:237-39; Lewis Morris, Memorial to Board of Trade, Aug. 5, 1701, ibid., 2:398.

10. Lewis Morris, Memorial to Board of Trade?, [1702?], Morris Papers, Box 1, Rutgers University Library; John Tatham et al., *The Case Put and Decided* (Philadelphia, 1699), pp. 7–8; Samuel Jennings, *Truth Rescued from Forgery and False-hood* (Philadelphia, 1699), pp. 22–23.

11. Depositions of William Bingla and Matthew Moore, May 12, 1698, *NJA*, 3:476–77, 482; Edsall, ed., *Journal of the Courts of Common Right and Chancery*, p. 311.

12. Lewis Morris, Letter to Elizabethtown, July 13, 1698, Sunderland Papers, New Jersey, 1698–1709. There are other texts of this letter in *NJA*, 3:487–91, and New Jersey Historical Society, *Proceedings*, 2d ser., 4 (1875–77): 182–86.

13. Address of Lieutenant Governor and Council of New Jersey to Lord Lovelace, [April 1709], *NJA*, 3:407.

14. Earl of Bellomont to Board of Trade, May 8, 25, Sept. 21, Dec. 14, 1698, Nov. 23, 1700, *NYCD*, 4:305, 314, 380–81, 438–39, 777–78; East Jersey Council Minutes, May 30, Nov. 26, Dec. 12, 1698, *NJA*, 13:241, 244; Proclamation of Jeremiah Basse, May 30, 1698, Petition of Jeremiah Basse and John Lofting to House of Commons, Feb. 23, 1700, ibid., 2: 227–28, 311–13.

15. Lewis Morris, "Memorial of the Proprietors of Jersey to the King," [1701], Morris Papers, Box 1.

16. Ibid.; East Jersey Council Minutes, March 2–4, 13, 1699, *NJA*, 13:255–58, 264–65; Miller, ed., *Minutes of the Board of Proprietors*, 1:223; Aaron Leaming and Jacob Spicer, comps., *The Grants, Concessions, and Original Constitutions of the Province of New Jersey* (Philadelphia, 1758), pp. 367, 368–72, 376–81.

17. Lewis Morris, "Memorial of the Proprietors of Jersey to the King," [1701], Morris Papers, Box 1; *NJA*, 2:106–113.

18. Lewis Morris, "Memorial of the Proprietors of Jersey to the King," [1701], Morris Papers, Box 1.

19. [Lewis Morris], Letter from Newark, Elizabethtown, Perth Amboy, and Freehold to East Jersey Proprietors, [April 21, 1699], *NJA*, 2:273–75. The stylistic similarities between this letter and Morris' second "Red-hott" letter to the East Jersey Council indicate that both were written by the same author. Ibid., 3:491–95. See also ibid., p. 478.

20. [Lewis Morris], Letter from Newark, Elizabethtown, Perth Amboy, and Freehold to East Jersey Proprietors, [April 21, 1699], *NJA*, 2:273–75; Depositions of Grimstone Boude and John Edsall, May 10, 1699, ibid., 3:477–79.

21. East Jersey Council Minutes, May 10, 1699, ibid., 13:266–67; Presentment of Joseph Woodrose et al., nd, ibid., 3:485–87; Edsall, ed., *Journal of the Courts of Common Right and Chancery*, pp. 318–19.

22. *NJA*, 13:269; Address of Lieutenant Governor and Council of New Jersey to Lord Lovelace, [April 1709], ibid., 3:407. Emphasis in original.

23. Lewis Morris to East Jersey Council, [ca. May 17, 1699], ibid., pp. 491–95.

24. East Jersey Council Minutes, May 16, 17, 18, 19, 1699, ibid., 13:269–73; Charles Goodman to Commissioners of Customs, June 27, 1699, ibid., 2:292.

25. *NYCD*, 4:546–47; *NJA*, 2:266–68, 294–97; Ned Earle, Jr., to Lewis Morris, Jan. 19, 1700, Morris Papers, Box 1.

26. *NJA,* 2:313–17, 322–27, 364–66, 439–42.

27. Lewis Morris to Board of Trade, Sept. 29, 1702, ibid., p. 502.

28. Deposition of Joseph Clark et al., July 5, 1700, Blathwayt Papers, vol. 7, Colonial Williamsburg, microfilm; Deposition of James Bollen, July 5, 1700, *NJA,* 3:485; Unknown to Jeremiah Basse, July 30, 1700, ibid., 2:329–30.

29. Andrew Bowne and Richard Hartshorne to [Jeremiah Basse], July 23, 1700, Unknown to Jeremiah Basse, July 30, 1700, ibid., pp. 327–31.

30. See Elizabethtown to other East Jersey Towns, July 31, 1700; Elizabethtown and Piscataway to Lewis Morris et al., July 31, 1700; and Middletown to Same, July 30, 1700, all in Blathwayt Papers, vol. 7. The only known text of Morris' last "Red-hott" letter, written to Elizabethtown on Aug. 2, 1700, is a brief fragment quoted in Address of Lieutenant Governor and Council of New Jersey to Lord Lovelace, [April 1709], *NJA,* 3:412.

31. Andrew Bowne and Richard Hartshorne to [Jeremiah Basse], July 23, 1700, ibid., 2:329.

32. Ibid., pp. 362–64, 366–67, 371–72.

33. Lewis Morris to Board of Trade, Sept. 29, 1702, ibid., pp. 505–506.

3 – "Their Champion Goliath"

1. William Penn to Andrew Hamilton, April 3, 1701, and to Unknown, April 29, 1701, William Penn Papers, Historical Society of Pennsylvania, microfilm; William Dockwra to Lewis Morris, Feb. 13, 1702, Morris Papers, Box 1, Rutgers University Library; Alison Gilbert Olson, "William Penn, Parliament, and Proprietary Government," *WMQ,* 3d ser., 18 (1961): 185–92.

2. *NJA,* 2:255–57, 294–97, 308–310; *Calendar of State Papers, Colonial Series, America and West Indies, 1699,* nos. 164, 225, 229, 249, 1006 (hereafter cited as *CSP*); *CSP 1700,* nos. 48, 70, 101, 670, 908, 937–38, 966–68, 973, 985, 1012, 1016; Charles M. Andrews, *The Colonial Period of American History,* 4 vols. (New Haven, 1934–38), 3:180–81; I. K. Steele, *Politics of Colonial Policy: The Board of Trade in Colonial Administration* (Oxford, 1968), pp. 63–81.

3. *NJA,* 2:385–86, 401–403, 445–46; *NJA,* 13:279, 282–92; William Dockwra to Andrew Bowne, Nov. 28, 1701, Stillwell Collection, New-York Historical Society; "A List of the Variety of Papers Sent . . . to Mr. Sonmans," Oct. 28, 1707, New Jersey MSS, 4, New Jersey Historical Society; Edwin Salter and George C. Beekman, *Old Times in Old Monmouth* (Freehold, N.J., 1887), pp. 282–83.

4. Frederick R. Black, "The Last Lords Proprietors of West Jersey: The West Jersey Society, 1692–1702" (Ph.D. diss., Rutgers University, 1964), pp. 305–310, 365–66, 369.

5. *CSP 1701,* nos. 651, 653, 663; *NJA,* 2:380–84, 394–97.

6. Lewis Morris to Board of Trade, Aug. 5, 1701, *NJA,* 2:398–403.

7. "The humble Representation of the case of the Proprietors of East new Jersey," June 1687, New Jersey MSS, 4; East Jersey Proprietors to Board of Trade, July 5, 1699, *NJA,* 2:294–97.

8. Memorial of East and West Jersey Proprietors to Lords Justices, Aug. 12, 1701, *NJA*, 2:404–408. Some vague hints about Morris' role in the formulation of these terms can be found in Lewis Morris to Earl of Sunderland, [1709], Morris Papers, Box 1; and *The Case of Lewis Morris, Esq.* (London, 1735), p. 1.

9. East and West Jersey Proprietors' Petition to Lords Justices, [Aug. 14, 1701], *NJA*, 2:408–411. Date supplied from *CSP 1701*, no. 745.i. See also William Dockwra to Andrew Bowne, Nov. 28, 1701, Stillwell Collection.

10. *CSP 1701*, nos. 786, 824; Lewis Morris, Memorial to Board of Trade, Sept. 13, 1701, *NJA*, 2:412–14.

11. Cornbury to William Blathwayt, Aug. 5, 1701, Blathwayt Papers, Henry E. Huntington Library, microfilm; Jeremiah Basse to Same, Aug. 20, 1701, Additional MSS 9747, fols. 38–39a, British Library, Library of Congress transcript; William Blathwayt to Cornbury, May 8, 1702, Blathwayt Papers, vol. 8, Colonial Williamsburg, microfilm; Stephen Saunders Webb, "William Blathwayt, Imperial Fixer: Muddling through to Empire, 1689–1717," *WMQ*, 3d ser., 26 (1969): 409–412.

12. Lewis Morris, Memorial to Board of Trade, Sept. 13, 1701, *NJA*, 2:412–14.

13. [Lewis Morris], "The Humble Memoriall of the Greatest Part of ye Proprietors of the Provinces of East and West Jersie," [Sept. 13, 1701], C.O. 5/1261/21i, Public Record Office, microfilm. Printed texts of this document and the proprietary list of conciliar nominees are in *NJA*, 2:415–17.

14. Records of the Society for the Propagation of the Gospel in Foreign Parts, Journal, 1:14–16, microfilm (hereafter cited as *RSPG*); C. F. Pascoe, *Two Hundred Years of the S.P.G.* (London, 1901), pp. 1–9, 932–35; Evarts B. Greene, "The Anglican Outlook on the American Colonies in the Early Eighteenth Century," *AHR* 20 (Oct. 1914): 64–83.

15. "The Memoriall of Col. Morris concerning the State of Religion in the Jerseys," ibid., Journal, 1, Appendix A, no. 2. This document has been printed in *Lewis Morris Papers*, pp. 7–10, where it is erroneously described as having been written to the Bishop of London in 1700 from East Jersey. On Nov. 18, 1701 Morris was made East Jersey "Correspondent" of the Society for Promoting Christian Knowledge, a slightly older Anglican mission organization which was interested in creating charity schools for the Christian education of youth, converting dissenters, especially Quakers, circulating religious works, and reforming prisons. Edmund McClure, ed., *A Chapter in English Church History, being the Minutes of the Society for Promoting Christian Knowledge for the Years 1698–1704* (London, 1888), pp. iii–vi, 154.

16. Board of Trade's Representation to Lords Justices, Oct. 2, 1701, *NJA*, 2:420–27; *CSP 1701*, nos. 870, 885, 907, 930, 965, 981, 994, 1001, 1005–1006.

17. Instructions to Lord Cornbury, Nov. 16, 1702, *NJA*, 2:506–537, articles 2, 14–15, 23, 36–38, 51–53.

18. Board of Trade to the Queen, June 25, 1702, ibid., pp. 484–85.

19. Same to Earl of Nottingham, Sept. 3, 1702, ibid., p. 503; George J. Miller, ed., *The Minutes of the Board of Proprietors of the Eastern Division of New Jersey, 1685–1764*, 3 vols. (Perth Amboy, 1949–60), 1:254; William Penn to James Logan, Dec. 4, 1703, Historical Society of Pennsylvania, *Memoirs* 9 (1870): 249 (hereafter cited as *HSP Memoirs*); Steele, *Politics of Colonial Policy*, pp. 76–77.

20. West Jersey Society's List of Proposed Governor and Councilors, nd, East Jersey Proprietors' List of Proposed Governor and Councilors, nd, *NJA*, 2:429-31; *CSP 1701*, no. 1055.

21. William Dockwra to Andrew Bowne, Nov. 28, 1701, Stillwell Collection; Same to Board of Trade, [Dec. 16, 1701], Lewis Morris to Same, [Dec. 31, 1701], Board of Trade to the King, Jan. 6, 1702, *NJA*, 2:432-36, 442-49; William Blathwayt to Cornbury, May 8, 1702, Blathwayt Papers, vol. 8, Colonial Williamsburg, microfilm; *CSP 1701*, no. 1108; *CSP 1702*, nos. 6-7, 71.

22. William Dockwra to Lewis Morris, Feb. 13, 1702, Lewis Morris, Petition to the King, [ante March 8, 1702], Morris Papers, Box 1; William Penn to James Logan, June 21, 1702, *HSP Memoirs*, 9:115; New Jersey Proprietors' Petition to the Queen, nd, William Dockwra and Peter Sonmans' Petition to Same, nd, William Dockwra and Peter Sonmans, Memorial to Board of Trade, May 28, 1702, *NJA*, 2:466-67, 469-72.

23. Lewis Morris' Bond with Paul Docminique, April 1, 1702, DePeyster Papers, 9, New-York Historical Society; Surrender of New Jersey Proprietors to the Queen, April 15, 1702, Privy Council Minutes, April 17, 1702, *NJA*, 2:456-62; *The Case of Lewis Morris, Esq.*, p. 1.

24. Lewis Morris to Earl of Sunderland, [1709], Morris Papers, Box 1; George Keith to SPG, June 12, 1702, *RSPG*, Ser. A, 1, no. 9.

25. Board of Trade to Earl of Nottingham, with a draft commission for Lewis Morris, June 1, 1702, *NJA*, 2:474; *CSP 1702*, nos. 561-62.1.

26. William Blathwayt to Lord Cornbury, May 8, 1702, Blathwayt Papers, vol. 8, Colonial Williamsburg, microfilm; Jeremiah Basse to William Blathwayt, Aug. 20, 1701, Additional MSS 9747, fols. 38-39a. Blathwayt revealed some of his concerns about New York's interests in his observations on the East Jersey proprietors' 1699 surrender terms. *CSP 1699*, no. 1006.

27. James Logan to William Penn, Dec. 1, 1702, *HSP Memoirs*, 9:148; *CSP 1702*, nos. 664, 783, 995; John Champante to Roger Mompesson, Oct. 10, 1707, Rawlinson MSS A, 272, fol. 237, Bodleian Library, Oxford, microfilm; Lewis Morris to Duke of Newcastle, June 2, 1732, *NJA*, 5:320; *The Case of Lewis Morris, Esq.*, p. 1.

28. [William Dockwra], "List of persons proposed to be of ye Councils of . . . New Jersey," [Aug. 3, 1702], Board of Trade to Earl of Nottingham, Sept. 3, 1702, *NJA*, 2:487-88, 502-503; *CSP 1702*, nos. 801, 824, 854.

29. Lewis Morris to Board of Trade, Sept. 29, 1702, *NJA*, 2:504-506.

30. Miller, ed., *Minutes of the Board of Proprietors*, 1:254-55; Indenture between Lewis Morris and East Jersey Proprietors, Dec. 10, 1702, Morris Papers, Box 1.

31. West Jersey Society Records, Treasury Solicitor 12/15/25, Public Record Office, microfilm; William T. McClure, Jr., "The West Jersey Society, 1692-1736," New Jersey Historical Society, *Proceedings* 74 (1956): 14-19; Black, "The Last Lords Proprietors of West Jersey," pp. 399-402.

32. George Keith to Bishop of London, Feb. 26, 1703, and to Thomas Bray, Feb. 24, 1704, Protestant Episcopal Historical Society, *Collections* (1851), pp. xxiii, xxvii.

33. Lewis Morris to Archdeacon William Beveridge, Sept. 3, 1702, July 12, 1703, *RSPG*, Ser. A, 1, nos. 45, 110.

34. Same to John Chamberlayne, 1702, ibid., no. 48; *Dictionary of National Biography*, s.v. "Chamberlayne, John." In 1709 Morris accepted Chamberlayne's "offer of Corresponding with you on a Philosophical Account," diffidently adding that he did so "always on Condition that you give great Allowances for a poor Americans want of that Judgment and parts requisite for such a Correspondence." Morris to Chamberlayne, May 30, 1709, *RSPG*, Ser. A, 4, no. 149. Unfortunately only four letters from Morris and Chamberlayne's private correspondence have survived, and they are all by Chamberlayne. See his letters to Morris of May 24, June 11, 1711, in Morris Papers, Box 1, as well as those of July 21, 1708, and Jan. 24, 1709, in SPG Papers, 14:107, 202, Lambeth Palace Library, microfilm.

4 – "Tricks upon Tricks"

1. Robert Quary to Board of Trade, June 16, Dec. 20, 1703, *NJA*, 2:544; *NJA*, 3: 14-16; Same to Same, July 20, 1703, Peter Force Collection, Ser. 9, Library of Congress.

2. West Jersey Society to Board of Trade, Jan. 27, 1704, William Dockwra to Same, Feb. 14, 1704, Daniel Coxe, Jr., to Same, Feb. 14, 1704, *NJA*, 3:35-47; "A List of the . . . Papers Sent . . . to Mr. Sonmans," Oct. 28, 1707, New Jersey MSS, 4, New Jersey Historical Society. For a different interpretation of the alliance between the English proprietors and the Nicolls patentees, see Donald L. Kemmerer, *Path to Freedom: The Struggle for Self-Government in Colonial New Jersey, 1703-1776* (Princeton, 1940), pp. 49-50.

3. Cornbury to William Blathwayt, Aug. 5, 1701, Blathwayt Papers, Henry E. Huntington Library, microfilm; James Logan to William Penn, Dec. 1, 1702, Sept. 3, 1703, William Penn to James Logan, May 10, 1705, Historical Society of Pennsylvania, *Memoirs* 9 (1870): 147, 227-28; *Memoirs* 10 (1872): 16 (hereafter cited as *HSP Memoirs*); Narcissus Luttrell, *A Brief Historical Relation of State Affairs from September 1678 to April 1714*, 6 vols. (Oxford, 1857), 2:51, 4:411; Thomas B. Macauley, *History of England from the Accession of James II*, ed. Charles H. Firth, 6 vols. (London, 1913-15), 3:1150; Keith Feiling, *A History of the Tory Party, 1640-1714* (Oxford, 1924), pp. 68, 122-24, 299; Geoffrey Holmes, *English Politics in the Age of Anne* (London, 1967), pp. 208-209, 270-79, 375-76.

4. Deposition of John Johnston, May 1, 1707, *NJA*, 3:207-209. Morris was the only person in New Jersey who is known to have had a copy of Cornbury's instructions at this time. Ibid., p. 2.

5. Robert Quary to Board of Trade, Dec. 7, 1702, *PMHB* 24 (1900): 74; Daniel Honan to Lewis Morris, Aug. 6, 1703, Morris Papers, Box 1, Rutgers University Library; James Logan to William Penn, Sept. 2, 1703, *HSP Memoirs*, 9:225-26; Cornbury to Board of Trade, Sept. 9, 1703, *NJA*, 3:1-3. Unfortunately there are no extant New Jersey Council records for Cornbury's administration after Aug. 25, 1703. Donald L. Kemmerer, "The Missing Journal of Lord Cornbury's Council," New Jersey Historical Society, *Proceedings* 57 (1939): 114-15.

6. Robert Quary to Board of Trade, Dec. 20, 1703, Cornbury to Same, Nov. 27, 1705, Address of Lieutenant Governor and Council of New Jersey to Lord Lovelace [April 1709], *NJA*, 3:14-16, 121, 392-93.

7. *Votes and Proceedings of the General Assembly of New Jersey*, Nov. 12, 16-18, 22, 24, 1703, Early State Records microfilm (hereafter cited as *N.J. Assem. Journ.*); *Anno Regni Reginae Annae . . . Secundo* [New Jersey Laws] (New York, 1703), pp. 3-4; Robert

Quary to Board of Trade, Dec. 20, 1703, Cornbury to Same, Jan. 14, 1704, Address of Lieutenant Governor and Council of New Jersey to Lord Lovelace, [April 1709], *NJA*, 3:17-19, 28-35, 404.

8. *N.J. Assem. Journ.*, Nov. 13, 23, Dec. 2-7, 1703; Robert Quary to Board of Trade, Dec. 20. 1703, Cornbury to Same, Jan. 14, 1704, Lewis Morris to Robert Harley, Feb. 9, 1708, *NJA*, 3:21, 35, 278.

9. Robert Quary to Board of Trade, Dec. 20, 1703; "A Collection of Affidavits," [April-May 1707], *NJA*, 3:16-17, 198-219.

10. The preceding account of Morris' differences with Cornbury is based on Cornbury to Board of Trade, Feb. 19, 1705, ibid., pp. 71, 74-75, 77-78. See also chaps. 7 and 9 of the present work for a description of Morris' criticism of provincial assemblies.

11. Depositions of John Fitzrandolph, Samuel Dennis, and John Pike, April 21, 29, 1707, *NJA*, 3:198-200, 204.

12. Andrew Bowne to Lewis Morris, Aug. 30, 1704, Morris Papers, Box 1; Cornbury to Board of Trade, Feb. 19, 1705, *NJA*, 3:75.

13. *N.J. Assem. Journ.*, Sept. 6, 12, 14, 28, 1704; James Logan to William Penn, Sept. 28, 1704, *HSP Memoirs*, 9:318; Cornbury to Board of Trade, Nov. 4, 1704, Lewis Morris to Robert Harley, Feb. 9, 1708, *NJA*, 3:65-66, 277-78.

14. *N.J. Assem. Journ.*, Nov. 14, 1704; Cornbury to Board of Trade, Feb. 19, 1705, *NJA*, 3:76.

15. James Logan to William Penn, Dec. 8, 1704, Isaac Norris to John Askew, July 13, 1705, *HSP Memoirs*, 9:348, 360. See also *N.J. Assem. Journ.*, Nov. 15-17, Dec. 6-7, 1704, Nov. 26, 1705; and *NJA*, 3:88-90, 137-38, 150-52, 278-80.

16. *N.J. Assem. Journ.*, Nov. 22-Dec. 12, 1704; *Anno Regni Reginae Annae . . . Tertio* [New Jersey Laws] (New York, 1704), pp. 1-5, 16-18.

17. Cornbury to Board of Trade, Feb. 19, 1705, *NJA*, 3:69-70, 76-77.

18. *N.J. Assem. Journ.*, Dec. 7, 9, 11-12, 1704, *Anno Regni Reginae Annae . . .Tertio* [New Jersey Laws], pp. 5-8; Lewis Morris to Robert Harley, Feb. 9, 1708, *NJA*, 3:280.

19. Cornbury to Board of Trade, Feb. 9, 1705, *NJA*, 3:77.

20. "Dates of Letters from Mr. Lewis Morris," West Jersey Society Records, Treasury Solicitor 12/4/23-24, Public Record Office, microfilm; West Jersey Society to Board of Trade, April 17, 1705, *NJA*, 3:86-95.

21. See *NJA*, 3:86-95, 117-18; and *Journal of the Commissioners for Trade and Plantations, 1704-1709*, pp. 184, 187-88, 190.

22. William Dockwra et al. to Board of Trade, April 5, 1705, Board of Trade to the Queen, April 20, 1705, *NJA*, 3:82-85, 96-98; *Journal of the Commissioners for Trade and Plantations, 1704-1709*, p. 126.

23. Cornbury to Board of Trade, Nov. 4, 1704, Feb. 19, 1705, William Dockwra et al. to Same, April 5, 1705, William Dockwra to Same, May 8, 1705, Board of Trade to Cornbury, Feb. 4, 1706, *NJA*, 3:66, 78-79, 83-84, 101-103, 125; *Journal of the Commissioners for Trade and Plantations, 1704-1709*, pp. 140-151, 153, 187, 192.

24. New Jersey Council Proceedings, Nov. 9, 1705, April 30, June 4, 1726, Morris Papers, Boxes 1 and 2; Miller, ed., *Minutes of the Board of Proprietors,* 1:259-63.

5—"To Obtain the Needful Certificats"

1. Lewis Morris to Unknown, [1705], William A. Whitehead, ed., "The Papers of Lewis Morris, Governor of the Province of New Jersey, from 1738 to 1746," New Jersey Historical Society, *Collections* 4 (1852): 12n.

2. *HSP Memoirs,* 10:16; Henry L. Snyder, ed., *The Marlborough-Godolphin Correspondence,* 3 vols. (Oxford, 1975), 1:548; Keith Feiling, *A History of the Tory Party, 1640–1714* (Oxford, 1924), p. 299; *Dictionary of National Biography,* s.v. "Hyde, Lawrence"; Henry Horwitz, *Revolution Politicks: The Career of Daniel Finch Second Earl of Nottingham, 1647-1730* (Cambridge, England, 1968), pp. 180-99; Stephen Saunders Webb, "William Blathwayt, Imperial Fixer: Muddling through to Empire, 1689-1717," *WMQ,* 3d ser., 26 (1969): 411-14.

3. Cornbury to William Blathwayt, Nov. 9, 1705, Blathwayt Papers, Henry E. Huntington Library, microfilm; John Johnston to Charles Dunster, Feb. 19, 1707, Rutherfurd Collection, 4:13, New-York Historical Society; John Champante to Roger Mompesson, Oct. 10, 1707, Rawlinson MSS A, 272, fol. 237, Bodleian Library, Oxford, microfilm; Cornbury to Board of Trade, June 7, 1707, *NJA,* 3:225-26; James Alexander to Robert Hunter, Nov. 20, 1728, Rutherfurd Collection, 1:95.

4. Lewis Morris to Robert Harley, Feb. 9, 1708, *NJA,* 3:281; James Logan to William Penn, Sept. 28, 1704, *HSP Memoirs,* 9:318.

5. *NJA,* 3:158-63, 221-23; John Clement, "An Old Ferry and an Old Post Road," *PMHB* 9 (1883): 441-44.

6. Lewis Morris to Robert Harley, Feb. 9, 1708, *NJA,* 3:284; Elias Neau to John Chamberlayne, Feb. 27, 1709, Records of the Society for the Propagation of the Gospel in Foreign Parts, Ser. A, 4, no. 121A, microfilm (hereafter cited as *RSPG*).

7. John Johnston to Charles Dunster, Feb. 19, 1707, Rutherfurd Collection, 4:13; James Logan to William Penn, April 2, 1707, *HSP Memoirs,* 10:208; Cornbury to Board of Trade, June 7, 1707, Robert Quary to Same, June 28, 1707, *NJA,* 3:225-26, 235-36; James Alexander to Robert Hunter, Nov. 20, 1728, Rutherford Collection, 1:95.

8. *N.J. Assem. Journ.,* April 7-10, 1707; Cornbury to Board of Trade, June 7, 1707, *NJA,* 3:226-27.

9. *N.J. Assem. Journ.,* April 21-30, 1707; *NJA,* 3:198-219, 227.

10. *N.J. Assem. Journ.,* May 5, 1707; Samuel Jennings to Robert Harley, May 5, 1707, C.O. 5/1091/38, Public Record Office, microfilm; New Jersey Assembly to Cornbury and to Queen Anne, May 5, 1707, Lewis Morris to Robert Harley, Feb. 9, 1708, *NJA,* 3:171-80, 274; Sheila Biddle, *Bolingbroke and Harley* (New York, 1974), pp. 124-30. For the evidence of Morris' authorship of the assembly's remonstrance, see James Logan to William Penn, May 20, 1707, *HSP Memoirs,* 10:226; and Cornbury to Board of Trade, June 7, 1707, *NJA,* 3:226.

11. *NJA,* 3:173-80.

12. Robert Quary to Board of Trade, June 28, 1707, Address of Lieutenant Governor and Council of New Jersey to Lovelace, [April 1709], ibid., pp. 237–38, 397.

13. Ibid., pp. 180–98.

14. Lewis Morris to Robert Harley, Feb. 9, 1708, ibid., p. 274; Same to John Chamberlayne, May 30, 1709, *RSPG*, Ser. A, 4, no. 149; Robert Quary to Earl of Rochester, June 28, 1709, Clarendon Family Papers, John Carter Brown Library, microfilm. The Board of Trade received Cornbury's June 7, 1707 letter and an enclosed copy of Morris' remonstrance on Jan. 27, 1708. *NJA*, 3:224. For the Board's generally favorable reaction to Morris' complaints, see ibid., pp. 323–27.

15. New Jersey Assembly to Cornbury, Oct. 24, 1707, ibid., 3:242–67; *N.J. Assem. Journ.,* Oct. 27, 31, 1707; Leonard W. Labaree, *Royal Government in America: A Study of the British Colonial System before 1783* (New Haven, 1930), pp. 343–44. The assembly's reply to Cornbury is unmistakably written in Morris' style; and since this lengthy document was approved on the second day of the legislative session, it is virtually certain that Morris wrote it before the assembly met.

16. Lewis Morris, "State of the Church in New York and the Jerseys," *RSPG,* Ser. C/Am, 1, no. 2.

17. Lewis Morris to Robert Harley, Feb. 9, 1708, *NJA*, 3:274–85; *Dictionary of National Biography,* s.v. "Heathcote, Sir Gilbert"; Dixon Ryan Fox, *Caleb Heathcote: Gentleman Colonist. The Story of a Career in the Province of New York, 1692–1721* (New York, 1926), passim.

18. Snyder, ed., *Marlborough-Godolphin Correspondence,* 2:876, 882, 902; John Champante to Roger Mompesson, Oct. 10, 1707, Rawlinson MSS A, 272, fol. 237; Board of Trade to Lovelace, June 28, 1708, *NJA*, 3:323–27; Robert Quary to Earl of Rochester, June 28, 1709, Clarendon Family Papers; Feiling, *History of the Tory Party,* pp. 391–401; I. K. Steele, *Politics of Colonial Policy: The Board of Trade in Colonial Administration, 1696–1720* (Oxford, 1968), pp. 109. 131–33; *Dictionary of National Biography,* s.v. "Lovelace, John."

19. Lieutenant Governor and Council of New Jersey to the Queen, [Feb. 1708], *NJA,* 3:287–90; Lewis Morris, Poem on verso of letter from John Corbett, [ante Aug. 1708], Same to Earl of Sunderland, [1709], Morris Papers, Box 1, Rutgers University Library.

20. *NJA,* 3:299–302, 309, 317, 328–29, 349–50.

21. "Address of Mr. Lewis Morris to the Lord Lovelace to which is annexed some Verses upon his addressing alone," [March 1709], ibid., pp. 380–83.

22. Ibid., pp. 362–63, 374–78, 385–88, 466.

23. Ibid., 13:367–69.

24. Lewis Morris to John Chamberlayne, May 30, 1709, *RSPG,* Ser. A, 4, no. 149; Same to Earl of Sunderland, [1709], Morris Papers, Box 1; William Dockwra, 1709 Marginalia on Lewis Morris to East Jersey Council, [ca. May 17, 1699], Sunderland Papers, New Jersey, 1698–1709, Henry E. Huntington Library, microfilm; Same to Board of Trade, Oct. 31, 1709, *NJA*, 3:475–76.

25. John Johnston to Lewis Morris, Oct. 8, 1710, Morris Papers, Box 1; Peter Sonmans to Robert Hunter, Oct. 12, 1710, Hunter to Sonmans, Oct. 18, 1710, Additional MSS

14034, fols. 128-30, British Library, Library of Congress transcript; *NJA,* 3:497-500, 4:15-16, 119-20; *Journal of the Commissioners for Trade and Plantations, 1709-1715,* pp. 107, 112.

26. New Jersey Assembly to Robert Hunter, Feb. 9, 1711, *NJA,* 4:24-48. There is a fragmentary draft of this representation by Morris in Morris Papers, Miscellaneous Folders. See also Peter Sonmans to Earl of Clarendon, Feb. 12, 1711, Same to William Dockwra, May 30, 1711, Additional MSS 14034, fols. 118-22, 135-37; [Daniel Coxe, Jr.] to Same, [March 27, 1711], Robert Hunter to Board of Trade, May 7, 1711, *NJA,* 4:49-61, 119-30. Although Coxe's letter is undated in *NJA,* a text of roughly the first half of it in Additional MSS 14034, fols. 137-42, bears the date given above.

27. *NJA,* 4:61-63, 125, 128-33; Peter Sonmans to Earl of Clarendon, Feb. 12, 1711, Same to William Dockwra, May 30, 1711, Additional MSS 14034, fols. 118-22, 135-37; Feiling, *History of the Tory Party,* pp. 417-18; George Macaulay Trevelyan, *England under Queen Anne,* 3 vols. (London, 1930-34), 3, chap. 4; Edwin P. Tanner, *The Province of New Jersey, 1644-1738,* pp. 271-73.

28. "Dates of Letters from Mr. Lewis Morris," West Jersey Society Records, Treasury Solicitor 12/4/23-24, Public Record Office, microfilm; Peter Sonmans to Earl of Clarendon, Feb. 12, and to William Dockwra, May 30, 1711, Additional MSS 14034, fols. 118-22, 135-37; *NJA,* 4:115-33, 140-41, 152-54; *CSP 1712-1714,* nos. 65, 315.

29. New Jersey Council Minutes, Jan. 18, 22, 28, March 4, 17, 1714, *NJA,* 13: 499-500, 504, 507-508, 534, 553.

6 – "The Governor's Perticular Favorit"

1. Robert Hunter to Joseph Addison, Nov. 8, 1714, Walter Graham, ed., *The Letters of Joseph Addison* (Oxford, 1941), p. 493.

2. Cadwallader Colden to Alexander Colden, Sept. 25, 1759, William Smith, Jr., *The History of the Province of New-York,* ed. Michael Kammen, 2 vols. (Cambridge, 1972), 1:299-302. See also E. B. O'Callaghan and Berthold Fernow, eds., *Documents Relative to the Colonial History of the State of New York,* 15 vols. (Albany, 1856-87), 5:451-55 (hereafter cited as *NYCD*); Henry L. Snyder, ed., *The Marlborough-Godolphin Correspondence,* 3 vols. (Oxford, 1975), 3:1212, 1227, 1237, 1339, 1346, 1355, 1366, 1381; Harold Williams, ed., *The Correspondence of Jonathan Swift,* 5 vols. (Oxford, 1963-65), 1:101-103, 119-23, 132-34; Walter A. Knittle, *The Early Eighteenth Century Palatine Emigration* (Philadelphia, 1936), chaps. 5-7; P. W. J. Riley, *The English Ministers and Scotland, 1707-1727* (London, 1964), pp. 21-23, 34, 98, 109, 117-18, 145-46, 150, 160, 246-47; Peter Smithers, *The Life of Joseph Addison,* 2d ed. (Oxford, 1968), pp. 144, 306-307; Jonathan D. Fiore, "Jonathan Swift and the American Episcopate," *WMQ,* 3d ser., 11 (1954): 425-33; James E. Scanlon, "British Intrigue and the Governorship of Robert Hunter," *New-York Historical Society Quarterly* 57 (1973): 199-211; Stephen Saunders Webb, "Officers and Governors: The Role of the British Army in Imperial Politics and the Administration of the American Colonies, 1689-1722" (Ph.D. diss., University of Wisconsin, 1965), pp. 23-24, 280, 300-301; and *Dictionary of National Biography,* s.v. "Arbuthnot, John," "Dalrymple, John, second earl," "Erskine, John, sixth or eleventh earl," "Hamilton, Lord George," "Philips, Ambrose."

3. *NYCD,* 5:423, 476.

4. *NJA,* 3:475-500; *Journal of the Commissioners for Trade and Plantations, 1709-1715,* pp. 107, 112.

5. Cadwallader Colden to Alexander Colden, Sept. 25, 1759, Smith, *History of New-York,* ed. Kammen, 1:300; [Robert Hunter and Lewis Morris], *Androboros: A Biographical Farce in Three Acts,* [New York, 1715]. I have relied on the text of this work in Lawrence H. Leder, ed., "Robert Hunter's *Androboros,"* New York Public Library, *Bulletin* 68 (1964): 153-90, although Leder disregards Cadwallader Colden's testimony that Morris and Hunter co-authored this play, not to mention the stylistic evidence indicating it was written by more than one person. Cadwallader Colden to Alexander Colden, Oct. 15, 1759, Smith, *History of New-York,* ed. Kammen, 1:306.

6. Smith, *History of New-York,* ed. Kammen, 1:140. John B. Owen, *The Rise of the Pelhams* (London, 1957), pp. 36-40, lucidly describes the office of prime minister in eighteenth-century England.

7. Lewis Morris, "A Dialogue between a South and a North Countryman," 14, [1727-28], Morris Papers, Box 2, Rutgers University Library; *Journal of the Votes and Proceedings of the General Assembly of the Colony of New York,* 2 vols. (New York, 1764-66), 1:170-71, 190, 197, 224 (hereafter cited as *N.Y. Assem. Journ.*); Leonard W. Labaree, *Royal Government in America: A Study of the British Colonial System before 1783* (New Haven, 1930), chaps. 7-8; Same, *Royal Instructions to British Colonial Governors, 1670-1776,* 2 vols. (New York, 1935), 1:172, 203-204, 371-72; Charles Worthen Spencer, *Phases of Royal Government in New York, 1691-1719* (Columbus, Ohio, 1905), pp. 120-28; Beverly McAnear, "Politics in Provincial New York, 1689-1761" (Ph.D. diss., Stanford University, 1935), pp. 217-22; Lawrence H. Leder, "The Politics of Upheaval in New York, 1689-1709," *New-York Historical Society Quarterly* 64 (1957): 425-27.

8. Patricia U. Bonomi, *A Factious People: Politics and Society in Colonial New York* (New York, 1971), pp. 56-75; Michael Kammen, *Colonial New York: A History* (New York, 1975), pp. 151-52, 159; McAnear, "Politics in Provincial New York," pp. 207-211. There are some sage comments by Cadwallader Colden about the competition between the landed and merchant interests to win the support of artisans, craftsmen, and farmers in "The Orig. of the Disp. with Mr. B.," [1728], Rutherfurd Collection, 1:63, New-York Historical Society.

9. Thomas J. Archdeacon, *New York City, 1664-1710: Conquest and Change* (Ithaca, N.Y., 1976), chaps. 5-6.

10. Quoted in Charles Worthen Spencer, "Sectional Aspects of New York Provincial Politics," *Political Science Quarterly* 30 (1915): 408.

11. *N.Y. Assem. Journ.,* 1:271-83; Robert Hunter to Board of Trade, Oct. 3, Nov. 14, 18, 1710, *NYCD,* 5:170, 177-79, 183-84; George Clarke to William Blathwayt, Nov. 15, 1710, George Clarke Papers, New-York Historical Society.

12. "Copy of Mr. Lewis Morris his Speech in the Assembly of New York," [Nov. 8, 1710], C.O. 5/1050/27-28, Public Record Office, microfilm.

13. *N.Y. Assem. Journ.,* 1:283; Robert Hunter to Board of Trade, Nov. 14, 1710, Board of Trade to the Queen, Feb. 16, 1711, *NYCD,* 5:178, 191; George Clarke to William Blathwayt, Nov. 15, 1710, George Clarke Papers; John Chamberlayne to Lewis Morris, June 16, 1711, Morris Papers, Box 1.

14. Robert Hunter to Board of Trade, Nov. 28, 1710, May 7, 1711, *NYCD,* 5:183–84, 209; *N.Y. Assem. Journ.,* 1:283–86.

15. Robert Hunter to Board of Trade, June 23, 1712, *NYCD,* 5:340; "Heads of an Act for Granting a Revenue to Her Majesty . . . [in] the Province of New York . . . for the Support of that Government," C.O. 5/1050/464–74; *NYCD,* 5:180, 190–92, 285, 287–88, 299, 351, 359–60, 366–67, 400.

16. [Lewis Morris], "To the Inhabitants and Free-holders of Westchester County," [New York, 1713], C.O. 5/1050/477–78; Same, "Dialogue Concerning Trade," 10, [1726], Morris Papers, Box 2.

17. Robert Hunter to Jonathan Swift, Nov. 1, 1712, Williams, ed., *Correspondence of Jonathan Swift,* 1:335; Same to Board of Trade, March 14, 1713, *NYCD,* 5:356; *N.Y. Assem. Journ.,* 1:287–88, 295–96, 306–309, 328–30; McAnear, "Politics in Provincial New York," pp. 237–41.

18. Alison G. Olson, "Governor Robert Hunter and the Anglican Church in New York," Anne Whiteman et al., eds., *Statesmen, Scholars and Merchants: Essays in Eighteenth-Century History Presented to Dame Lucy Sutherland* (Oxford, 1973), pp. 45–56.

19. "Memorial of the Clergy &c Relating to Mr. Poyer and the Church of Jamaica," Nov. 13, 1711, Lewis Morris to John Chamberlayne, Jan. 1, Feb. 20, 1712, Caleb Heathcote to Same, Jan. 5, 30, 1712, Robert Hunter to Same, Feb. 25, 1712, Thomas Poyer to Same, Feb. 28, 1712, John Sharpe to Same, June 23, 1712, Records of the Society for the Propagation of the Gospel in Foreign Parts, Ser. A, 7:149–73, 177–83, 192, 214–17, 295–304, microfilm (hereafter cited as *RSPG*).

20. Lewis Morris and Caleb Heathcote to Jacob Henderson and William Vesey, Feb. 20?, 1712, ibid., pp. 240–41; Robert Hunter to New York Clergy, Feb. 20, 1712, ibid., Ser. B, 1, no. 123; New York Clergy to Robert Hunter, Feb. 20, 1712, ibid., no. 122; Caleb Heathcote to John Chamberlayne, March 6, 1712, ibid., Ser. A, 7:189.

21. Lewis Morris to John Chamberlayne, Jan. 1, Feb. 20, 1712, ibid., Ser. A, 7:159–73; Robert Hunter to John Chamberlayne and to Bishop of London, Feb. 25, March 1, 1712, *NYCD,* 5:310–17.

22. SPG to Robert Hunter and to New York Clergy, July 25, 1712, *RSPG,* Ser. A, 7: 263–66; Same to Queen, Aug. 26, 1712, Order in Council, Jan. 8, 1713, *NYCD,* 5:345–46, 352–53.

23. "A short State of the Church of England planted in . . . New York and New Jersey," June 2, 1712, *NYCD,* 5:334–35.

24. Robert Hunter to New York and New Jersey Clergy, Feb. 27, 1713, New York and New Jersey Clergy to Robert Hunter, March 4, 1713, *RSPG,* Ser. A, 8:219–23; Lewis Morris to New York and New Jersey Clergy, Feb. 27, 1713, Clarendon MSS, 102, fol. 212b, Bodleian Library, Oxford, Library of Congress transcript; New York and New Jersey Clergy to Lewis Morris, nd, ibid., fol. 213b; Robert Hunter to SPG, March 14, 1713, *RSPG,* Ser. A, 8:123–25.

25. Horatio O. Ladd, *The Origin and History of Grace Church, Jamaica, New York* (New York, 1914), p. 77; Olson, "Governor Hunter and the Anglican Church," pp. 59–63.

26. Lewis Morris to John Morris, Nov. 4, 1732, Morris Papers, Box 2; Same to Bishop of London, May 17, 1741, Fulham Papers, 7:267–68, Lambeth Palace Library, microfilm. See also Jacob Henderson to SPG, July 1, 1712, *RSPG,* Ser. C/Am, 1, no. 27.

27. [Lewis Morris], "To the Inhabitants and Free-holders of Westchester County," [New York, 1713], C.O. 5/1050/477–78. The writer's description of himself as a resident of Westchester, the striking similarities in economic philosophy between this work and Morris' 1710 address to the assembly, and the antimercantile sentiments of both—all these point to Morris as the author of this pamphlet. Herbert L. Osgood, *The American Colonies in the Eighteenth Century,* 4 vols. (New York, 1924), 2:109n3, also attributes it to Morris. See also [Robert Hunter], *To All whom these Presents may Concern* (New York, 1713), p. 7.

28. [Robert Hunter], *To All whom these Presents may Concern* (New York 1713), passim.

29. Robert Hunter to William Popple, May 11, 1713, Same to Board of Trade, July 18, 1713, *NYCD,* 5:364, 367; *The Colonial Laws of New York from the Year 1664 to the Revolution,* 5 vols. (Albany, 1894–96), 1:779–80; "Captain Mulford's Speech to the General Assembly the Second of April 1714," Horsemanden Papers, no. 1, New-York Historical Society; Lewis Morris, "A Dialogue between a South and a North Countryman," 24, [1727–28], Morris Papers, Box 1; Kammen, *Colonial New York,* pp. 161–63.

30. Robert Hunter to William Popple, Oct. 10, 1715, *NYCD,* 5:447–50; Report of Edward Harley, March 31, 1724, C.O. 5/1050/266–67; Robert Hunter, Petition to the King, Nov. 15, 1727, ibid., fol. 264; Spencer, *Phases of Royal Government,* p. 123.

31. May Bickley to Earl of Clarendon, Nov. 10, 1714, Clarendon Family Papers, John Carter Brown Library.

32. Robert Livingston to Alida Livingston, May 19, 1714, Livingston-Redmond Papers, Franklin D. Roosevelt Library, microfilm.

33. Same to Same, April 17, 1714, ibid.

34. May Bickley to Earl of Carendon, Nov. 10, 1714, Clarendon Family Papers.

35. Ibid.; *N.Y. Assem. Journ.,* 1:346–64; *The Laws of His Majesties Colony of New-York* (New York, 1719), pp. 239–87.

36. "Captain Mulford's Speech to the General Assembly the Second of April 1714," Horsemanden Papers, no. 1.

37. [Lewis Morris], "To the Inhabitants and Free-holders of Westchester County," [New York, 1713], C.O. 5/1050/478; May Bickley to Earl of Clarendon, Nov. 10, 1714, Clarendon Family Papers; *Laws of . . . New-York* (New York, 1719), p. 285; Spencer, *Phases of Royal Government,* pp. 147–48.

38. Robert Hunter to Board of Trade, March 28, July 25, 1715, Charles Lodwick to Same, Aug. 23, 1715, Board of Trade to Secretary Stanhope, Aug. 31, 1715, *NYCD,* 5:400, 419, 423, 429; *CSP 1714–1715,* no. 630. Texts of Morris' commission as chief justice are in Morris Papers, Box 1, and Lewis Morris Papers, New-York Historical Society.

39. Cadwallader Colden to Board of Trade and to Earl of Egremont, Jan. 11, 12, 1762, New-York Historical Society, *Collections* 9 (1876): 149, 152; Same, *History of Governor William Cosby's Administration,* ibid., 68 (1935): 299; Paul M. Hamlin and Charles E. Baker, eds., *Supreme Court of Judicature of the Province of New York, 1691–1704,* ibid., 78 (1952): 67–77.

40. May Bickley to Earl of Clarendon, Nov. 10, 1714, Clarendon Family Papers; *N.Y. Assem. Journ.,* 1:372; Indictment of Samuel Mulford, June 10, 1715, Horsemanden Papers, no. 2; Robert Hunter to Board of Trade, July 25, 1715, *NYCD,* 5:416; Samuel Mul-

ford, *An Information,* [1717], *Documentary History of New York,* 3:380–81; Julius Goebel and T. Raymond Naughton, *Law Enforcement in Colonial New York: A Study in Criminal Procedure (1664–1776)* (New York, 1944), pp. 313–14.

41. Robert Hunter to Board of Trade, May 21, July 25, 1715, *NYCD,* 5:403–404, 416–17; *Colonial Laws of New York,* 1:847–63; Lewis Morris, "A Dialogue between a South and a North Countryman," 23, [1727–28], Morris Papers, Box 2.

42. Horace Walpole to Lords of the Treasury, June 28, 1720, Robert Hunter's Observations on Same, Aug. 18, 1720, *NYCD,* 5:546, 558–59; Lewis Morris, Speech to New York Assembly, June 17, 1726, C.O. 5/1093/58–64; Same to James Alexander, March 29, 1729, Rutherfurd Collection, 1:113; Cadwallader Colden to Alexander Colden, Jan. 31, 1760, Smith, *History of New-York,* ed. Kammen, 1:319.

43. Lewis Morris, "Dialogue between a South and a North Countryman," 4–5, [1727–28], Morris Papers, Box 2.

44. Lewis Morris, Speech to New York Assembly, [post June 17, 1726], C.O. 5/1093/65–66.

45. Leder, ed., "Robert Hunter's *Androboros,*" pp. 165, 168, 170, 173, 177. Although Leder states that this play was written in the fall of 1714, it must have been composed a year later because the prologue refers to William Vesey's appointment as commissary of the Bishop of London—a fact of which Hunter did not become aware until November 1715. *NJA,* 4:219–20. See also Cadwallader Colden to Alexander Colden, Oct. 15, 1759, Smith, *History of New-York,* ed. Kammen 1:306.

46. Robert Hunter to William Popple, Nov. 22, 1717, *NYCD,* 5:493; *Colonial Laws of New York,* 1:938–91; Bonomi, *A Factious People,* pp. 86–87.

47. "Humble Representation of the Grand Jury for the City and County of New York," Nov. 29, 1717, "Some Considerations to be humbly offered to the Lords of Trade," [Dec. 1717], Jay Papers, Box 3, New-York Historical Society; *N.Y. Assem. Journ.,* 1: 410–12; Robert Hunter to William Popple, Dec. 3, 1717, and to Board of Trade, Jan. 27, 1718, *NYCD,* 5:494–95, 499–500.

48. Lewis Morris, "A Dialogue between a South and a North Countryman," 26, [1727–28], Morris Papers, Box 2; "The Case of the Inhabitants of . . . New York, 1718," "The Case of the Inhabitants . . . 1718," Letter about the Long Bill, [1718], Jay Papers, Box 3; Robert Hunter to Board of Trade, Jan. 27, 1718, *NYCD,* 5:497; McAnear, "Politics in Provincial New York," pp. 296–97, 306–313.

49. *Colonial Laws of New York,* 1:847–57, 898–901; Board of Trade to Robert Hunter, Feb. 25, 1718, *NYCD,* 5:501; *CSP 1717–1718,* no. 662.

50. Lewis Morris, Representation of New York Assembly, Oct. 9, 1718, *N.Y. Assem. Journ.,* 1:422–25; *Colonial Laws of New York,* 1:1010–12; Robert Hunter to Board of Trade, Nov. 3, 1718, *NYCD,* 5:519–20.

7 — "A Wise Man Sick of Publick Employs"

1. Lewis Morris, "The Opinion of the Chief Justice," [ca. Sept. 24, 1720], C.O. 5/1052/93, Public Record Office, microfilm; "Province of New York," [1720], "Abt Parliaments in Ireland," [1720], Jay Papers, Box 3, New-York Historical Society.

2. Lewis Morris, "The Opinion of the Chief Justice," [ca. Sept. 24, 1720], C.O. 5/1052/93-96; William Burnet to Board of Trade, Sept. 24, 1720, *NYCD,* 5:573; "Province of New York," [1720], Jay Papers, Box 3; Cadwallader Colden to Robert Hunter, [1725], Rutherfurd Collection, 1:47, New-York Historical Society.

3. William Burnet to Board of Trade, Sept. 24, 1720, *NYCD,* 5:573; Copy Letter on the State of New York, [1720], Jay Papers, Box 3.

4. James Alexander to Robert Hunter, Nov. 20, 1728, Rutherfurd Collection, 1:95. See also William Burnet to Board of Trade, Nov. 27, 1720, *NYCD,* 5:578-79; Cadwallader Colden to Robert Hunter, [1725], and Same, "The Orig. of the Disp. with Mr. B.," [1728], Rutherfurd Collection, 1:47, 63.

5. "Province of New York," [1720], Jay Papers, Box 3; "The Opinion of the Attourney Generall," Sept. 24, 1720, Andrew Hamilton, Legal Opinion, Sept. 27, 1720, C.O. 5/1052/97-99.

6. Copy Letter on the State of New York, [1720], Jay Papers, Box 3; William Burnet to Board of Trade, Nov. 26, 1720, *NYCD,* 5:576; *Colonial Laws of New York,* 2:16-32.

7. *N.Y. Assem. Journ.,* 1:441-45; *Colonial Laws of New York,* 2:8-12; Lawrence H. Leder, *Robert Livingston 1654-1728 and the Politics of Colonial New York* (Chapel Hill, 1961), pp. 250-56; Thomas Elliot Norton, *The Fur Trade in Colonial New York 1686-1776* (Madison, 1974), pp. 121-38.

8. William Smith, Jr., *The History of the Province of New-York,* ed. Michael Kammen, 2 vols. (Cambridge, 1972), 1:167; "Province of New York," [1720], Copy Letter on the State of New York, [1720], Jay Papers, Box 3.

9. Copy Letter on the State of New York, [1720], Jay Papers, Box 3.

10. William Burnet to Board of Trade, March 9, 1721, *NYCD,* 5:584; *CSP 1720-1721,* nos. 470, 475, 492; Cadwallader Colden to Robert Hunter, [1725], Rutherfurd Collection, 1:47.

11. Horatio Walpole to Lords of the Treasury, June 28, 1720, *NYCD,* 5:545-48; Charles Stanhope to Charles Delafaye, Aug. 4, 1720, C.O. 5/1085/77; Lord Carteret to William Burnet, May 16, 1721, ibid., fol. 127.

12. Lewis Morris, "The humble Representation of the General Assembly," June 30, 1721, *N.Y. Assem. Journ.,* 1:459-62.

13. Horatio Walpole to Lords of the Treasury, April 26, 1722, Lords of the Treasury to William Burnet, April 28, 1722, C.O. 5/1085/143-50.

14. George Clarke to Horatio Walpole, Oct. 10, Dec. 12, 1724, ibid., fols. 187-90; Leder, *Robert Livingston,* pp. 262-65. For a different interpretation of the outcome of the audit dispute, see James A. Henretta, *"Salutary Neglect": Colonial Administration under the Duke of Newcastle* (Princeton, 1972), pp. 16-17.

15. *N.Y. Assem. Journ.,* 1:472-75; *Colonial Laws of New York,* 2:98-105; Norton, *Fur Trade in Colonial New York,* pp. 138-40.

16. "Province of New York," [1720], Jay Papers, Box 3; William Burnet to Duke of Newcastle, Nov. 17, 1725, George Clarke to Horatio Walpole, Nov. 24, 1725, *NYCD,* 5:766, 768-70; Cadwallader Colden to Robert Hunter, [1725], Rutherfurd Collection, 1:47; Lewis Morris, "Dialogue on Trade," pp. 6-7, [1726], Morris Papers, Box 2, Rutgers University Library; James Alexander to Robert Hunter, Nov. 20, 1728, Rutherfurd Collection, 1:95.

17. Lewis Morris, "A Dialogue between a South and a North Countryman," 30, [1727–28], Morris Papers, Box 2; William Burnet, *An Essay on Scripture Prophecy* (New York? 1724); Cadwallader Colden to Alexander Colden, Dec. 31, 1759, Smith, *History of New-York,* ed. Kammen, 1:314–15; Beverly McAnear, "Politics in Provincial New York, 1689–1761" (Ph.D. diss., Stanford University, 1935), pp. 275–77, 342–44; Sung Bok Kim, "A New Look at the Great Landlords of Eighteenth-Century New York," *WMQ,* 3d ser., 27 (1970): 593–94.

18. Cadwallader Colden to Alexander Colden, nd, Smith, *History of New-York,* ed. Kammen, 1:311–12; *N.Y. Assem. Journ.,* 1:515.

19. Lewis Morris, Legal Opinion, Sept. 19, 1725, *N.Y. Assem. Journ.,* 1:518–19; Philip Livingston to Robert Livingston, Sept. 23, 1725, Livingston-Redmond Papers, Franklin D. Roosevelt Library, microfilm; George Clarke to Horatio Walpole, Nov. 24, 1725, *NYCD,* 5:769.

20. Cadwallader Colden to Alexander Colden, nd, Smith, *History of New-York,* ed. Kammen, 1:312; William Burnet to Duke of Newcastle, Nov. 17, 1725, George Clarke to Horatio Walpole, Nov. 24, 1725, *NYCD,* 5:765–66, 768–70; *N.Y. Assem. Journ.,* 1:525.

21. Lewis Morris, *The Chief Justice's Speech to the General Assembly . . . of New York the third of May 1726* (New York, 1726), pp. 1–2; *N.Y. Assem. Journ.,* 1:534, 536, 544.

22. Same, "A Second Speech made by the chief Justice to the general Assembly of New York on friday the 17th day of June 1726," C.O. 5/1093/64–65.

23. Same, Speech to New York Assembly, [post June 17, 1726], ibid., fols. 65–66.

24. McAnear, "Politics in Provincial New York," pp. 335–45.

25. Lewis Morris to James Alexander, March 31, 1729, Rutherfurd Collection, 1:117; New York Council to William Burnet, Oct. 21, 1726, New-York Historical Society, *Collections* 50 (1917): 191–93; William Burnet to Duke of Newcastle, Dec. 20, 1726, *NYCD,* 5: 805; Cadwallader Colden to Alexander Colden, Jan. 31, 1760, Smith, *History of New-York,* ed. Kammen, 1:319.

26. Lewis Morris, "Dialogue on Trade," [1726], Morris Papers, Box 2.

27. Same, *The Charge Given by the Chief Justice of the Province of New York, to the Grand Jury of the City of New York, in March Term, 1726–1727* (New York, 1727), pp. 3–5, 17–18.

28. Same, "A Dialogue between a South and a North Countryman," pp. 4–5, 35, [1727–28], Morris Papers, Box 2.

29. Cadwallader Colden to Alexander Colden, Jan. 31, 1760, Smith, *History of New-York,* ed. Kammen, 1:318; John Montgomerie to the King, [1728], C.O. 5/1092/48; John M. Beattie, *The English Court in the Reign of George I* (Cambridge, England, 1967), pp. 268–71.

30. James Alexander to Cadwallader Colden, May 5, 1728, New-York Historical Society, *Collections* 50 (1917): 260; John Montgomerie to Board of Trade and to Alured Popple, May 30, 1728, *NYCD,* 5:856–57; Cadwallader Colden to Alexander Colden, Jan. 31, 1760, Smith, *History of New-York,* ed. Kammen, 1:318.

31. Cadwallader Colden to James Alexander, May 17, June 21, 30, 1728, Lewis Morris, Jr., to Same, [June 1728], James Alexander to Cadwallader Colden, Nov. 25, 1728, Rutherfurd Collection 1:49, 53, 97, 105.

32. Cadwallader Colden to James Alexander, March 1, 4, 1729, Lewis Morris to Same, March 9, 29, 31, 1729, James Alexander to John Montgomerie, March 28, 1729, Rutherfurd Collection, 1:107, 109, 111, 113, 117; Same to Cadwallader Colden, March 26, April 14, 1729, New-York Historical Society, *Collections* 50 (1917): 277–79; New York Council Minutes, June 12, 1729, C.O. 5/1055/81; *N.Y. Assem. Journ.,* 1:579–80.

33. "Reasons humbly offered by Lewis Morris Junr.," [June 13, 1729], New York Council Minutes, June 13, 1729, C.O. 5/1055/66–69; James Alexander to Cadwallader Colden, June 18, 1729, New-York Historical Society, *Collections* 50 (1917): 281–86; Cadwallader Colden to James Alexander, June 22, 1729, Rutherfurd Collection, 1:125.

34. Unknown to William Burnet, March 25, 1729, William Burnet to James Alexander, June 2, 1729, Rutherfurd Collection, 1:117, 121; James Alexander to Cadwallader Colden, June 18, 28, 1729, New-York Historical Society, *Collections* 50 (1917): 280, 287–88; William Cosby to Duke of Newcastle, May 3, 1733, *NYCD,* 5:946; *Journal of the Commissioners for Trade and Plantations, 1729–1734,* pp. 16–18; Henretta, *"Salutary Neglect",* pp. 61–82.

35. Lewis Morris, Jr., "May it Please Your Excellency," [June 26, 1729], New York Council Minutes, June 26, 1729, C.O. 5/1055/71–78.

36. Lewis Morris, Jr., to Duke of Newcastle and to Board of Trade, July 15, 19, 1729, C.O. 5/1093/46–48, *NYCD,* 5:882–88.

37. John Montgomerie to Board of Trade, June 30, 1729, *NYCD,* 5:877–82; Duke of Newcastle to Board of Trade, Nov. 6, 1729, C.O. 5/1055/48; Lewis Morris to John Morris, April 22, 1730, Morris Papers, Box 2; *Journal of the Commissioners for Trade and Plantations, 1729–1734,* pp. 72–73, 77–78, 80–81, 83, 85, 122; Henretta, *"Salutary Neglect",* pp. 52, 95–101.

38. Lewis Morris to John Morris, April 22, 1730, Morris Papers, Box 2.

39. James Alexander to Cadwallader Colden, June 5, 1730, New-York Historical Society, *Collections* 51 (1918): 15; George Miller, ed., *The Minutes of the Board of Proprietors of the Eastern Division of New Jersey,* 3 vols. (Perth Amboy, 1949–60), 2:1–42; William T. McClure, "The West Jersey Society, 1692–1736," New Jersey Historical Society, *Proceedings* 74 (1956): 14–20.

40. New Jersey Council to Lewis Morris, July 18, 1731, Lewis Morris to Duke of Newcastle, July 19, 1731, June 2, 1732, Richard Partridge to Same, Sept. 15, 1731, William A. Whitehead et al., eds., *Documents Relating to the Colonial History of the State of New Jersey,* 43 vols. (Newark, 1880–1949), 5:295–301, 303–304, 314–20.

8—"An Interest for the Cause"

1. Cadwallader Colden, *History of Governor William Cosby's Administration and of Lieutenant-Governor George Clarke's Administration through 1737,* New-York Historical Society, *Collections* 68 (1935): 286 (hereafter cited as Colden, *History of Cosby and Clarke*).

2. James Alexander to Alured Popple, Dec. 3, 1733, Rutherfurd Collection, 1:107, New-York Historical Society; Colden, *History of Cosby and Clarke,* pp. 283–86; William

Smith, Jr., *History of the Province of New-York,* ed. Michael Kammen, 2 vols. (Cambridge, 1972), 2:1–2; Stanley N. Katz, *Newcastle's New York: Anglo-American Politics, 1732–1753* (Cambridge, 1968), pp. 23–24, 32; James A. Henretta, *"Salutary Neglect": Colonial Administration under the Duke of Newcastle* (Princeton, 1972), pp. 120–21.

3. James Alexander to Ferdinand John Paris, March 19, 1733, Rutherfurd Collection, 1:158; Joseph H. Smith and Leo Hershkowitz, "Courts of Equity in the Province of New York: The Cosby Controversy, 1732–1736," *American Journal of Legal History* 14 (1972): 16–20.

4. Lewis Morris, *The Charge Given by the Chief Justice . . . in March Term, 1726–1727* (New York, 1727), pp. 7–8; William A. Whitehead et al., eds., *Documents Relating to the Colonial History of the State of New Jersey,* 43 vols. (Newark, 1880–1949), 14:461, 465, 475 (hereafter cited as *NJA*); Colden, *History of Cosby and Clarke,* p. 291.

5. Lewis Morris, "Dft of Opinion . . . [in] King agt Van Dam," [1732–33], James Alexander, "The Plea and Demurrer of RVD," [1733], Morris Papers, Box 2, Rutgers University Library; William Cosby to Duke of Newcastle, May 3, 1733, *NYCD,* 5:945; Smith and Hershkowitz, "Courts of Equity," 24n61.

6. New York Supreme Court Minutes, March 15, 1733, New York City Hall of Records, Office of the County Clerk, microfilm; James Alexander to Ferdinand John Paris, March 19, 1733, Rutherfurd Collection, 1:158; William Cosby to Duke of Newcastle, May 3, 1733, *NYCD,* 5:944.

7. Lewis Morris, *The Opinion and Argument of the Chief Justice of the Province of New-York concerning the Jurisdiction of the supream Court of the said Province, to determine Causes in a Course of Equity,* 1st ed. (New York, 1733), 2,5–13; Smith and Hershkowitz, "Courts of Equity," pp. 5–16; Leonard W. Labaree, *Royal Government in America: A Study of the British Colonial System before 1783* (New Haven, 1930), pp. 379–80.

8. "Some extracts from the annexed Letter from Governr Cosby relating to Morris and Courts of Equity in New York," [April 20, 1733], *NJA,* 5:345; Stanley N. Katz, "The Politics of Law in Colonial America: Controversies over Chancery Courts and Equity Law in the 18th Century," *Perspectives in American History* 5 (1971): 273–79.

9. Joseph Warrell, Deposition, Dec. 16, 1733, C.O. 5/1093/237–38, Public Record Office, microfilm.

10. Lewis Morris, *Opinion and Argument of the Chief Justice,* p. 14; New York Supreme Court Minutes, April 17, 1733; William Cosby to Duke of Newcastle, April 20, 1733, *NJA,* 5:333–34; Smith and Hershkowitz, "Courts of Equity," pp. 30–31.

11. William Cosby to Duke of Newcastle, April 20, 1733, *NJA,* 5:343; Lewis Morris to Board of Trade, Aug. 27, 1733, *NYCD,* 5:951–52, 955; Colden, *History of Cosby and Clarke,* pp. 297–99.

12. "Paper on the removall of Lewis Morris Esqr.," Robert Hunter Morris Papers, 2, no. 17, New Jersey Historical Society.

13. Katz, *Newcastle's New York,* pp. 78–79, 85–90.

14. Ibid., pp. 11–13, 23–24, 111–13.

15. Colden, *History of Cosby and Clarke,* pp. 286–87; Smith, *History of New-York,* ed. Kammen, 2:23.

16. Beverly McAnear, "Politics in Provincial New York, 1689–1761," (Ph.D. diss., Stanford University, 1935), pp. 356–67.

17. Lewis Morris to Board of Trade, Oct. 4, 1733, C.O. 5/1056/148–51; William Cosby to Same, Dec. 15, 1733, *NYCD*, 5:960–61; Smith, *History of New-York*, ed. Kammen, 2:23; Philip J. Schwarz, *The Jarring Interests: New York's Boundary Makers, 1664–1776* (Albany, 1979), chap. 4.

18. *New York Weekly Journal*, Nov. 5, 1733 (hereafter cited as *N.Y. Journal*); James DeLancey to Sir John Heathcote, Dec. 9, 1734, Ancaster Papers, i/X1/B/4s, Lincolnshire Archives Committee, microfilm; Thomas Marsh, Deposition, Dec. 30, 1734, Rutherfurd Collection, 2:103; Archibald Foord, *His Majesty's Opposition* (Oxford, 1964), pp. 113–21.

19. James Alexander to Robert Hunter, Nov. 8, 1733, Rutherfurd Collection, 1:163; Cathy Covert, "'Passion is Ye Prevailing Motive': The Feud Behind the Zenger Case," *Journalism Quarterly* 50 (1973): 3–10. There are draft articles for the *Journal* by Lewis Morris, Lewis Morris, Jr., James Alexander, Cadwallader Colden, and William Smith in Rutherfurd Collection, 2:109, 151, 153, 159, 161, 163, 165, 169.

20. *N.Y. Journal*, Nov. 26, Dec. 3, 10, 17, 1733, Feb. 4, 11, 25, March 18, April 1, 1734. William Cosby to Board of Trade, Dec. 6, 1734, *NYCD*, 6:21, and Francis Harison to Henry Grey, March 9, 1736, Audley End Papers, D/DBy/o31, County of Essex Record Office, microfilm, strongly reject the country party's charges against Harison.

21. *N.Y. Journal*, April 8, 29, 1734.

22. Ibid., April 29, 1734.

23. Ibid., March 18, April 8, 22, May 20, July 8, 1734; Gary B. Nash, "Social Change and the Growth of Pre-revolutionary Urban Radicalism," Alfred F. Young, ed., *The American Revolution: Explorations in the History of American Radicalism* (DeKalb, Ill., 1976), pp. 13–14.

24. *N.Y. Journal*, Jan. 21, 1734; Bernard Bailyn, *The Ideological Origins of the American Revolution* (Cambridge, 1967), chap. 3.

25. *N.Y. Journal*, June 10, 17, 1734; *N.Y. Assem. Journ.*, 1:654, 660–80; Colden, *History of Cosby and Clarke*, pp. 322–23; Smith, *History of New-York*, ed. Kammen, 2:15–16; George W. Edwards, "New York City Politics before the American Revolution," *Political Science Quarterly* 36 (1921): 586–91.

26. Lewis Morris to Board of Trade, Aug. 27, Oct. 4, Dec. 15, 1733, *NYCD*, 5:951–55, 957–59, C.O. 5/1056/148–51; *Journal of the Commissioners for Trade and Plantations, 1729–1734*, pp. 363–64, 407.

27. Matthew Norris to Lewis Morris, Jan. 28, 1734, Morris Papers, Box 2; James Alexander to Ferdinand John Paris, March 19, 1733, Rutherfurd Collection, 1:158; *CSP 1733*, no. 329; Katz, *Newcastle's New York*, pp. 102–104; J. H. Plumb, *Sir Robert Walpole: The King's Minister* (London, 1960), pp. 266, 277–78, 308; John B. Owen, *The Rise of the Pelhams* (London, 1957), pp. 16–17.

28. Matthew Norris to Lewis Morris, Jan. 28, Feb. 7, 1734, Morris Papers, Box 2; *CSP 1733*, nos. 324i–ii, 351i–v, 44li–v.

29. Order in Council, Jan. 8, 1734, Ferdinand John Paris to Matthew Norris, Feb. 1734, Morris Papers, Box 2; W. L. Grant and James Munro, eds., *Acts of the Privy Council, Colonial Series, 1613–1783*, 6 vols. (Hereford and London, 1908–1912), 3:397–98.

30. *NYCD*, 6:8–14; William Cosby to Duke of Newcastle, June 19, 1734, Additional MSS 32689, fols. 278–79, British Library, Stanley N. Katz transcript.

31. William Sharpe to Duke of Newcastle, Dec. 11, 1734, C.O. 5/1093/305; *Journal of the Commissioners for Trade and Plantations, 1729–1734*, p. 408; *Acts of the Privy Council*, 3:398.

32. *N.Y. Assem. Journ.*, 1:677; Adolph Philipse, Affidavit, Nov. 28, 1734, C.O. 5/1057/47; Sarah Kearny to Robert Hunter Morris, Jan. 5, 1735, Morris Papers, Box 2.

33. James Alexander, "Instructions proposed for the method of Coll Morris' Conduct in Great Britain," Nov. 19, 1734, Rutherfurd Collection, 2:75. For the draft instructions for Morris that Lewis Morris, Jr., and William Smith prepared about this time and submitted to Alexander, see ibid., pp. 71, 73.

34. James Alexander to Lewis Morris, Jan. 6, 1735, ibid., p. 95.

35. Ibid., p. 105; Lewis Morris to Duke of Newcastle, Jan. 7, 1735, C.O. 5/1093/336; Same to John Morris, Feb. 9, 1735, Morris Papers, Box 2.

36. Same to James Alexander, March 31, 1735, Rutherfurd Collection, 2:117.

37. Same, *The Case of Lewis Morris, Esq. . . . To be heard before the Right Honourable the Lords of his Majesty's most Honourable Privy Council, for Plantation Affairs* (London, 1735); Same to James Alexander, Feb. 8, 1735, Rutherfurd Collection, 2:105; Same to Marquis of Lothian, March 26, 1735, and to Cadwallader Colden, April 11, 1735, New-York Historical Society, *Collections* 51 (1918): 124–28, 136; Beverly McAnear, ed., "An American in London, 1735–1736," *PMHB* 64 (1940): 179–80, 204–205, 207–208 (hereafter cited as Robert Hunter Morris, "Diary").

38. Katz, *Newcastle's New York*, pp. 102–107; Lewis Morris to James Alexander, Feb. 8, 1735, Rutherfurd Collection, 2:105; Same to John Morris, Feb. 9, 1735, Morris Papers, Box 2; John Norris to Robert Hunter Morris, "Sund. the 11th" [1735], ibid., Box 4.

39. Lewis Morris to James Alexander, Feb. 24, March 31, 1735, Rutherfurd Collection, 2:113, 115; Same to Cadwallader Colden, April 11, 1735, New-York Historical Society, *Collections* 51 (1918): 136–37; Euphemia Norris to Lewis Morris, June 15, 1742, Morris Papers, Box 2; Robert Hunter Morris, "Diary," p. 189; Plumb, *Sir Robert Walpole: The King's Minister*, pp. 200, 207–219, 312–24.

40. Lewis Morris to James Alexander, Feb. 8, March 31, 1735, Rutherfurd Collection, 2:105, 115; Robert Hunter Morris, "Diary," pp. 182, 203, 369, 395.

41. Lewis Morris to James Alexander, Feb. 8, Aug. 25, 1735, Rutherfurd Collection, 2:105, 129; Robert Hunter Morris, "Diary," pp. 206–207, 364–66; Katz, *Newcastle's New York*, pp. 126–28.

42. Lewis Morris to James Alexander, Feb. 24, March 31, 1735, Rutherfurd Collection, 2:113, 115.

43. Robert Hunter Morris, "Diary," p. 384; Same to Lewis Morris, Jr., Jan. 3, 1736, *N.Y. Journal*, April 19, 1736.

44. Robert Hunter Morris, "Diary," pp. 384–85; Lewis Morris to James Alexander, Jan. 11, 1736, Rutherfurd Collection, 2:171; *NYCD*, 6:39–42; Labaree, *Royal Government in America*, pp. 160–63.

45. Robert Hunter Morris, "Diary," p. 386; Matthew Norris to Lewis Morris, Jan. 5, 1735, Lewis Morris, "List of the Most Honble Privy Council taken in 1736," Morris Papers, Box 2; Katz, *Newcastle's New York,* pp. 113–14.

46. The foregoing account of Morris' hearing before the Privy Council is based mainly on Robert Hunter Morris, "Diary," pp. 385–88. See also Peter Collinson to James Alexander, Nov. 8, 1735, Rutherfurd Collection, 2:145; Samuel Baker to Sir John Heathcote, Nov. 8, 1735, Ancaster Papers, i/XI/B/2s; Ferdinand John Paris to James Alexander, Nov. 21, 1735, Rutherfurd Collection, Small Scrapbook, no. 67; *NYCD,* 6:36–37; *Acts of the Privy Council,* 3:398.

47. Samuel Baker to Sir John Heathcote, Nov. 8, 1735, Ancaster Papers, i/XI/B/2s; Lewis Morris to James Alexander, March 31, 1735, Rutherfurd Collection, 2:115; Robert Hunter Morris, "Diary," pp. 395–96.

48. "A State of the Case between Governor Cosby and Lewis Morris Esquire," [1734], C.O. 5/1093/363–66; Robert Hunter Morris, "Diary," pp. 392–98; Same to Lewis Morris, Jr., Feb. 13, 1736, Morris Papers, Box 2; Lewis Morris to Duke of Newcastle, March 21, 1736, C.O. 5/1093/386.

49. Lewis Morris to James Alexander, Jan. 11, 1736, Rutherfurd Collection, 2:171; Robert Hunter Morris to Lewis Morris, Jr., Feb. 13, 1736, Morris Papers, Box 2; Same, "Diary," pp. 393–95; *Acts of the Privy Council,* 3:486.

50. "Abstract of Lewis Morris' Petition complaining of Colo Cosby Governor of New York," [ca. Feb. 5, 1736], Privy Council Papers 1, 57/85a, Public Record Office, microfilm; Robert Hunter Morris to Lewis Morris, Jr., Feb. 13, 1736, Morris Papers, Box 2; *Acts of the Privy Council,* 3:486.

51. Sir Charles Wager to Duke of Newcastle, Feb. 12, 1736, State Papers Domestic Naval, 22:1, Public Record Office, microfilm; Lewis Morris to James Alexander, Jan. 11, 1736, Rutherfurd Collection, 2:171.

52. Lewis Morris, "The Dream and Riddle, a Poem," [1736], Morris Papers, Box 2.

53. West Jersey Society to Lewis Morris, Feb. 24, 1718, Feb. 5, 1719, May 10, June 1, 1727, March 25, 1728, May 8, 1729, Jan. 22, 1736, West Jersey Society Records, Treasury Solicitor 12/4/1, 3–4, 12/5/1–6, 12–13, Public Record Office, microfilm; Lewis Morris to West Jersey Society, Dec. 14, 1727, ibid., 12/6/1–4; Same to Adolph Philipse, April 3, 1732, ibid., 12/1/np; Same to Lewis Morris, Jr., Aug. 1, 1735, ibid., 12/5/8–9.

54. West Jersey Society Business Minutes, March 4, 1735–Aug. 12, 1736, passim, ibid., 12/16/11–24; West Jersey Society to Lewis Morris, Jan. 22, April 8, May 13, Aug. 26, 1736, ibid., 12/5/12–21.

55. Lewis Morris, "The Dream and Riddle, a Poem," [1736], Morris Papers, Box 2.

56. *NYCD,* 6:44–47, 49–50, 63–64, 72–80.

57. *New York Gazette,* Sept. 20–27, 1736; *NYCD,* 6:85; Colden, *History of Cosby and Clarke,* p. 348.

58. Smith, *History of New-York,* ed. Kammen, 2:27; *NYCD,* 6:76–80; *New York Gazette,* Oct. 11–18, 1736; Colden, *History of Cosby and Clarke,* p. 349.

59. Colden, *History of Cosby and Clarke,* p. 350; *NYCD,* 6:81–87; James Alexander to Lewis Morris, Oct. 19, 1736, Morris Papers, Box 2.

60. Abigail Franks to Napthali Franks, Oct. 25, 1736, Leo Hershkowitz and Isidore S. Meyer, eds., *The Lee Max Friedman Collection of American Jewish Colonial Correspondence: Letters of the Franks Family (1733–1748)* (Waltham, Mass., 1968), pp. 52–53.

61. Most of the relevant documentation on the Morris-Hamilton affair is in *NJA*, 5: 455–508, passim, 14:538–44. See also Lewis Morris to John Kinsey, Nov. 13, 1736, *Historical Magazine*, 1st ser., 10 (1866): 42–44, and Feb. 14, 1737, Gratz Collection, Historical Society of Pennsylvania.

62. Lewis Morris to John Kinsey, Feb. 14, 1737, Gratz Collection.

63. "Memo. abt. New York," [1737], C.O. 5/1092/166; Lewis Morris to John Kinsey, Feb. 14, 1737, Gratz Collection; Same to Robert Hunter Morris, Dec. 14, 1737, Morris Papers, Box 2.

64. Euphemia Norris to Lewis Morris, June 15, 1742, Morris Papers, Box 2. See also Lewis Morris to Robert Hunter Morris, Dec. 14, 1737, ibid.; and Same to Sir Charles Wager, May 10, 1739, William A. Whitehead, ed., "The Papers of Lewis Morris, Governor of the Province of New Jersey, from 1738 to 1746," New Jersey Historical Society, *Collections* 4 (1852): 45.

65. West Jersey Society to John Hamilton, Sept. 14, 1738, TS 12/5/40; *CSP 1738*, nos. 19, 38, 64, 150, 354, 429.

9 – "I Think I Have Acted Rightly"

1. Lewis Morris to Francis Gashery, May 27, 1739, William A. Whitehead, ed., "The Papers of Lewis Morris, Governor of the Province of New Jersey, from 1738 to 1746," New Jersey Historical Society, *Collections* 4 (1852): 58 (hereafter cited as *Lewis Morris Papers*).

2. Same, Address to New Jersey Assembly, Nov. 15, 1738, William A. Whitehead et al., eds., *Documents Relating to the Colonial History of the State of New Jersey,* 1st ser., 43 vols. (Newark, 1880–1949), 15:4 (hereafter cited as *NJA*). See also Robert Hunter Morris, Commission as Chief Justice, March 17, 1739, Robert Hunter Morris Papers, 1, no. 3, New Jersey Historical Society.

3. Lewis Morris to Board of Trade and to Duke of Newcastle, Sept. 11, 1738, *NJA*, 6:56–58; Same to Sir Charles Wager, May 10, 1739, *Lewis Morris Papers,* p. 41.

4. Same, Address to New Jersey Assembly, Nov. 15, 1738, *NJA*, 15:2–9.

5. *Votes and Proceedings of the General Assembly of New Jersey,* Dec. 15, 1738, Early State Records microfilm (hereafter cited as *N. J. Assem. Journ.*).

6. Lewis Morris, Address to New Jersey Assembly, Jan. 15, 1739, ibid.

7. Ibid., Feb. 3, 1739; *A Letter to B. G. from one of the Members of Assembly of the Province of New Jersey, dissolved March 15, 1738/39* (Philadelphia, 1739), pp. 1–2.

8. Lewis Morris to Board of Trade, May 26, 1739, *Lewis Morris Papers,* p. 49.

9. *N. J. Assem. Journ.,* Feb. 15, 24, March 2, 3, 6, 1739; New Jersey Council Minutes, March 6, 13, 1739, *NJA*, 15:57–58, 61–68.

10. Lewis Morris, Address to New Jersey Assembly, March 15, 1739, *NJA*, 15:79-84; Same to Sir Charles Wager, May 10, 1739, and to Board of Trade, May 26, Oct. 4, 1739, *Lewis Morris Papers,* pp. 41-43, 49-52, 58-61.

11. Same to Benjamin Smith, Jan. 3, 1740, *Lewis Morris Papers,* pp. 73, 76; New Jersey Assembly, Representation, Oct. 17, 1749, *NJA,* 7:337.

12. *A Letter to B. G.,* pp. 1-2; Lewis Morris to Benjamin Smith, Jan. 3, 1740, *Lewis Morris Papers,* pp. 73-80.

13. Lewis Morris to Sir Charles Wager, May 10, 1739, *Lewis Morris Papers,* p. 40.

14. Same to Board of Trade, Oct. 4, 1739, ibid., pp. 61-62.

15. *NJA,* 15:112-17; *Lewis Morris Papers,* pp. 87-90, 94-95, 102-104, 107, 114-15.

16. Lewis Morris, Address to New Jersey Assembly, April 16, 1740, *N. J. Assem. Journ.*

17. Ibid., June 27, 28, July 4, 1740; Lewis Morris, Address to New Jersey Assembly, June 26, 1740, *NJA,* 15:126-27; Same to Duke of Newcastle, Oct. 18, 1740, *Lewis Morris Papers,* pp. 116-17.

18. Same to George Thomas, July 16, 1740, *Lewis Morris Papers,* p. 98.

19. Same to Andrew Johnston, Aug. 26, Sept. 4, 22, 30, Oct. 22, 1740, ibid., pp. 105-113, 115-16; Same to Robert Hunter Morris, Sept. 1, 1740, Morris-Popham Papers, Box 1, Library of Congress.

20. Same to William Gooch, July 14, 1740, *Lewis Morris Papers,* p. 96; Same to George Thomas, July 16, 1740, ibid., p. 97; Same, "The Soldiers Case," [1740], William Smith Papers, 2:284-89, New York Public Library; Richard B. Morris, *Government and Labor in Early America* (New York, 1946), pp. 282-84.

21. Lewis Morris to William Blakeney, Aug. 21, 1740, *Lewis Morris Papers,* p. 104; B. Mcl. Ranft, ed., "The Vernon Papers," *Navy Records Society* 99 (1948): 6-20; Albert Harkness, Jr., "Americanism and Jenkins' Ear," *MVHR* 37 (1950): 61-90; Russell W. Ramsey, "The Defeat of Admiral Vernon at Cartagena in 1741," *Southern Quarterly* 1 (1963): 332-55.

22. *N. J. Assem. Journ.,* April 18-June 10, 1740; Lewis Morris to Board of Trade, Oct. 25, 1740, *Lewis Morris Papers,* pp. 123-24.

23. Lewis Morris to Duke of Newcastle, Oct. 18, 1740, *Lewis Morris Papers,* pp. 117-18; Same to Board of Trade, Oct. 25, 1740, ibid., p. 123.

24. Same to Board of Trade, Aug. 16, 1741, ibid., pp. 136-37.

25. Ibid., 138n.

26. Lewis Morris, Address to New Jersey Assembly, Oct. 3, 1741, *NJA,* 15:199-204.

27. *N. J. Assem. Journ.,* Oct. 12, 13, 23, 24, 29, 1741.

28. Lewis Morris to Board of Trade, Dec. 16, 1741, *Lewis Morris Papers,* p. 140.

29. Same to Euphemia Norris, May 14, 1742, ibid., p. 145; John B. Owen, *The Rise of the Pelhams* (London, 1957), pp. 33-35.

30. Euphemia Norris to Lewis Morris, June 15, 1742, Morris Papers, Box 1, Rutgers University Library. Euphemia Norris' assessment of Morris' prospects was remarkably perceptive. After Walpole's fall from power there was only one recorded instance of an attempt in England to find a replacement for Morris in New Jersey. On Jan. 25, 1744, the Duchess of Richmond wrote to the Duke of Newcastle and solicited an appointment as governor of New Jersey for one "Mr. Gouldworthy." Additional MSS 32702, fol. 27, British Library, Stanley N. Katz transcript. But as the Duchess only made her request after hearing an unfounded rumor of Morris' death, the matter went no further.

31. *N. J. Assem. Journ.,* Oct. 25, 28, Nov. 3, 1742; New Jersey Council Minutes, Oct. 29–Nov. 15, 1742, *NJA,* 15:250–57.

32. *N. J. Assem. Journ.,* Oct. 20, 27, Nov. 10, 17, 19, 25, 1742; Lewis Morris to Board of Trade, Dec. 15, 1742, *Lewis Morris Papers,* p. 152.

33. *N. J. Assem. Journ.,* Oct. 21, 26, 27, Nov. 3, 8, 16, 17, 1742; Lewis Morris to Board of Trade, Dec. 15, 1742, *Lewis Morris Papers,* pp. 154–55; Leo Francis Stock, ed., *Proceedings and Debates of the British Parliament Respecting North America,* 5 vols. (Washington, D.C., 1924–41), 5:42, 47–51, 99–100; Donald L. Kemmerer, "A History of Paper Money in Colonial New Jersey, 1668–1775," New Jersey Historical Society, *Proceedings* 74 (1956): 107–21.

34. Lewis Morris, Address to New Jersey Assembly, Nov. 25, 1742, *NJA,* 15:268–79.

35. Same to Board of Trade, June 10, 1743, *Lewis Morris Papers,* p. 162.

36. Same to Board of Trade, Dec. 15, 1742, ibid., p. 155. The imperial administration did give belated consideration to Morris' proposal for appointing his son lieutenant governor of New Jersey. Among the Newcastle Papers in the British Library is a commission for Robert Hunter Morris to serve in this office dated "1746" but probably made out in 1747. Additional MSS 33029, fol. 34, microfilm. Unfortunately for young Morris, the imperial administration never did more than consider him for service in this capacity.

37. Lewis Morris, Address to New Jersey Assembly, Oct. 10, 1743, *NJA,* 15:279–80.

38. *N. J. Assem. Journ.,* Dec. 5, 7–10, 1743; New Jersey Council Minutes, Dec. 7, 1743, *NJA,* 15:312–14; Lewis Morris, Address to New Jersey Assembly, Dec. 10, 1743, ibid., pp. 315–21; Same to Board of Trade, March 3, 1744, *Lewis Morris Papers,* pp. 181–84.

39. *NJA,* 15:322; Lewis Morris to George Clinton, May 23, 31, 1744, *Lewis Morris Papers,* pp. 187–89; *A Dialogue between two Gentlemen in New York . . . relating to the publick Affairs of New Jersey* (Philadelphia, 1744), p. 1; Walter Dorn, *Competition for Empire* (New York, 1940), pp. 147–53.

40. Lewis Morris, Address to New Jersey Assembly, June 22, 1744, *NJA,* 15:322–25.

41. *A Dialogue between two Gentlemen,* pp. 4–5; *N. J. Assem. Journ.,* June 26–27, 30, July 2, 1744; New Jersey Council Minutes, June 27, 1744, *NJA,* 15:325; Lewis Morris, Addresses to New Jersey Assembly, June 29, July 2, 1744, ibid., pp. 329–33, 335–36; Same to Board of Trade, Jan. 28, 1745, *Lewis Morris Papers,* pp. 213–14.

42. *N. J. Assem. Journ.,* Oct. 4–Nov. 12, Nov. 14–Dec. 8, 1744; Lewis Morris to Euphemia Norris, Jan. 22, 1745, *Lewis Morris Papers,* p. 205; Same to Board of Trade and to Duke of Newcastle, Jan. 28, 1745, ibid., pp. 214–28; Same to Richard Partridge, Jan. 31, 1745, ibid., p. 229.

43. Lewis Morris to Richard Partridge, Jan. 31, 1745, *Lewis Morris Papers,* p. 229; *N. J. Assem. Journ.,* Nov. 9, 1744.

44. Lewis Morris to Euphemia Norris, Jan. 22, 1745, *Lewis Morris Papers,* p. 206; Same to Board of Trade, Jan. 28, 1745, ibid., pp. 216-17, 225.

45. Same, Address to New Jersey Assembly, April 5, 1745, *NJA,* 15:393-408.

46. New Jersey Assembly to Lewis Morris, April 18, 1745, ibid., pp. 410-18.

47. Lewis Morris, Address to New Jersey Assembly, May 2, 1745, ibid., pp. 418-37; *N. J. Assem. Journ.,* May 28-30, 1745; Robert Hunter Morris to James Alexander, April 30, 1745, Rutherfurd Collection, Small Scrapbook, no. 11, New-York Historical Society.

48. Robert Hunter Morris, Poem on Land Riots, [1745?], Morris Papers, Box 2; Gary Horowitz, "New Jersey Land Riots, 1745-1755" (Ph.D. diss., Ohio State University, 1966), pp. 48-61.

49. Lewis Morris, Address to New Jersey Assembly, Sept. 26, 1745, *N. J. Assem. Journ.,* Sept. 28, 1745.

50. Ibid., Sept. 28-Oct. 18, 1745; Lewis Morris to Board of Trade, Oct. 23, 1745, *Lewis Morris Papers,* p. 282.

51. Lewis Morris, Address to New Jersey Assembly, March 4, 1746, *N. J. Assem. Journ.*

52. Ibid., March 5-April 29, 1746.

53. Ibid., April 30, May 1, 7-8, 1746.

54. *Lewis Morris Papers,* p. 314.

55. New Jersey Assembly, Representation, Oct. 17, 1749, *NJA,* 7:336-43.

Bibliography

PRIMARY SOURCES

A. Manuscripts

Bodleian Library, Oxford, England
  Ashmolean Manuscripts, Library of Congress transcripts
  Clarendon Manuscripts, Library of Congress transcripts
  Rawlinson Manuscripts A 272, microfilm
British Library, London, England
  Additional Manuscripts 9747, American Papers, 1698–1705, Library of Congress transcripts
  Additional Manuscripts 14304, Board of Trade Papers, 1696–1786, Library of Congress transcripts
  Additional Manuscripts 15895, Clarendon Papers, Library of Congress transcripts
  Additional Manuscripts 33028–33030, Newcastle Papers, America and West Indies, 1701–1802, microfilm
John Carter Brown Library, Providence, Rhode Island
  Clarendon Family Papers
Colonial Williamsburg Inc., Williamsburg, Virginia
  William Blathwayt Papers, microfilm
County of Essex Record Office, Chelmsford, England
  Audley End Papers, microfilm

Historical Society of Pennsylvania, Philadelphia, Pennsylvania
    Gratz Collection
Henry E. Huntington Library, San Marino, California
    William Blathwayt Papers, microfilm
    Sunderland Papers, New Jersey, 1698–1709, microfilm
Lambeth Palace Library, London, England
    Fulham Papers, Bishop of London Manuscripts, microfilm
    Society for the Propagation of the Gospel in Foreign Parts Papers, micro-
        film
Library of Congress, Washington, D.C.
    Peter Force Collection
    Morris-Popham Papers
Lincolnshire Archives Committee, Lincoln, England
    Ancaster Papers, microfilm
New Jersey Historical Society, Newark, New Jersey
    East Jersey Manuscripts
    Lewis Morris Papers
    Robert Hunter Morris Papers
    New Jersey Manuscripts
New Jersey State Library, Trenton, New Jersey
    New Jersey Assembly Journal, 1703–46, Early State Records microfilm
New York City Hall of Records, New York City
    New York Supreme Court Minutes, 1715–33, microfilm
New-York Historical Society, New York City
    James Alexander Papers
    George Clarke Papers
    Cadwallader Colden Papers
    DePeyster Family Papers
    Daniel Horsemanden Papers
    Jay Papers
    Miscellaneous Manuscripts, Henry Ludlow
    Lewis Morris Papers
    Rutherfurd Collection
    John E. Stillwell Collection
New York Public Library, New York City
    William Smith, Jr., Papers
Public Record Office, London, England
    Colonial Office Papers, Class 5, vols. 1050–1058, Board of Trade Papers,
        microfilm
    Colonial Office Papers, Class 5, vols. 1090–1093, Secretary of State Papers,
        microfilm
    Treasury Solicitor Papers, Class 12, vols. 1–100, West Jersey Society Rec-
        ords, microfilm
Franklin D. Roosevelt Library, Hyde Park, New York
    Livingston-Redmond Papers, microfilm

Rutgers University Library, New Brunswick, New Jersey
  Broadside Collection
  Indenture Collection
  Morris Family Papers
Mrs. Lawrence M. C. Smith, Germantown, Philadelphia
  Morris Family Papers
Society for the Propagation of the Gospel in Foreign Parts, London, England
  SPG Records, microfilm
    1. Series A, Letters received, 1701–36
    2. Series B, Letters received, 1701–86
    3. Series C, Miscellaneous Manuscripts, 1630–1811
    4. Journal, 1701–15

B. Public Records: England

Acts of the Privy Council, Colonial Series, 1613–1783, ed. W. L. Grant and James
  Munro, 6 vols. (Hereford and London, 1908–1912).
Calendar of State Papers; Colonial Series, America and West Indies, ed. W. N.
  Sainsbury et al., 44 vols. (London, 1860–   ).
Journal of the Commissioners for Trade and Plantations, 1704–1782, 14 vols.
  (London, 1920–38).
*Proceedings and Debates of the British Parliaments Respecting North America,
  1542–1754,* ed. Leo F. Stock, 5 vols. (Washington, D.C., 1924–41).
Royal Instructions to British Colonial Governors, 1670–1776, ed. Leonard W.
  Labaree, 2 vols. (New York, 1935).

C. Public Records: New Jersey

Documents Relating to the Colonial History of the State of New Jersey, ed. William A. Whitehead et al., 1st ser., 43 vols. (Newark, 1880–1949).
*Journal of the Courts of Common Right and Chancery of East New Jersey, 1683–
  1702,* ed. Preston Edsall (Philadelphia, 1937).
*The Grants, Concessions, and Original Constitutions of the Province of New Jer-
  sey,* comp. Aaron Leaming and Jacob Spicer (Philadelphia, 1758).
*The Minutes of the Board of Proprietors of the Eastern Division of New Jersey,
  1685–1764,* ed. George J. Miller, 3 vols. (Perth Amboy, 1949–60).

D. Public Records: New York

Calendar of Council Minutes, 1668–1783, ed. Berthold Fernow, New York State
  Library, *Bulletin* 58 (1902).
*Colonial Charters, Patents and Grants to the Communities Comprising the City
  of New York,* ed. Jerrold Seymann (Albany, 1939).

Documentary History of the State of New York, ed. E. B. O'Callaghan, 4 vols. (Albany, 1849–51).

Documents Relative to the Colonial History of the State of New York, ed. E. B. O'Callaghan and Berthold Fernow, 15 vols. (Albany, 1856–87).

Ecclesiastical Records, State of New York, ed. Edward T. Corwin, 7 vols. (Albany, 1901–1916).

Journal of the Votes and Proceedings of the General Assembly of the Colony of New York, 2 vols. (New York, 1764–66).

Supreme Court of Judicature of the Province of New York, 1691–1704, ed. Paul M. Hamlin and Charles E. Baker, New-York Historical Society, *Collections* 78–80 (1952–59).

The Colonial Laws of New York from the Year 1664 to the Revolution, 5 vols. (Albany, 1894–96).

The Records of New Amsterdam from 1653 to 1674, ed. Berthold Fernow, 7 vols. (New York, 1897).

E. Histories, Letters, and Pamphlets: England and the West Indies

A Chapter in English Church History, being the Minutes of the Society for Promoting Christian Knowledge for the Years 1698–1704, ed. Edmund McClure (London, 1888).

Addison, Joseph. *The Letters of Joseph Addison,* ed. Walter Graham (Oxford, 1941).

Luttrell, Narcissus. *A Brief Relation of State Affairs from September 1678 to April 1714,* 6 vols. (Oxford, 1857).

Morris, Lewis. *The Case of Lewis Morris, Esq; Late Chief Justice of the Province of New York* (London, 1735).

Swift, Jonathan. *The Correspondence of Jonathan Swift,* ed. Harold Williams, 5 vols. (Oxford, 1963–65).

"The Early Days of the Morris Family," *Historical Magazine,* 3d ser., 1 (1872), p. 118.

The Marlborough-Godolphin Correspondence, ed. Henry L. Snyder, 3 vols. (Oxford, 1975).

"The Narrative of General Venables," ed. Charles H. Firth, *Camden Society,* new ser., 60 (1900).

"The Vernon Papers," ed. B. Mcl. Ranft, *Navy Records Society,* 99 (1958).

"The Voyages of Captain William Jackson (1642–1645)," ed. Vincent T. Harlow, *Camden Miscellany* 13 (1923).

F. Histories, Letters, and Pamphlets: New Jersey

A Dialogue between two Gentlemen in New York . . . relating to the publick Affairs of New Jersey (Philadelphia, 1744).

A Letter to B. G. from one of the Members of Assembly of New Jersey, dissolved March 15, 1738/39 (Philadelphia, 1739).

A Modest Vindication of the Late New Jersey Assembly (Philadelphia, 1745).

Correspondence between William Penn and James Logan, Historical Society of Pennsylvania, *Memoirs* 9-10 (1870-72).

Jennings, Samuel. *Truth Rescued from Forgery and Falsehood* (Philadelphia, 1699).

Morris, Lewis. "A Scrap of New Jersey History," *Historical Magazine,* 1st ser., 10 (1866), pp. 42-44.

_____. *Extracts from the Minutes and Votes of the House of Assembly of the Colony of New Jersey . . . To Which are Added some Notes and Observations upon the Said Votes* (Philadelphia, 1743).

_____. "The Papers of Lewis Morris, Governor of the Province of New Jersey, from 1738 to 1746," ed. William A. Whitehead, New Jersey Historical Society, *Collections* 4 (1852).

Revell, Thomas et al. *The Case Put and Decided* (Philadelphia, 1699).

Smith, Samuel. *The History of the Colony of Nova-Caesaria, or New Jersey* (Philadelphia, 1765, 2d ed. Trenton, 1890).

The Interest of New Jersey Considered, with Regard to Trade and Navigation by Laying of Duties, &c. (Philadelphia, 1743).

The Note-Maker Noted, and the Observer Observed Upon (Philadelphia, 1743).

G. Histories, Letters, and Pamphlets: New York

Bobin, Isaac. *Letters of Isaac Bobin, Esq.; Private Secretary of Hon. George Clarke, Secretary of New York, 1718-1730* (Albany, 1872).

Colden, Cadwallader. *History of Gov. William Cosby's Administration and of Lt. Gov. George Clarke's Administration through 1737,* New-York Historical Society, *Collections* 68 (1935), pp. 283-355.

_____. *The Letters and Papers of Cadwallader Colden,* New-York Historical Society, *Collections* 50-56, 67-68 (1918-23, 1935-37).

DeLancey, James. *The Charge of the Honourable James DeLancey Esq; Chief Justice of the Province of New York, to the Gentlemen of the Grand Jury for the City and County of New York* (New York, 1734).

Franks, Abigail. *The Lee Max Friedman Collection of American Jewish Correspondence: Letters of the Franks Family (1733-1748),* ed. Leo Hershkowitz and Isidore S. Meyer (Waltham, Mass., 1968).

Hunter, Robert. *To All Whom these Presents may Concern* (New York, 1713).

Hunter, Robert and Lewis Morris. "Robert Hunter's *Androboros,*" ed. Lawrence H. Leder, New York Public Library, *Bulletin* 48 (1964), pp. 153-90.

Morris, Lewis. "Petition to the King for a Redress of Grievances in New York," *Historical Magazine,* 2d ser., 1 (1866), pp. 68-79.

_____. *Some Observations on the Charge Given by the Honourable James DeLancey* (New York, 1734).

_____. *The Chief Justice's speech to the General Assembly . . . of New York the third of May, 1726* (New York, 1726).

_____. *The Charge Given by the Chief Justice of the Province of New York, to the Grand Jury of the City of New York, in March Term, 1726-1727* (New York, 1727).

_____. *The Opinion and Argument of the Chief Justice of the Province of New York, concerning the Jurisdiction of the Supream Court of the said Province, to determine Causes in a Court of Equity* (New York, 1733).

_____. "To the Inhabitants and Free-holders of Westchester County" (New York, 1713).

Morris, Robert Hunter. "R. H. Morris: An American in London, 1735-1736," ed. Beverly McAnear, *PMHB* 64 (1940), pp. 164-217, 356-406.

Smith, William, Jr. *The History of the Province of New-York,* ed. Michael Kammen, 2 vols. (Cambridge, 1972).

H. Newspapers

New York Gazette, 1725-38.

New York Weekly Journal, 1733-38.

For a list of most of the secondary sources used in connection with this study, see Eugene R. Sheridan, "Politics in Colonial America: The Career of Lewis Morris, 1671-1746" (Ph.D. diss., University of Wisconsin, 1972), pp. 464-472.

Index

West Jersey Society (*cont.*)
LM business agent, 50–51; supports LM, 54, 66, 87–88, 94; intercedes with Board of Trade, 66, 82, 86, 87–88; opposes Lord Cornbury, 78; disenchanted with LM's performance as business agent, 145–46, 175; dismisses LM, 175; dislikes LM's appointment as governor of New Jersey, 180

Whigs: LM's ties with, 55; mentioned, 80, 81, 87, 88, 92, 93, 114

Whitefield, George: criticized by LM, 107

Willes, John, represents LM, 166, 171

William III, 47, 55, 56

Willocks, George: expelled from East Jersey Assembly, 29; opposes Gov. Basse, 30–31; helps draft "Long Bill," 59; mentioned, 26

Wilmington, Spencer Compton, Earl of: meets with LM, 166, 173; attends LM's Privy Council hearing, 170–71

Woodbridge, N.J., 20

Wright, Joshua, 64

York, James Stuart, Duke of: grants rights of government to New Jersey proprietors, 20, 26, 45; disavows Nicolls patentees, 20; mentioned, 4. *See also* James II

Zenger, John Peter: prints *New York Weekly Journal,* 157; arrested, 160; mentioned, 125

LEWIS MORRIS, 1671-1746

was composed in 10-point Compugraphic Times Roman and leaded two points
by Metricomp Studios,
with display type in Americana and with Clearcut initials
by Partners Composition;
printed on 55-lb. acid-free Perkins & Squier Offset Vellum,
Smythe-sewn and bound over boards in Joanna Arrestox B,
by Maple-Vail Book Manufacturing Group, Inc.;
and published by

SYRACUSE UNIVERSITY PRESS
SYRACUSE, NEW YORK 13210